Scale Up Your Trading Skills

A Definitive Guide for Aspiring Stock Traders

Govindarajan Muthusamypillai

ISBN 979-8-88749-960-4

TABLE OF CONTENTS

CHAPTER 1   Trading Stocks-Basic 5

CHAPTER 2   Fundamental Analysis... 29

CHAPTER 3-A   Technical Analysis-Single & Multiple Candlestick Pattern 51

CHAPTER 3-B   Technical Analysis Tools for Trading (1) 71

CHAPTER 4   Intra Day Trading 105

CHAPTER 5   Trading Futures 117

CHAPTER 6   Trading Options I 135

CHAPTER 7-A   Trading Options II – Single Leg Strategy.. 171

CHAPTER 7-B   Trading Option III – Multi Leg Option Strategies 175

CHAPTER 8   Economic Calendar of Events That Impact Indian Stock Market 209

CHAPTER 1

TRADING STOCKS-BASIC

CONTENTS

1 Investments, investments in stocks, why in stocks

2 Know about market participants

3 Depository, Depository participant, Opening Demat account, trading account, buying/selling a stock

4 Holding a stock and related benefits

5 Know about stock market

6 Terms commonly used in stock trading

7 Events that impact stock market

8 Bid/Ask spread-Narrow-wide bid/ask spread-Comparison

9 Various order forms for stock trading

10 Market order, Stop loss Market order, Limit order, Stop loss limit order-Example

11 How to set Market order, Limit order with Stop loss order-Examples

12 Comparison between Stop loss Market order and Stop loss Limit order

13 How to place Stop loss order and key points while placing Stop loss-Example

14 GTT order/Bracket order/Cover order/OCO

WHAT IS INVESTMENT	An investment is an asset acquired with the aim of generating income through it`s appreciation. Surplus money, if invested, creates wealth for one`s future needs. A person needs to forecast future financial needs like housing, children` education expense, medical expenses etc and plan his investment accordingly. Investment in stock is one among the various other forms of investment like Bank FDs, debentures, real estate, gold &silver. Just like any other investments, investment in stocks too has it`s own risks. Hence, before proceeding to invest, one must have adequate knowledge and skill to avoid risks involved with the aim of protecting his money from loss in value.
WHAT IS STOCK	Corporate/Companies issue stock to raise funds to operate their businesses A stock is, therefore, a form of security that indicates the holder`s proportionate ownership in the issuing corporate. There are two types of stock: common and preference. Stocks are bought and sold predominantly on stock exchanges, though stocks can also be bought and soldout of exchange.
TRADING IN STOCK	Trading in stock is different from investing in stock as trading usually involves one`s focused attempt to make money from market`s or stock`s price movement in the short run, usually with speculative mindset. Investment is, rather, a long term plan to earn money with portfolio of stocks.
WHAT IS REQUIRED TO TRADE IN STOCK	To invest and trade in stock, trader needs to open with a stock broking house, a Demat a/c & a Trading a/c and link the Bank a/c he has earlier opened in a Bank, with Trading a/c, for the purpose of deposit and withdrawal of money. Demat a/c is similar to normal Bank a/c, difference between them being, in a Bank a/c money is deposited and withdrawn while in Demat a/c, stocks, are held in dematerialized form or digitized form that are deposited and withdrawn.
TYPES OF INVESTORS	There are two types of investors, viz institutional investor & retail investor. An institutional investor is a professional or an organization who trades in securities in large quantities, by investing either their own money for profit or other people`s money for commission. A retail investor, on the other hand, is an individual or non-professional investor who buys and sells securities through brokerage firms for investing for themselves.
TYPE OF TRADERS	Scalp trader, Swing Trader, Day trader and Trend trader. Please follow various notes hereunder to know more about these traders.
TYPES OF MARKET	Bull Market refers to a stock market in which prices are rising or expected to rise shortly.
	Bear Market refers to a stock market in which prices are falling or expected to fall shortly.
WHY BULL/ BEAR	Both Bull and Bear are cyclical in nature because Bull or Bear, the market is determined by demand & supply of stocks under trade. Hence, both Bull or Bear can sustain for prolonged period or be a short-lived one, depending on the pulls and pressures of buying & selling.

VARIOUS TYPES OF ANALYSIS OF STOCK	Qualitative analysis	Means looking at a company that has issued stocks, through the eyes of a customer and understanding its competitive advantage such as management expertise, industry cycles, strength of research and development, labor relations etc which one can not measure on quantifiable terms.
	Financial analysis	There are 2 types of financial analysis: fundamental analysis (also called Quantitative analysis) and technical analysis.
	Fundamental analysis	Fundamental analysis uses ratios and financial statement data to determine the intrinsic value of a security and to analyze whether a company is stable, solvent and earns adequate profit, cash flow etc to share the profit with investors
	Technical Analysis	Technical analysis assumes a security's value is already determined by its price and therefore it focuses on trends to predict its` value over time, by deploying various tools like Candlestick pattern, Oscillators, Moving Averages etc,.
	Note	For detailed study on Technical Analysis see Part 3A, 3B, & 4 & for Fundamental Analysis, see Part 2.
EXCHANGES	In India, there are two stock exchanges namely, NSE & BSE who are conducting trade in stocks. Regulatory control over these two Exchanges is vested with SEBI. In India, T+2 is the norm for settlement of stocks, meaning stock will be delivered into Demat a/c as at the close of second day from trading day (T). So a stock that was bought, say on Monday, is ready for trade on Thursday morning session.	

TRADING STOCKS-BASIC

VARIOUS FORMS OF INVESTMENT, THEIR RETURNS & RISKS PERCEPTION	
Holding Period	If you think about return on investment, your thinking process will be incomplete if you do not take into account the holding period of investments. Holding period is what an investor intends to hold on the investment and this varies person to person depending on risk perception or the returns appetite, one expects from holding it. In stock marker, long term investment is said to be 20 years or more, though many investors treat long term as 3 to 5 years. That said, money markets are characterized by the fact that returns are directly proportional to risks, meaning higher risk higher return and lower risk lower return.
Investments opportunities	While investment in Bank FDs is safe with less risk, return is low. Return from Investment in real estate is high although from risk`s point, investor needs to thoroughly check the documents of title to property beforehand to avoid impersonation. Post registration, you have to be alert about potential encroachments etc. Investment in Gold & silver returns good yield, however with the risk of theft etc. Investing in stocks is safe as you hold it in demat form and it yields a solid return of around 15 to 18% when you hold it at least for 5 years. So, in terms of returns, stock is a good investment option.

KNOW ABOUT MARKET PARTICIPANTS	
Market participants	For a market to be active, there must be buyers & Sellers, Brokers/Banks, medium of Exchange through which trades to be executed, intermediaries to settle the flow of funds between buyer & seller, clearing houses for the movement of scripts from one person to another, a depository to hold the stock scripts in dematerialized form, shortly called Demat and finally a regulator to monitor all these activities and safeguard the interest of all the participants especially those of small retail investors.
Traders	Traders are the core people creating the demand and supply of stock in the market. They are (i) Retail traders who are so called because of their involvement with low capital (ii) Non resident Indians, who by their status of residency and with higher capital involvement, trade usually through their advisors (iii) Institutions like Domestic institutional investors (DII) / Foreign Institutional Investors (FII) who are registered as such and invest their surplus money for the purposes of higher return and Asset Management Companies (AMC) known as Mutual fund operators, for their investment in stock/debt and building up their funds on behalf of their clients. Though all are called so by their needs of investments, the urge for all is the same viz income generation from investments.
Depositories	In India there are two Depositories –CDSL & NSDL-who play the role of (i) exchanging securities based on Stock brokers` advice of transactions put through them by way of selling & buying and corroborated so by Clearing Houses and (ii) safekeeping stocks in electronic form in demat accounts of traders. Traders cannot deal directly with Depositories.
Brokers/Banks	A trader cannot execute their trades directly with stock Exchanges without intermediaries like broking houses/Banks who offer trading platforms for execution of trade. It is through the platforms of these intermediaries that trades are filled to Stock Exchange. Brokers/sub Brokers/ Banks are all registered with SEBI. They are called Depository Participants or DPs for their liaison role in assisting traders to open Demat account and enabling movement of stock scripts in Demat form to Depositories based on the trades executed through them.
Clearing Houses	Two clearing houses, called NSCCL – National Security Clearing Corporation Ltd and ICCL-Indian Clearing Corporation are wholly owned subsidiaries of National Stock Exchange and Bombay Stock Exchange respectively, operate for smooth conduct of operations in clearing and settling funds between exchanges and also to ensure that no defaults occur between traders while buying and selling. A trader cannot interact with these clearing houses.
Stock Markets	In India, there are two stock exchanges National Stock Exchange (NSE) & Bombay Stock Exchange (BSE) which are stock markets. It is through these markets that an investor/trader executes his trade of buying and selling of a listed stock

TRADING STOCKS-BASIC

Regulator	The Securities and Exchange Board of India, called shortly SEBI, is the regulator of the overall activities. SEBI`s role is developing stock exchanges, protecting interest of traders, monitoring performance of depository participants and intermediaries and keeping vigilance over the listed Companies` action, with the aim of securing the interest of traders.
Traders` requirement	From the foregoing, an investor can understand that he needs to open a Trading account& Demat account and link his Bank account to Trading account to facilitate flow of funds for trading. In order to make you understand with more clarity, action flow is given below on how a single buy trade by a trader will activate every one of the market participants.

BUYING A STOCK

1. Contact via online or offline a stock broker (known as Depository participant or simply DP) of your choice to open a Demat a/c with him.
2. Comply with KYC norms etc as prescribed by him
3. Pay appropriate charges for maintenance of your Demat a/c and other charges for opening trading a/c
4. Link your own mobile number, E-mail, and your Bank a/c with Trading a/c for the purpose of flow of funds for trade.
5. Get cleared with DP of all your doubts that will arise while opening a/cs
6. After satisfying himself about your identity, authenticity etc, DP will open a Demat a/c & a Trading a/c in your name and ask you to confirm through a OTP linked to your mobile. Confirm
7. Note your Demat a/c number which will have 16 digits. The first 8 digits represent your DP`s ID (stock broker`s identification number with depository i.e., CDSL/NSDL which is common for all the trading members of stock broker) and the remaining 8 digits which is unique to yourself, represent your BO ID. So, all 16 digits combined i.e., DP ID & BO ID represent your Demat ID.
8. Please be clear that your Depository is here either CSDL or NSDL, DP (depository participant) is your stock broker and BO (beneficial owner) is yourself and you are maintaining demat a/c with NSDL/CDSL through your stock broker (DP).
9. Set your User ID & Pass word for the trading a/c that has been sent to your E-Mail by DP.
10. You will also receive a confirmatory e mail advice from CDSL/NSDL for having opened a Demat a/c in your name as advised by your DP.
11. (Assuming that you want to buy one TCS stock on Monday) Remit adequate fund to your Trading a/c to buy one stock plus appropriate charges of Security Transaction Tax plus GST
12. DP, after close of trading session, reports your trade of buying one stock to NSE or BSE as appropriate including the amount settled, not later than 9.30 AM Tuesday.
13. (Assuming your trade is done in NSE) NSE will send the report with DP no. to NSSCL,(Clg. Corporation)& Depositories.

14. NSSCL in turn, receives the amount, clears the trade and remits to the appropriate Broker/ Exchange, the amount to be settled, to the seller.
15. (Assuming Depository is CDSL) NSSCL reports Depository CDSL on Tuesday evening/ Wednesday morning to enable them for credit of the stock in Buyer`s Demat a/c
16. CDSL processes the report and credits the script to the Buyer`s Demat a/c while sending simultaneously an email advice to the buyer on deposit of script in his Demat a/c on Wednesday evening.
17. This cycle of settlement is referred as T+2, meaning you will receive Demat script at the end of T+2 (T refers to transaction day).
18. Buyer is entitled to trade the stock, if he so wishes, on Thursday trading session.
19. Buyer will also receive a daily report on purchase transaction of one TCS stock from NSE that has taken place, with transaction number.
20. DP will send a Contract note to the buyer with details of the time & date, the price at which the stock was bought and Security Transaction Tax and GST levied by NSE on the purchase. This is important one and the buyer should keep all such contract notes as they are legally admitted document for the transaction.
21. DP will also send an email to the buyer, a weekly/monthly report on Demat holding. Periodicity of reports may vary from DP to DP.

TRADING STOCKS-BASIC

SELLING A STOCK

The same process happens for selling a script. The difference between buying & selling is that (i) instead of depositing the script, CDSL will now withdraw the script from trader`s Demat a/c to transfer it to buyer now and (ii) the seller will be charged additional levy as DP charges for the sale.

Delivery Trade	The activity flow described above is called delivery trade because of involvement of physical delivery of script in Demat form between buyer & seller. In Futures & Options trade, there will not be any physical delivery of scripts because they are derivative contracts on the underlying securities. Traders may find more details on F & O in another chapter.

HOLDING STOCKS AND THE RELATED BENEFITS

Benefits of holding	By holding a share in TCS now, you are entitled to Dividend, Rights issue, Bonus share, Split stock, and voting rights.
Face value	Just like our currency having face value, denominated in Rs 10, or Rs 100/- etc, stocks are issued with face value of Rs 2/ or Rs 5/-or Rs 10/- Face value in stocks is the fixed denominated value whereas it`s market value is assessed value that an investor is willing to pay in the market, based on it`s anticipated future earnings in relation to it`s past performance. When a Co., declares 100 % dividend on the face value of a stock at Rs 10/-, it means Dividend declared is Rs 10/-.

Dividend	This is your share of profit per share as per the Co.`s announcement on dividend for the year. So, if a Co, declares 100% dividend on it`s share whose face value is Rs 10/-, it means your share of profit declared as dividend per share is Rs 10/-. Normally all the profit amount is not distributed to share holders. The Co,. may retain some amount for it`s future needs. Dividend represents the share of profit being distributed to each share holder after it`s retention of some amount as Reserves & Surplus.
Rights issue	Rights issue means share holder`s entitlement of additional share allotment that the Co may offer to it`s existing share holders at the price per share and at the ratio of allotment, set by it and approved by it`s Board. For ex. If TCS declares rights issue at a ratio of 1:1, it means if you hold one TCS share, you are eligible to apply for one share under rights allotment at the price set by the Co,. which is normally less than it`s current market price. In other words, rights issue means offering share to existing share holders at a discounted price, instead of going to Public.
Bonus issue	Bonus issue means offering free shares to existing share holders out of it`s Reserves &Surplus. Bonus issue may also be termed as dividend share owing to it`s no cost offer. Ratio of allotment is done as per approval of the Board of the Co. For ex. If TCS declares bonus issue at a ratio of 1:4, you are entitled to receive one free share if you hold 4 shares. Bonus offer normally will not lead to any increase in market price of the share. Second, bonus issue increases the share holding structure of the Co., without any increase in the equity capital. Hence, it may decrease the future dividends
Stock split	Stock split refers to splitting the face value of the stock from Rs10/- to Rs 1/- or from Rs 5/- to Rs 1/- as per the ratio approved by the Board. If you own one share, the face value of which is Rs 10/- and stock split is announced at 1:2, you will now own 2 shares at the face value of Rs 5/- each. There will not be any change in the value of the share.
Buy back	Buy back means buying back shares from the Public by the Co., when it has surplus cash to dispose. The Co may announce buying back it`s own shares at a fixed price or under a tender process whereby share holder can sell their shares back to the Co. Normally, the offer price set by the Co., is less than it`s market price. Buying back is an initiative to restructure the capital of the Co., and also to prevent other Companies from acquiring majority holdings. Buy back is a reverse process of IPO.

TRADING STOCKS-BASIC

Primary & Secondary market	Primary market refers to trade of allotment to Public, by the Co., pending listing process. Once allotments to Public through the process of Initial Public offer (IPO) is over, scripts are listed by the Co., in Stock Exchanges for enabling trades on stocks by all stake holders. Secondary market, rather, refers to trades on scripts after their listing. In effect all trades in Stock Exchanges are secondary market trades including the one above

IPO (Initial Public offer) & FPO (Follow on Public offer)	Whenever an existing Co., need funds, say for it`s new project or Fixed Asset, it may get the funds (i) from Internal accruals (ii) Loans from Banks (iii) borrow from market by debts like Bonds etc (iv) issue shares to public. For a new Co, source from internal accruals is limited. Availing heavy borrowings from Banks may also position it in excess leverage. So, the Co., may opt for raising equity capital from Public. Initiating the process of IPO for Co., starts from appointing a Merchant Banker to issue, valuing the Co, fixing price band and getting SEBI nod. Allotments are made as per SEBI norms. After the allotments, shares are listed in the Stock exchange. Having raised capital through IPO, a Co., in later year, may raise additional fresh equity capital from Public which is called FPO. Both IPO & FPO are called book building exercise while Buy back is called reverse book building exercise.
OFS	In addition to IPO& FPO, Companies are allowed to raise capital through Offer For Sale route by which promoters off load their shares to public through bidding process for sale to retail & non retail investors. OFS may be done on stand alone or as a part of shares on sale along with the process of IPO/FPO.

KNOW ABOUT YOUR STOCK MARKETS

Market Capitalization	Market capitalization refers a company `s worth with respect to it`s outstanding shares and their current market value in the stock market. To calculate a company's market capitalization, multiply the number of outstanding shares by the current market value of share. For Ex. If a Co`s total outstanding shares in the market is say 10,00,000 shares and the current market value of a share is Rs 80/- it`s market cap is Rs 8 crores.
Market index	Market index is an index of market behavior with assessments based on daily price movement of selective stocks from different sectors in relation to their different weight-age assigned according to their market capitalization. So, higher the price movement of weighted stocks, higher the index and vice versa. Market index simply says how it reacted to pulls and pressures of buyers/sellers by their trading activity on the day. So, if Index is up, market is said to be in boom and if it is down, it indicates it`s fall.
How market Index is derived	A trader need not track the price movement of each and every stock in the market to assess the market behavior. Instead, a basket of high value stocks based on their market cap and earnings performance in each sector is created as benchmark stocks. Price movement of these benchmark stocks are taken as the overall market movement. Bombay Stock Exchange has 30 stocks from different sectors while NSE has 50 stocks from different sectors. These are value based stocks and assigning weight-age are reviewed or stocks are removed from the basket, depending on their changing values and volume traded. For Ex. Assume a stock X has weight-age of 7%. If Market index moves up say by 2%, you may take it that in 2% up move, 7% is attributable to X. In other words, index is sensitive to price changes of a stock according to their assigned weight-age.

Sector specific index	Market index refers to entire market while sector index refers to the specific sector. Index is arrived for each sector based on their price changes in the stocks of that sector. NSE has sector index on Bank, IT, Pharma, Infrastructure, Large cap, Mid cap or Small cap and so on
Bull market	Bull Market refers to a stock market in which prices are rising or expected to rise. Bull market does not mean that prices of all stocks that have been traded on the day are rising.

TRADING STOCKS-BASIC

Bear market	Bear Market refers to a stock market in which prices are falling or expected to fall. Bear market does not mean that prices of all stocks that have been traded on the day are falling. Both Bull and Bear are cyclical in nature because Bull or Bear, the market is determined by demand & supply of stocks. Hence, both Bull or Bear can sustain for prolonged period or be a short lived one, depending on the pulls and pressures of buying & selling.
Market trend	Market trend is the overall direction of a market in a given time/period.
Trending market	Trending market is when the price is making sustained moves in one direction or the other.
Market breadth	Market breadth is analyzer of the number of stocks that are advancing to the number of stocks that are declining in a given index or Stock Exchange in a bull or bear market. In a bull market advancing stocks are high and declining stocks are low. In a bear market it is vice versa.
Market depth	Market depth refers to a market's ability to sustain relatively large market orders without much impact on the price of a stock. This goes to say that if a trader places a buy order of say 20,000 shares of stock X, the market should be able to absorb the trade without much impact of that stock on the market.
Market cycle	Market cycle refers to cyclical changes in the market. This is when the market is at the bottom, buyers start buying as the prices are very low. By doing so, buyers, in effect, push the market up as demands rise, prices also rise. So there is an up move. When the market is at peak, sellers start booking profit by selling the stock at higher price. This pulls down the market as supply overlap demand resulting in fall in prices. Uptrend and downtrend, thus, evolve into market cycle.
Market correction	A correction is a decline of 10% or more in the price of a stock. Corrections can last anywhere from days to months, or even longer. While incurring heavy losses in the short term, a correction can be healthy since in a way this adjusts overvalued asset prices and provides buying opportunities for stocks that are available at rock bottom prices. Normally correction may not last for more than 3/4 months.

<table>
<tr><td colspan="2" align="center">TERMS COMMONLY USED IN STOCK TRADING</td></tr>
<tr><td>OHLC</td><td>OHLC stands for Open, High, Low and Close. It refers to the opening price of a stock, it`s highest price during the day, it`s lowest price during the day and it`s closing price at the end of the day. OHLC helps in predicting the price behavior of the stock. If opening & closing prices indicate higher gap, the stock`s price momentum is said to be stronger while the opening price & closing price is very close, the stock`s momentum is said to be weak. Range between high & low indicates the volatility. An illustration below:-

<table>
<tr><td>Opening price</td><td>Rs 450/-</td><td rowspan="4">1. As the closing price is far higher than the opening price, stock momentum is strong.
2. Difference between high & low is Rs 110/- which indicates the stock is volatile.
3. Closing price is the most important data for technical analysis in charts etc based on which direction of stock`s price is predicted.</td></tr>
<tr><td>Lowest price</td><td>Rs 410/-</td></tr>
<tr><td>Highest price</td><td>Rs 520/-</td></tr>
<tr><td>Closing price</td><td>Rs 500/-</td></tr>
</table>

<table>
<tr><td>Opening price</td><td>Rs 450/-</td><td rowspan="4">1. As the closing price is higher by fewer amount than the opening price, stock momentum is weak.
2. Difference between high & low is Rs 7/- indicates the stock is less volatile.</td></tr>
<tr><td>Lowest price</td><td>Rs 449/-</td></tr>
<tr><td>Highest price</td><td>Rs 456/-</td></tr>
<tr><td>Closing price</td><td>Rs 452/-</td></tr>
</table>
</td></tr>
</table>

TRADING STOCKS-BASIC

Last traded price (LTP)	LTP represents the price at which the stock was lastly traded in the exchange on the day. Do note that LTP is different from closing price as closing price is weighted price, weight being the buy & sell trade and it`s volume on the stock in the last 30 minutes of the closing session.
Bid/Ask price	Ask price is the price at which a seller is ready to sell the stock to you- the buyer. So, when you buy a stock you look at the askprice and buy it. Bid price is the price at which a buyer is ready to buy the stock from you- the seller. So, when you sell a stock, you look at the bidding price and sell the stock. See more details below.
Bid/Ask spread	The gap between the bid and Ask price is called spread. Learn more on spread below.
Momentum	Momentum is the speed at which the price is changing in a stock. This is a trading technique used by traders to take long (buy) position when the change is accelerating up or short (sell) position when the change is accelerating down.
Trend	Trend is the general direction of the price of the asset or market. An uptrend or downtrend are marked by data in Technical Analysis on which you can learn more in later chapters
Volatility	Volatility occurs when a stock`s price moves with big swings either up or down over a sustained period.

Liquidity	Liquidity refers to an asset or a stock which can easily be bought or sold in the stock market
closing price	Closing price is the day`s closing price of a stock. Closing price is important data as various chart analysis are done based on this.
Position Open position Close the position	Position may be said as a condition in which, by trading a stock, a trader creates his market exposure to open until he initiates an opposite trade to close the position. For ex. If an investor owns 100 shares of a stock, he is in open position until it is sold. Open position exists following a buy, called long position and following a sell, called short position. Open positions are closed when opposite trade takes place to nullify the market exposure. Thus long position is nullified by a sell or short position is nullified by a buy. Open position may exist from a minute to months or years while short position cannot exist for more than a day`s trading session except under derivatives contract.
Long- Long position	In stock trading, when you buy a stock with a bullish view, you are said to be long on the stock. Note that when buying a stock to square off existing short position, it is not long. If you buy stocks expecting appreciation in the long run say 3 to 5 years, you are still said to be on long position. Hence long is reference to measurement of time.
Short Intra day Trade	Shorting or short refers to a trade in which a trader sells, first, a stock that he does not own, anticipating fall in it`s price later in the day and squares it off by buying it back. Any nature of trade entails in buying first at low, and selling later at high. Shorting is a reverse of this- meaning, selling first at high, and buying later at low. By employing this strategy trader generates profit in a falling market. Shorting requires high skill in choosing the right time to enter the trade and the right stock that a trader expects will fall later. However, the trader has to square off/ cover the earlier sale by buying the same stock within such time that stock brokers allow for square off or in any case not later than the day`s closing session, failing which stock brokers will square it off at the prevailing market price on that day at the risk and responsibility of the trader, regardless of any loss that may befall on the trader. Short trades, selling, first, and buying it, later, both happening in the same day, is known as intra day trades.
Short position	Short position refers to a position that a trader is exposed to, by virtue of his shorting, means selling a stock and open position caused by such selling, the cover to which is as yet not executed by buying it back.
Square-off	Square off means closing the existing position. In a short trade where selling is executed first, square off is done to close the position by buying it back. In a long trade square off is done to close his existing open position by selling it.
Freak trade	A trade is called a freak trade when it gets executed at a price far away from the current market price, which may happen due to low liquidity

TRADING STOCKS-BASIC

Risk	Risk is the possibility of losing some or all amount invested, depending on various events or market forces that may befall. Risk is an associated feature directly proportionate to expected returns. Higher the return higher the risk and lower the return lower the risk.
52 week high/Low	52 week high/low refers to stock's highest and lowest price in a year.
All time high/low	All time high/low refers to stock's highest/ lowest price in it's history since it's listing in the Stock Exchange.
Upper/lower circuit	A stock may be susceptible to very high volatility owing to corporate news/ policy announcements etc,. In such situations, Stock Exchanges fix price band by which it places restrictions on it's trade with the highest price or lowest price at which a stock can be traded on the day. Through this action, stock Exchanges attempt to protect the interests of retail and small investors.
Volume	Volume is an important data as it's impact on stock's price is more visible. Volume traded on a stock is calculated based on both buy & sell transactions on that stock on a day.
T+2	T+2 represents settlement cycle, T being the transaction day. When a trader buys a stock say on Monday, script will be delivered in his Demat a/c on the evening of Wednesday. So the buyer of the stock can start trading on that stock on Thursday trading session. For a seller, stock script will be withdrawn from his Demat a/c by the close of the session as his buyer is now under T+2 cycle.
Record date Ex-Dividend	Corporate/ Companies declare benefits to its' share holders like dividend/rights issue/bonus issue/ stock split/ voting rights. You are considered eligible for these benefits if only you are a stock holder on a given date which is known as record date. By announcing record date, a Co., determines your eligibility as on that date. Here, settlement cycle T+2 needs to be factored into while arriving at record date. Assume a Co., announces on say 2nd June `19 dividend @ 100% to it's share holders with record date 13th June `19. This means you should have bought their shares on 11th June`19 or earlier since as per settlement cycle your script bought on 11th June will be delivered in your Demat a/c only on 13th June `19. Simply put, your eligibility is determined as per your holding status in Demat a/c. Stocks that are traded after 11th June`19 will be Ex-date/ Ex-dividend /Ex-benefits. Ex means "without".
Cum Dividend	Cum means "with " In the above example, stocks traded between 2nd June to 11th June will be known with cum-dividend.
Settlement Holiday	In the above example, if 13th June`19 falls on settlement holiday, you will be ineligible for the benefit even if you have bought the share on 11th June`19 as your Demat a/c will be delivered only on 14 th June`19.

T+3	In the above example, there is another possibility that you may not be eligible for benefits even if you have bought the share on 11th June `19. In cases of rare occurrence in delivery trade, a seller may not be able to deliver the stock the day he has sold it, which is called short delivery. In such situations, Exchange initiates auction proceedings to procure the stock from the market and arrange delivery of the script to you on T+3 viz one more day from the normal cycle, resulting in your ineligiblity for the benefit.
Large/Mid/ Small cap	Size of the companies is classified as per their market capitalization. Shares of Companies having market cap of Rs 20,000 crores & above are large cap stocks, mid cap with market cap between Rs 5000 crores to 20000 crores & Small cap with market cap below Rs 5000 crores
Blue Chip stocks	Blue chip stocks are shares of very large & well recognized Companies with a long history of sound financial performance
Penny stocks	Penny stocks, also called illiquid stocks whose market price is Rs 10/- & below for which Buyers are very few.
Liquidity	Liquidity refers to an asset or a stock which can easily be bought or sold in the stock market
Return	Return on an asset or stock is the money gained or lost on investment with reference to holding period of the investment
Portfolio	Portfolio refers to collection of various financial investments like stock, bonds, ETFs, Mutual Funds, Sovereign Gold Bonds etc in diversified manner with the intention of earning returns by holding them in a long term perspective.

TRADING STOCKS-BASIC

EVENTS THAT IMPACT YOUR STOCK MARKET
An investor should know that stock markets reflect the strength and weakness of overall economy of the nation by their movements of index. Hence, stock market is prone to impact from policy initiatives, like RBI monetary Policy, Govt., budgets, Govt. spending policy, inflationary pressures, Nation`s trade imbalance, Foreign Exchange reserves implying foreign Currency movements in relation to local currency, stability of the Banking system, status of money markets, Household savings, Corporate savings, Stability of the Govt., Corporate` earnings and their ease of doing business, effect & counter effect of policy announcements on the economy etc. As the scope of the book is limited to stock trading, few important events are listed below which are very likely to impact stock markets. However, any impact cannot prolong for sustained period as markets adjust themselves to such events by self-correction and reflecting their correction in price movements of stocks/assets in the short or medium term. Eventually, any prudent government will aim at framing and implementing economic policies that it hopes will sustain growth of economy without yielding to inflationary pressures because inflation erodes value of investment

Reserve Bank of India`s Repo rate, Reverse Repo rate	RBI`s role in economy is formulating monetary policy to control money supply and inflation. Repo rate is a rate at which RBI lends money to commercial Banks for short term, by purchasing collateral securities offered by commercial Banks. Reverse repo rate is the rate at which RBI accepts funds from commercial banks, by repurchasing collateral securities offered by commercial Banks and pay interest on them. So, purchase and repurchase are facilities from RBI intended to lend/accept emergency funding arrangement for commercial banks. Increase in repo rate generally leads to increase in cost of borrowing to public. So, by increasing or decreasing Repo rate and reverse repo rate, RBI performs balancing act to control money supply/liquidity in the economy and inflation through banking operations of commercial banks. Other measures that RBI employ to control liquidity include changing commercial Banks` reserve requirements, supporting/regulating fund markets/ buying & selling Government bonds/Bills, regulating NBFCs/Co-operative Societies engaged in banking, regulating forex rates etc.
Govt., budget	While RBI`s policy measures come under monetary policy initiatives, those announced usually, in Union Govt.`s budget session fall under fiscal policy initiative. Govt`s announce their spending programme and/or tax policies and other measures based on their assessment of economy. In stagnating or falling economy Govts., spend more on infrastructure projects/Schemes to create more jobs and raise demand for goods and services. Another measure is offer of incentives on tax rates in personal/Corporate taxes in order to fuel demand. In rising economy policies are moderated to suck in excess liquidity like by higher tax rates or by slowing it`s spending with a view to control inflationary pressures. Govt`s fiscal policy measures have direct influence on creation of jobs, income, consumer spending etc,. and hence more sensitive to public debates/ criticism. Measures to fuel economy and it`s growth has positive effect on stock markets as these measures lead to higher corporate / personal/household savings and stimulate stock markets investments.
Corporate` Performance	Corporate` earning play an important role in stock markets. Corporate cannot earn profit unless it has supporting policy roles from Govt., like infra structure creation, clear taxation policy, smooth labor policy, enhancing / facilitating supply chains from local/abroad, Macroeconomic policies to augment income/ disposable income to fuel consumer spending, creating a favorable international market by open/transparent policies, besides, initiating flexible/ appropriate trade agreements with other nations, etc. Increased corporate earnings will spur growth by plough back their profit in expansion or new ventures. Thus, higher earnings of Corporate lead to higher dividends and more investor in stock trade.

TRADING STOCKS-BASIC

SPREADS

BID-ASK SPREAD

Bid- Ask spread refers to difference between bidding price and asking price of an asset in the market. If you want to buy a stock you buy it at ask price (quoted by a seller of that stock) Similarly, when you sell, you sell at the bidding price (quoted by a buyer of your stock). A tabular below will enhance your understanding:-

Buyer X quotes say Rs 500/-to buy stock A in the market		Seller Y quotes say Rs 501/-to sell stock A in the market	
Now bidder is	Now his Bid price is	Now seller is	Now his ask price is
Buyer X	Rs 500/-	Seller Y	Rs 501/-*
When you sell, you place order to sell at BID price		When you buy, you place order to buy at ask price	
You sell to buyer X at BID price of Rs 500/-		You buy from seller Y at ASK price of Rs 501/-	

Note:-*Logic of selling at higher price is due to the fact that a seller, here Y, will always like to sell, at a price, as high as possible, while, a buyer, here X, will always like to buy at a price, as low as possible because motive of both buyer & seller is to maximize their profit. In the above example, spread is Rs1/ -. To keep in memory, to buy just know "ask to buy" i.e., a to b, the remaining one i.e., bid to sell to sell.

KNOW ABOUT BID-ASK SPREAD

Knowledge on Bid-Ask spread is essential for your regular trading activity. Bid-Ask spread in the above example is Rs 1/- which is narrow. It means the stock`s liquidity is high owing to heavy demand and supply for the stock. By quoting it with two way quote, it is 500/501 meaning bid price is Rs 500/-(demand for the stock) and ask price (supply of the stock) is Rs 501/-It further indicates that swing in stock`s price is high, besides, being with great liquidity. On the other hand, if in the above example, bid/ask quote is say Rs 499/502 It means spread has widened indicating change in demand and supply. Widening spread may happen (i) when professionals deliberately create it to trade on spread trading in Options contract (ii) when stock is a penny stock and illiquid one (iii) when stock is a small cap stock with less demand. Hence narrow spread is a signal to a stock`s liquidity. Having said that, bid-ask spread also gets widened If a stock is highly volatile or the market is volatile. A stock is said to be volatile when there is rapid fluctuations in it`s price action for unspecific duration of time. Please learn more on various types of orders below.

Narrow Bid-ask spread	Wide Bid-ask spread
1. Narrow spread shows that the stock`s liquidity is high and actively traded in the market with high demand and supply for that stock	1. Wide spread shows that the stock is not actively traded in the market with investors showing less interest in trading the stock
2. Narrow spread stocks, due to their high liquidity, have higher possibilities of executing your various orders placed in the market	2. Wide spread has a less possibility of executing your orders in full because of the low liquidity of the stock

3. If large volume of stocks is on trade, you have a probability of executing the trade in a price advantageous to you.	3. Owing to less liquidity of the stock, it may not be possible to trade in an advantageous price as much as a liquid stock does.

VARIOUS ORDER FORMS FOR STOCK TRADING
As a trader and a reader as well, you are entering into a very important portion of study. Your success of trade is decisive on proper understanding of various orders and its` effectiveness on your trade. Hence, a trader should know the following order types thoroughly and their merits & demerits on its` deployment in the stock trading. Ultimately, suitability of deployment of one or the other order rests with the trader`s view on the market and price reaction of a stock.

TRADING STOCKS-BASIC

MARKET ORDER & LIMIT ORDER	
Market order	There are two basic orders, market order and limit order. Market order is the most basic order of simply buying and selling a security or a stock at the current market price. In a market order a trader places a buy order at the offer price and a sell order at the bid price. As this order involves no complexities and a straight forward one, it is filled at the Exchange immediately by stock brokers and orders are executed in the quickest possible time. In market order trader`s prime desire is it`s execution at any price in the market.
How market orders are executed	Market orders are executed by the Stock Exchange at the available offer/ bid price at the moment of time For ex. if you place market order to buy, Stock exchange will execute your buy order at the lowest offer price of a seller at that time. Similarly, in a sell order, Stock exchange will execute your sell order at the highest price quoted by a buyer at that time.
When market order is suitable	If in a trader`s view the stock is not volatile and he minds only execution of trade and not the price, he can place market order. This order is suitable for highly liquid stocks with less volatility. If a stock is too volatile, market order is not the right order to place. In essence, in market order, trader has no control over the stock`s price while, at the same time, execution of trade is certain.
Limit order	By Limit order trader sets a specific price or better price at which he intends to buy or sell the stock. This order, however, does not give guarantee that the order will be executed at the set price. Execution of your order depends on your set price hitting or breaching the last traded price with adequate volume at the given time. So, in a trade with limit order, trader`s prime concern is the price and it`s execution is secondary. Note that you cannot set a limit order to buy above the market price or to sell below the market price as better prices are available at the current trading itself. For Ex. current market price to buy a stock is say Rs 200/- and you set a limit price to buy at Rs 210/-Exchange will execute your trade at Rs 200/- i.e., at market rate and not at Rs 210/-as the market price is more beneficial to you than your set price by Rs 10/-

How limit orders are executed	Limit orders are executed when the set price hits or breaches last traded price. For ex. if a stock`s current market price is say Rs 250/- and a seller sets a sell limit order say at Rs 260/-, stock exchange will not execute his order till the stock`s market price hits at Rs 260/-and also till a bid price at Rs 260/- is available. Assuming adequate bidders for the stock@ Rs 260/-, Exchange will execute the trade @ Rs 260/- or higher. On the other hand, if his sell limit price is say Rs 249/-, order will be executed at market rate of Rs 250/, since best bids are available at higher price than his limit price.
When limit order is suitable	If, in a trader`s view, the stock is volatile with high swings, he may specify the price at which he intends to trade the stock. However, even if limit price is hit, limit order may not be executed owing to fast movs in price. In such trades trader may use stop loss order or GTT order.

	Market order	Limit order
Comparison of market order vs limit order	1. Trade is executed instantly at market price 2. Trade execution is fast and guaranteed 3. Market order is not the right choice for high volatile stock 4. For large volume trades, market order is right choice as there is no fear of non execution 5. Market order cannot be visible in the market as the order is executed instantly	1. Trade is executed at market rate after hitting set price 2. Trade execution is only when the set price hits last traded price and so not guaranteed. 3. Limit order is right one for volatile stock, preferably with Stop loss 4. For large volume trade, limit order may go unfilled and lead to partial execution or non- execution 5. Limit order with set price can be visible in the market till it is executed.

TRADING STOCKS-BASIC

STOP LOSS ORDER (SL)

In order to give more choices on placing order, Stock Exchanges offer two more types called Stop-loss (SL) order and GTT (Good Till Triggered) order. Stop Loss order is intended to limit your loss. By placing stop loss order, either in the market order or limit order, a trader protects himself against high fluctuations in the price in the short term and gets an opportunity to enter or exit the trade when it is suited to him. Placing Stop Loss is desirable but equally desirable is choosing the appropriate Stop Loss price. Learn more below, on how to choose stop loss price in various order types. For trading large volume of stocks, Stop loss order may not be the right choice. Stop Loss orders are valid for the day only.

Stop Loss price	Normally, when quarterly or annual results are likely to be announced shortly or when stocks` performance have beaten or dumped street estimates or when, in traders` opinion, few Govt., policy changes or new technology advancements will spoil or spur a company`s future performance, stocks of that Company are swiftly traded with heavy demand and supply, resulting in huge swings in price action. For instance, assume, a trader wants to buy a stock at Rs 190/- while it`s current market price is Rs 200/-. If the price of the stock falls to Rs 190/-, jolly well, he will buy it. Contrary to it, if, due to swift price action, his trade went against him, i.e., if the price rises instead of falling and if, still he wants to buy, he may place SL at Rs 210/-. By placing SL, he instructs his stock brokers not to buy it at a price above Rs 210/-
Trigger price	A trader may note the difference between Market order &Limit order with SL and without SL. Market order & Limit orders are filled by stock brokers to Exchanges instantly whereas in orders with stop loss, stock brokers fill only trigger price i.e., Stop Loss price to Exchanges. Only when trigger price hits LTP, stock brokers fire the full order to Exchanges for execution. So, stop Loss price is also called trigger price.
Execution with SL	Prices may move so fast that after hitting trigger price but before filing the full order, price may surge past your stop loss price. Chances of non execution of your trade are possible in such volatile stock/market. So, while placing SL, a trader should take into account potential profit or loss and stock`s volatility and try to set SL in such a way that the order does not go unfilled and he does not miss a chance of gaining potential profit also.
STOP LOSS MARKET ORDER	
When it is suitable to placeSL with market order	Stop loss in market order is suitable in intra-day trading. For ex., intra-day trader, anticipating fall in price of a stock, may sell first, say at Rs 120/-(current market rate) hoping to repurchase it to square off later in the day at lower price, say at Rs 100/- If he fears that the trade may go against him later with surge in buy price above Rs 120/-he may restrict his loss by placing stop loss buy order say at Rs 130/-Reversely, in a rising market an intra-day trader may buy a stock first, say at Rs 120/-(current market rate) hoping to sell it later in the day say at Rs 140/- to square off. If he fears that the trade may go against him later with fall in sell price below Rs 120/-he may place stop loss sell order,say at Rs 110/-to restrict his loss. (Note buying first and selling later within the day has few restrictions as per SEBI)
How SL with market order is executed	In the above example, your stock broker will fill the Exchange, with your SL price Rs 130/- as trigger price for buy and Rs 110/-as trigger price for sell. When the trigger price hits LTP, stock broker will fire your order to Exchange and Exchange, in turn, executes your buy or sell order at available price at MARKET RATE, depending on availability of the offer price from sellers at that time and volume on offer. Note that in a stop loss market order, trader chooses just stop loss price only.
Risks involved in SL Market orders	When Stop Loss is hit and Exchange is filled, trade is executed as market order i.e., at the market rate or at the next available bid/offer price in the market. If the fall or rise in prices is sharp, you may be put to further loss, by buying at higher price or selling at lower price than what you try to control by stop loss. To protect against these losses, Stop Loss Limit order is a better option for a trader.

TRADING STOCKS-BASIC

STOP LOSS LIMIT ORDER

Stop loss market orders are risky due to the fact that once SL is hit and filled in the Exchange, it becomes market order where prices may move in any direction. In order to avoid such unforeseen risks, SL may be set with a limit price. Stop loss limit order has, thus, one more option for a trader that allows him to choose two prices, (i) stop loss price (trigger price)(ii) specific, limit price. By doing so, he conditions his trade within a range of price i.e., between stop loss price (trigger price) and limit price. Upon hitting SL, his order becomes a limit order.

When SL limit order is suitable	Assume a stock is trading say @ Rs 658/- You have missed an opportunity to get allotment in it`s recent IPO and, therefore, you like to buy the stock now. You are doubtful about the stability of the price as you feel it is highly volatile with indications like (ii) opening price is say 5% higher than it`s previous day`s closing price (ii) candle formation is long blue in a time frame of say 15 minutes (ii) you are convinced that the volatility is due to a positive announcement from the Company and the surge in price will be sustained for few more days. At the same time, you feel the price is quite expensive as it`s fundamentals are yet to hit the market. In such scenario or similar to it, you may place SL limit order. Predicting price action through candle formation is a part of technical analysis on which learn more in another chapter
Placing SL limit order	As said earlier, a trader needs to choose two prices. Revisit the above example where stock is trading @ Rs 658/-. Here, he may set SL @ 660/- & limit price say @ Rs 662/- in a buy order-i.e.,658 (CMP)-660 (SL)-662 (LIMIT) in ascending order for buy trade. Trader, by placing this type of order, indicates that he is ready to buy the stock at a price between Rs660/- to Rs 662/- and not above Rs 662/-On placement of order, stock broker will fill trigger price i.e SL to Stock Exchange. Upon hitting the SL, stock broker will fire the order to Exchange. Exchange will execute the limit order @Rs 662/- or below, subject to availability of offers at the limit price or lower and the volume on offer. Similarly, trader, in sell order, will set, say Rs 656/-as SL &say, Rs 655/- as limit price-i.e., 658 (CMP)-656 (SL)-655 (LIMIT) in descending order for sell trade. Sale, upon hitting Rs 656/-, will be executed @ Rs 655/-or above.

HOW TO SET LIMIT ORDER (WITHOUT STOP LOSS)–INDICATIVE

Assuming Current market price of a stock @ Rs 250/-(CMP)	
To BUY	To SELL
Limit price may be set at above or below CMP-Here@Rs245/-	Limit price may be set at above or below CMP-Here @Rs 255/-
Limit price is 2% below CMP	Limit price is 2% above CMP
1. Select appropriate Limit as per your view on stock- here 2% below CMP	1. Select appropriate Limit as per your view on stock- here 2% above CMP
2. Place the order and it is filled instantly to Stock Exchange	2. Place the order and it is filled instantly to Stock Exchange
3. When limit price Rs 245/-is hit, limit order becomes buy market order	3. When limit price Rs 255/-is hit, limit order becomes sell market order

4. Upon hitting limit price, current market is now at Rs 245/-	4. Upon hitting limit price, current market is now at Rs 255/-
5. Exchange will execute the order at the available best offer price @Rs 245/- or below	5. Exchange will execute the order at the available best bid price @Rs 255/-or above
Disadvantage:-	
Order may NOT be executed (i) if, during the entire day`s trading session, stock`s LTP does not hit the limit price or (ii) if LTP has already crossed above your limit price in buy order and below your limit price in sell order due to sharp price movements.	

TRADING STOCKS-BASIC

HOW TO SET MARKET ORDER WITH STOP LOSS–INDICATIVE	
Assuming current market price (CMP)@ Rs 456/-	
To BUY	To SELL
Assume setting Stop Loss price @Rs 460/- (0.87% above CMP)	Assume setting Stop Loss price @Rs 450/-(1.31 % below CMP)
1. Select appropriate SL as per your view on stock- here 0.87 % above CMP	1. Select appropriate SL as per your view on stock- here 1.31% below CMP
2. Stock broker fills SL as trigger to Stock Exchange	2. Stock broker fills SL as trigger to Stock Exchange
3. When trigger is hit @Rs 460/,-Broker fires the order to Exchange	3. Whentrigger is hit @Rs 450/,-Broker fires the order to Exchange
4. Upon hitting trigger price, current market is now at Rs 460/-	4. Upon hitting trigger price, current market is now at Rs 450/-
5. The order becomes now Market buy order	5. The order becomes now Market sell order
6. Exchange will execute the order at the available best offer price	6. Exchange will execute the order at the available best bid price
Disadvantage:-	
1. Order may not be executed if, at the end of the day, LTP of the stock does not hit the trigger price.	
2. If the price climbs up or down sharply before Broker fires the order to Exchange, It may happen that you end up buying at Rs 460/- or at any rate and selling at Rs 450/- or at any rate i.e., both trades at current market rate.	
HOW TO SET LIMIT ORDER WITH STOP LOSS–INDICATIVE	
To BUY	To SELL
Assume Stop Loss price @Rs 660/-	Assume Stop Loss price @Rs /-656/-
Assume Limit price @Rs 662/-(0.61% above CMP)	Assume Limit price @Rs 655/-(0.46% below CMP)
1. Select appropriate limit price as per your view on stock- here 1.06 % above CMP	1. Select appropriate limit price as per your view on stock- here 0.91% below CMP

2. Select SL aligned to limit price and place the order	2. Select SL aligned to limit price and place the order
3. Stock broker fills SL as trigger to Stock Exchange	3. Stock broker fills SL as trigger to Stock Exchange
4. When trigger is hit @Rs 660/,-Broker fires the order to Exchange	4. When trigger is hit @Rs 656/,-Broker fires the order to Exchange
5. Upon hitting trigger price, current market is now at Rs 660/-	5. Upon hitting trigger price, current market is now at Rs 656/-
6. The order becomes now Limit buy order	6. The order becomes now limit sell order
7. Exchange will execute the buy order in the price range of Rs 660/- to Rs 662/-& not above @ Rs 662/-	7. Exchange will execute the sell order in the price range of Rs 656/- to Rs 655/- & not below Rs 655/-

Stop Loss setting:-
If SL is far from CMP like Rs 670in buying & Rs 640/- in selling-you pay higher price to buy & sell at too low price. On the other hand, if you set SL too close like Rs 658.50/-in buy & Rs 657.80/- in sell,you may miss the trading opportunity also, if the price movement is too swift and sharp,
Disadvantage:-
Assuming current market price (CMP)@ Rs 658/-
1. Order may not be executed if, at the end of the day, stock does not hit the trigger price i.e., stop loss price
2. If, after hitting and before firing the order by Broker to Exchange, stock crosses already above Rs 662/-in buy order and below Rs 655/- in a sell order owing to sharp rise and fall in price, your order is vulnerable to still open position. In such scenario, your loss may be higher.

TRADING STOCKS-BASIC

COMPARISON BETWEEN STOP LOSS MARKETORDER&STOP LOSS LIMIT ORDER	
SL Market Order	SL Limit Order
1. Trader sets SL (Trigger price) only	1. Trader sets two prices: SL (Trigger price)& Limit price
2. Upon hitting SL, order becomes market order	2. Upon hitting SL, order becomes a normal limit order
3. Upon hitting SL, possibility of execution is reasonably high	3. Upon hitting SL, possibility of execution depends on price qualifying limit price
4. Trader has less control over the price after hitting SL	4. Trader continues to hold control over the price with limit price

POINTS TO KEEP IN MIND WHILE PLACING STOP LOSS

1. Loss in trade occurs when your trade goes against your anticipation i.e., price falls when you anticipate rise in price or vice versa. In order to protect from such trends, you put stop loss in opposite price action i.e., loss from rising price in buy order and loss from falling price in sell order. So, you fix SL price above current market price (CMP) in buy order and below current market price (CMP) in sell order. Having fixed SL price, your limit order price should be above SL price in buy order and below SL price in sell order. If SL prices are not set properly, chances are there that trading platforms of stock brokers reject your SL order showing error message. Hence know the correct way of setting SL Price and Limit price, indicative example of which is as under:-

Type of order	If CMP Is	Set buy SL Price @	Set buy Limit Price @	Order to buy	If CMP is	Set sell SL Price @	Set sell Limit Price @	Order to sell
SL Market order	100	101	NA	SL should be above CMP	100	99	NA	SL should be below CMP
SL Limit order	100	101	102	Set ascending-100-101-102	100	99	98	Set descending-100-99-98

In other words, SL Price (trigger price) < limit price in buy order. SL Price (trigger price) > limit price in sell order.

2. In stop loss limit order, SL price may also be set to be equal to limit price in both buy or sell order. However, it is preferable to set a gap between SL price & Limit price because, with gap in price, chances of sudden surge past the limit price is less than that in case of both SL & Limit price being equal, leaving non- execution or partial execution of trade less probable to occur.

3. SL price is picked in the above example for the purpose of illustration. In actual trade, Trader, however, needs to set SL Price through S&R, Candlestick patterns Moving average etc which are meant to predict the price action of a stock in advance, the study on which is called Technical Analysis. Learn Technical Analysis in the following chapters.

4. Placing stop loss orders is convenient way of trading to restrict your loss in a volatile stock / market. If you find the market is too volatile to predict sustained price action, exit the market for the time being or till the time volatility is off and enter the market later, instead of deploying stop loss.

5. By placing SL order, Trader should not assume that his trade will be executed. Instead, it is good for him to wait for confirmation on execution of his trade.

6. In the event of non execution or partial execution, options before a trader is (i) modify SL price & limit price according to current trend or (ii) wait till the price climbs up or down to meet your limit price (iii) exit the trade. Note that SL is valid for the day only.

TRADING STOCKS-BASIC

GOOD TILL TRIGGERED (GTT) ORDER

GTT is another specific order available for a trader, which is as good as SL Limit order, except with a few differences.

(1) In GTT order, trader sets trigger price & limit price. When trigger price is hit GTT order is filed in Exchange. However, GTT order cannot be executed for any reason, trader has to replace the order afresh manually again. Once trigger price is hit, GTT order will become limit order

(2) In GTT order too, trader needs to set trigger price like in SL limit order i.e., trigger price < limit price in buy order & trigger price > limit price in sell order.

(3) GTT order is valid for one year (SL Limit order is valid for a day) At the end of one year, GTT order will be cancelled.

(4) GTT can be placed in percentage terms.

(5) Before placing GTT order, check with your brokers if they are offering it in their trading platform. If offered, check with various terms and conditions they stipulate for placing GTT orders. Note that terms and conditions for GTT orders may vary among stock brokers.

BRACKET ORDER (FOR INTRA DAY TRADE)

(i) Bracket order allows you to place 3 orders in ONE GO. Order no.(1) is to create buy or sell position. Order no.(2) is for profit booking, indicating a price at which you want to book profit on opposite trade of your Order no.(1) to square off/cover the position. Order no.(3) Stop loss price at which you want to cut loss on your order no.(1). For Ex. **If order no 1 is to buy, order no. 2 is high side sell limit order & order no.3 is low side sell stop loss order. Similarly, If order no1 is to sell, order no.2 is low side buy limit order & order no.3 is low side buy stop loss order**

(ii) Order no (2) & (3) are ALWAYS in the opposite direction of Order no (1), meaning If order no (1) is for BUY, orders no. (2) & (3) for SELL and vice versa

(iii) On successful completion of the Order no.(1),orders (2) & (3) are triggered. If profit booking price of square off/cover is reached FIRST, Order no.(2) will be executed & position squared off. So, order no.(3) viz Stop loss will be cancelled

(iv) If stop loss is reached FIRST, Order no.(3) will get executed & your position is squared off. So, order no.(2) for profit booking will be cancelled.

(V) Bracket order cannot be placed in BSE trades.

(vi) Bracket orders are for intra-day trades and only few Stock brokers offer this.

Disadvantages	By placing BO, you cannot exit position partially. You have to exit all at once. BO cancellation is not possible once entered. BO can be closed only by closing the position. Limit orders are not possible during exit. Executed exit price will be done at market price. BO is not permitted in stock option.
Caution	BO can be used ONLY for Intra-day trades. All BO s are squared off automatically before market close. BO s are banned in BSE in stock, stock option, currency option & Multiple Commodity Exchange. Factoring into various restrictions on exit and others, experienced traders may use BO.

	COVER ORDER (FOR INTRA DAY TRADE)
Cover order is an opposite order to close the existing open position. For example, if one`s existing open position is long, his cover order will be a sell order and if open position is short, cover order will be a buy order.	
Caution	CO` s are banned in BSE in stock, stock option, currency option & Multiple Commodity Exchange
Advice to traders	Bracket & Cover orders are for intra-day trades and only few stock brokers offer this orders because of too many complexities involved. Hence trader are advised to use these orders only when they have sufficient experience.
	ONE CANCELLS OTHER ORDER (OCO)
This order allows placing two orders in one pair. When one order is executed, the other order is automatically cancelled.	

CHAPTER 2

FUNDAMENTAL ANALYSIS

CONTENTS

1 Investment class/Non-investment class stocks
2 Quarterly/Annual reports/Know your Corporate-Important Aspects to check
3 Leveraged funds-How It is useful
4 Model Balance sheet, Assets & Liabilities
5 Cash Flow Statement-Indicative example of how Cash Flow Statement is arrived
6 Operational Activity, Investing Activity, Financing Activity
7 Notes on why changes are made in CFS and what Cash Flow Statement discloses
8 Profitability Ratios
9 Leverage ratios
10 Operational Efficiency Ratios
11 Valuation Ratios

WHAT IT NEEDS TO IDENTIFY INVESTMENT CLASS STOCK	An investment is an asset acquired with the aim of generating income through it`s appreciation. Stocks are instruments of investment Not all stocks but only those which are fundamentally strong tend to appreciate and create wealth in the long run ie more than 3 years. So, knowledge on quantitative analysis, also known as Fundamental Analysis, is essential for both Long term investors & short term traders, in order to identify and segregate stocks which are fundamentally strong and worth investing known as investible grade stock and other stocks which give less or no return..
WHAT IS INVESTIBLE AND NON-INVESTIBLE GRADE STOCK	An investible grade stock which yields higher annual return year on year compared to other stocks with less or no return, is characterized by two attributes called Qualitative aspect & Quantitative aspect. Qualitative aspect deals with analyzing the Company`s background, business profile, management expertise, business ethics, competitive advantage, R &D efforts etc Quantitative analysis also known as Fundamental analysis, deals with various financial parameters like operational efficiency, earnings, profit, cash flow, dividend pay out earning per stock, book value to stock etc
WHAT IS ANNUAL REPORT	Annual report is a document that a corporate must publish and provide annually to shareholders, spelling out their operations and financial conditions in the past year with forecasts for the future operations. Annual report contains corporate information, operating & financial highlights, Management discussion and analysis, Financial section including the balance sheet, income statement, and cash flow statement, Notes to the financial statements, Auditor's report, Directors report, Report on Corporate Governance. Publication of Annual report is mandatory and must be submitted to shareholders, Registrar of Companies, Ministry of Company Affairs, Stock Exchanges and SEBI. All the data and statements from Annual report are critically analyzed from the perspective of Qualitative & Quantitative analysis to grade the stocks and award ratings by rating Agencies.
QUARTERLY REPORTS	Corporate are mandated to release quarterly reports about their performance usually quarter ending June, Sept, Dec & March. An investor can go through such reports besides Annual reports to take an informed decision.

IMPORTANT SECTIONS IN ANNUAL REPORT

Operating &financial Highlights report about the financials of the company in the year gone by with comparison over a longer period of time. Management statement often called as Chairman`s report gives details about the positioning of the business. Management discussion and analysis reports economy at macro level, trends in Industry, outlook/forecast for the business in domestic/ international level

Profit & Loss a/c	Is a report of income and expenses over a given period time normally for the year end. This a/c details source of income, earned from various operations & expenses or loss that have been met in the process of earning such income, arriving the net surplus or deficit called Profit or Loss. This a/c is the base document from which flows all other statements- Balance sheet & Cash flow statement

Balance Sheet	Is a financial statement that reports how much it owns (Asset) & how much it owes to others (Liability) and how much it holds as shareholders equity at a specific point of time, normally, as at the end of a particular financial year, indicating also it`s previous year`s position side by side. It is a financial statement based on which various ratios including rate of return to shareholders are computed to assess the financial health of the corporate.
Cash flow statement	One of the important statements that one has to go through to see whether cash flow from operations, increases in comparison with industry average/ peers before adding cash flow from Investment & financial activity.
Auditors` report	Perusing the Auditor`s report one can find any lapses/defaults/commissions/ omissions that will have an impact on the financial condition of the Company. Especially, qualitative Comments of Auditors should be looked into from the angle of impact that may cause or alter financial health of the Co.
NOTE 1	All ratio analysis of any Company that has released recently it`s Annual report/ Quarterly report can be seen in website screener.in. Trader need not calculate ratios.

FUNDAMENTAL ANALYSIS

KNOW YOUR CORPORATE (KYC)

Before choosing a stock, an investor must have knowledge on the Co., and their background on various aspects briefly detailed below:

Background	1. Who are the promoters?	2. Their educational qualification	3. Prior experience in the field	4. Credit worthiness &capacity
	5. Core competence to highlight	6. Seamless& clean chit character	7. Resident or non-resident	8. Non political affliation
	9. New or old entrepreneurs	10. Financially sound	11. Promoters from one family	
Constitution	1. Listed Co since when	2. Small or mid or large cap Co	3. Stand alone or subsidiary Co	4. Subsidiary/ parent/Holding Co
	5. Promoters` capital	6. Shareholding pattern	7. Holding % of FII, DII,MF	8. Corporate & Regd.office
	9. Auditors to the Co.	10. Corporate Governance policy	11. Transparency	12. Declared mission of the Co
Capital	1. Authorised, issued &Paid up	2. Promoters share capital	3. Tier 2 capital/ Bond/Debentur	4. Bank Loan funds
	5. General Reserves & surplus	6. Specific reserves, if any		

Business Activity	1. Sector-IT/ FMCG/Infra/etc	2. Manufacturing or Services	3. Tech or non tech	4. Location of Plant/factory
	5. Supply chain-Local/Abroad	6. Import substitution	7. Entry in new or existing field	8. Product-existing /new market
	9. Competitors/ Rivals	10. Maket share of the Co.	11. Entitlement to Govt. subsidy	12. Organic/ inorganically grown
	13. Technology/ Franchisee agrmt	14. Royalty Pay out	15. Performance growth	16. Principal Banker to the Co
	17. R & D effort			
Management Team	1. CEO & his leadership profile	2. Profile of all Directors	3. Salary & perqs of Directors	4. Independent Directors
	5. CSR Policy approved by Board	6. Compliance of BSE/NSE/SEBI	7. Growth Co or mature Co	8. Dividend policy
	9. Compliance of Govt. directives	10. Submission of Qly/Anl. report	11. Labor relations	12. Awards achieved if any

An investor cannot gather the above information at one go. The brief description is to highlight its` importance and make an investor conscious of the above in more detailed fashion because it is his money that an investor is going to invest in the Co.

FUNDAMENTAL ANALYSIS

LEVERAGE

Leverage refers to use of borrowed funds to finance Project expansion or for any purpose of investing activity with the aim of increasing the return to share holders. Instead of raising capital through additional equity offer to public, a Co., leverages it`s activity by borrowed funds. So, leverage may be termed as a Co.,`s strategy in relation to it`s capital funding structure. Positive effect of leveraged funds is enhanced return by way of dividend to share holders, besides, increase in value of the Co. On the other hand, highly leveraged position means enjoying large loan inconsistent to it`s earnings that may pull down it`s debt servicing. Thus, while Leverages appear to increase the financial obligation of the Co., it is quite possible that it increases returns to shareholders. For example, If two Companies have the same capital structure, one with equity alone and another with equity and loan funds, the Co., with the leveraged funds could yield higher return to shareholders because the leveraged Co., can claim tax benefit on interest paid on loan funds. An illustration below highlights the point.

Gross profit :-40%	Tax on profit:-40%	Interest on loan:-14%

Company X		Company Y	
Equity	10,00,000	Equity	4,00,000
Debt	Nil	Debt	6,00,000

Profit before Tax	4,00,000	Profit before Tax	4,00,000
		Less interest on Debt	84,000
Profit before Tax	4,00,000	Profit before Tax	3,16,000
Tax on profit @ 40%	1,60,000	Tax on profit @ 40%	1,26.400
Profit after Tax	2,40,000	Profit after Tax	1,89,600
Return on equity-24%		Return on equity-47.4%	

FUNDAMENTAL ANALYSIS

BALANCE SHEET (BS)	
Before proceeding to analyze balance sheet, an investor should know it`s fundamentals so that it is easier for him to disseminate further. Balance sheet is a statement of assets and liabilities disclosing the Co.`s financial health.	

TWO SIDES OF B/S	Balance sheet has two sides, viz Assets and Liabilities each of which is equal in value to the other in aggregate
WHAT THEY INDICATE	Assets are those owned by the Co., while liabilities are those that the Co. owe to others
FINANCIAL OBLIGATIONS	Balance sheet is a report of financial condition or status of a Co. In another way, Balance sheet tells the financial obligation of the Co, to it`s shareholders and general public, by way of what it owns and what it owes to others, segregating them into long term & short term obligations that have potential impact on it`s operational activity in the long and short run. Long term are those that obligate the Co after 1 year or more while short term does so within 12 months

WHAT ARE LONG TERM & SHORT TERM ASSETS & LIABILITES	**LIABILTIY**		**ASSET**
	<u>Share holders` funds</u> 1. Share Capital 2. Reserves & surplus <u>Long Term Liability</u> 1. Debentures/Bonds 2. Long Term Debt (Repayable after 1 year or more) 3. Prepaid advance received) (For services to be rendered after 1 year) 4. Defrred Tax Liability		<u>Long Term Asset</u> <u>Tangible asset</u> 1. Land & Building (Gross block &Net block) 2. Plant &Machinery (Gross block &Net block) 3. Capital work in progress 4. Fixtures &Vehicles (Gross block &Net block) 5. Investments on long term maturity 6. Investments in other Cos <u>Intangible asset</u> 1. Patent 2. Good will 3. Copy right 4. Trade mark

	Current Liability	Current Asset
	1. Short Term Bank loan	1. Cash & Bank balance
	2. Accounts Payable	2. Short term investments
	3. Dividends payable	3. Accounts Receivable
	4. Advance received	4. Inventory
	(For Goods & Services to be rendered in future)	5. Advances paid to suppliers
	5. Current year dues of principal & interest	6. Advance paid to Contractors
	(Due during the year on outstanding long term Debts)	7. Advance Tax paid
	6. Income taxes due on current year earnings and payable within the next year provided for	

FUNDAMENTAL ANALYSIS

ASSET & LIABILITY	Long term asset &Long term Liability may also be mentioned as non-current asset (or fixed asset) and non-current liability respectively. Value of Asset & Liability must be equal because of double entry accounting practices. Double entry book keeping involves a Debit entry off setting a Credit entry or Credit entry off setting a Debit entry for the same value or aggregated value. For example, if an asset is purchased with Bank loan, it is a credit entry for the amount in Liability under Bank loan a/c and a debit entry in asset a/c. If an Asset is purchased out of cash, it is a credit entry to cash a/c and debit entry to asset a/c.
INVESTMENT	Investments under Long Term Asset shall be shown at cost price and if market price of the investment is less than it`s cost, loss on such investment should be adequately provided for by creating provision a/c and shown net of investment
ACCOUNTS RECEIVABLE	Accounts receivable shall be shown net of receivables if, any of it`s credit sales is over-aged or non collectible as per the Co`s view, with adequate provision.
TANGIBLE ASSET	Tangible asset is a physical asset like Plant, Machinery, Vehicle, Computers etc which have economic value. Economic value, in contrast to market value, is a measure of benefit one gets from goods or services. Market value is driven by supply and demand while economic value is tangible value that is derived from that products` function.
INTANGIBLE ASSET	Intangible Assets are Patent, Goodwill, Trade mark, Copy right. Intangible asset, though having economic value value like tangible asset, is non-physical asset. It`s economic value is linked to weight-age of brand value. Intangibles are shown in B/S only when these are acquired from other Co, or if the Co., has incurred expenditure on them. For example- Patent Fee & Lawyer fees etc which the Co., has incurred to create patent. Such expenses may be spread over a longer or shorter period of time as per the policy of the Company.

CARRY OVER VALUE	Long term assets are running accounts and shown with carry over value while Current assets are not, because current assets are working capital assets, the profit or loss on which is determined for a given period of time to arrive P &L a/c for the year ending while B/S is evolving one as at the date of the year.
CAPITAL & COST OF CAPITAL	Capital is a financial resource in the form of fund or any seed asset to generate profit or augment income by running economic activity sourced from it. All capitals have a cost attached to it. There are three types of capitals. Equity capital, Debt capital and working capital. Cost of Equity capital is dividend payable on it. A Co, in the event of winding up, has to pay the residual amount to Share holders after paying off of all it`s debts. From this perspective, Equity is also a long term liability. Debt capital owes it`s cost to interest payable on it while working capital is sourced either from internal accruals or a short term debt like cash credit loan from Banks. Working capital sourced from internal accrual too has a cost to it because it is a fund earned after spending for expenses of value addition like cost of processing, selling cost etc.
CONTINGENT LIABILITY	A contingent liability is one which is potential to alter or impact, directly or indirectly, financial obligation of a Co., upon outcome of an unforeseen action of law from a party to contract or warranty involving the Co. This is shown as a footnote in the Balance sheet, with or without mentioning the potential liability amount, that the Co, may incur, with Auditors` comments thereon. In India, Inland/Foreign Letter of Credits for Imports & Exports, Inland/foreign Guarantees are shown under this head.
LAW SUITS	This is another foot note that describes pending suits against the Co., and suits filed by the Co., against any person or a Co.,. Foot note briefly describes the current status of the suit with the likely amount, if any, that may accrue to or drain the finances of the Co.
AUDITOR`S REPORT	Before concluding the study of B/S, an investor should go through Auditor`s report to see whether he has commented on any accounting practices of the Co, and given any general or qualifying comment. Find whether the Co., has addressed and rectified qualifying comments to the satisfaction of the Auditors. One must also study Directors` report/reply on such comments.

FUNDAMENTAL ANALYSIS

CASH FLOW STATEMENT (CFS)
All the Companies are following accrual accounting method, whereby, while arriving P&L, few Income & expenditure transactions are taken on accrual basis even though real cash is not involved in such transactions. As the Cos may boost their performance by inflating accrued income or deflating accrued expenses, cash flow statement is considered more revealing on the true health of the Co. CFS is mandated for submission along with P&L a/c, Balance sheet. Core concept of cash flow statement is that Income & expenditures are recorded only when cash is received and paid respectively. In other words, cash flow statement excludes accrual accounting.

WHY CASH FLOW IS IMPORTANT?
Cash flow of a Co., provides insight to an investor to assess the ability of the Co, in generating cash and cash equivalents and how the Co., utilizes those cash flows. While cash means cash on hand & Bank, cash equivalent means those held in Bank deposits, short term securities which can be converted into cash in the market i.e., highly liquid. For the purpose of easy understanding, Cash flow statement is divided into three different sections called cash flow from Operational activity, investing activity, and financing activity. Operating activity indicates cash flow from it`s ongoing business operations. Investing activity includes purchase of physical assets, Capital Expenditure, Investment in securities and sale of assets or securities. Financing activity includes transaction on Equity, Debt, Dividend and related transactions. This tells an investor increase or decrease in cash flow in each activity and all collectively put, indicate the overall picture on liquidity and value of the Co. So, Cash Flow Statement is considered the most important one.
WHAT CFS DISCLOSES TO AN INVESTOR
1. Cash Flow is the net amount of cash and cash-equivalents being transferred in and out of a company.
2. Positive cash flow indicates that a company's liquidity is increasing and so do it`s ability to settle debts, reinvest in its business, return money to shareholders, pay expenses, and to face any financial challenges in future. On the other hand a Co., may generate negative cash flow, if it`s business cycle is decreased as evidenced by delay in collection of receivables, higher stocking period of it`s inventory and/ or Co, is highly leveraged for it`s funding requirements leading to it`s struggle to service it`s debts.
3. When used in conjunction with the other financial statements, Cash flow information is useful in assessing the ability of the Co., to generate cash and cash equivalents.
4. It enhances the comparable standards in analyzing operative performance of different Cos, because it eliminates the effects of using different accounting treatments for the same transactions and events.
5. It is useful in examining the relationship between profitability and net cash flow
WHERE AN INVESTOR MUST BE CAUTIOUS WHILE STUDYING CFS
1. In order to retain cash, a Co., can manipulate working capital by delaying the bill payments to suppliers and delaying the purchase of inventory.
2. Capital work in progress indicates construction of building/ erection of pant & machinery or any capital asset in progress. Delaying the work means financial drain on the Co., due to likely cost overrun.
3. Check on Promoters` capital and whether their shares in the Co are unencumbered.
4. Intangible assets are either acquired when merging with another Co., or created for brand value, normally without disclosing their book value, the assessment of which is difficult. Expenses on this head are spread over a period by way of amortization
5. Check inter corporate transfers or transfers between subsidiary Companies/Holding Companies which happen by raising invoices, investing funds etc.
6. Only brief notes are given here as elaborate details may divert the scope of this book.

KNOW HOW CFS ARE PREPARED
Learning how CFS is prepared is good for you to know cash & cash equivalent of a Co., and take an informed decision on investing. Here is how CFS is arrived.

FUNDAMENTAL ANALYSIS

A-INDICATIVE NET CASH FLOW FROM OPERATIONAL ACTIVITY	
1.	Take down Net profit before Tax for the reporting year
2.	Adjustment Entries:- ADD BACK transaction of non- cash nature that has been debited earlier to P&L a/c as expenses **Depreciation/Goodwill/Amortization of expenses** **Loss on sale of asset written off** **Bad debts written off** **Provisions for diminution in value of asset** **Provision for taxes** **Proposed dividend** **All new provisions** **Net Increase in existing provisions**
3.	Adjustment Entries :- LESS:- Transactions of accrued income, but not received that have been credited earlier to P&L a/c as income Net Decrease in existing Provision Provision & Credit balance written back Decrease in Provision Accrued Interest on trade advances Any other income taken on accrual basis Profit on sale of fixed asset –This is a cash inflow in investing activity-Add in IA Dividend received- This is a cash inflow in Investing Activity-Add in IA Interest received on Investment- This is a in Investing Activity-Add in IA
4.	1+2-3=4Net profit before taxes & working capital changes
5.	Working Capital Changes:-Difference between the one reporting year and the last year ADD:-Increase in Accounts Payable (CL) & Decrease in Accounts Receivable (CA) & Decrease in Inventories (CA)
6.	LESS:- Decrease in Accounts Payable (CL) & Increase in Accounts Receivable (CA) & Increase in Inventories (CA)
7.	LESS:-Taxes paid in Cash for the year
8.	4+5—6—7 =8 Net Cash Flow from Operating Activity- See whether this is increasing or decreasing

FUNDAMENTAL ANALYSIS

B-INDICATIVE NET CASH FLOW FROM INVESTING ACTIVITY	
1.	ADD:-Cash received from Sale of Fixed Asset including Intangible asset, Sale of invested securities, Interest Received on Investment, Dividend Received
2.	LESS:- Cash payments made to Purchase of fixed assets including Intangibles assets, Purchase of investments, lending money
3	1-2=3 Net Cash Flow from Investment Activity- See whether this is increasing or decreasing
Note	Investment In assets and securities relate to acquisition and disposal of LONG TERM assets
C-INDICATIVE NET CASH FLOW FROM FINANCING ACTIVITY	
1.	ADD:-Cash received from Issue of Shares/Debts, Profit on redemption of Share
2.	LESS:-Cash paid for Redemption of shares, Repayment of Loan, Interest paid, Dividend paid, Buy back of shares
3	1-2=3 Net Cash Flow from Investment Activity- See whether this is increasing or decreasing
Note	Financing involves owners capital & borrowing of the Co on LONG TERM nature.
INDICATIVE NET CASH FLOW	
1.	ADD:-A+B+C This is Net increase/decrease in cash & cash equivalent for the current year before extraordinary event
2.	ADD or LESS:-Other items that can not be strictly classified in A or B or C, like Contingent cash receipts/cash Payments, Cash Receipts or Cash Payments on extraordinary items that arise as one time event
3.	ADD:- 1+2 =3 This is Net increase/decrease in cash & cash equivalent for the current year after extraordinary event
4.	ADD:- Cash & cash equivalent at the beginning of the year
5*	3+4=5 This is Closing Cash & Cash equivalent at the end of the year*
*	5-This must be equal to Cash & Cash balance appearing in Current Asset column of Balance Sheet of the year
Note 1	The concept of cash and cash equivalent is that revenues & expenditures are recorded only when cash is received and paid respectively. In other words, cash flow statement excludes accrual accounting.
Note 2	(i) Cash comprises cash on hand and demand deposits with banks. (ii) Cash equivalents are short term, highly liquid investments that are readily convertible into known amounts of cash and which are subject to an insignificant risk of changes in value. (iii) Cash flows are inflows and outflows of cash and cash equivalents. Short term investments are those that can be converted into cash within 3 months or less
Note 3	In cash flow statement B & C, transactions of only long term nature are shown as those of short term are accounted in Operational activity-A
Note 4	Income Tax payment or refund should be reported under OA. If the same is related to FA or IA, then, it should be shown under the appropriate head

Note 5	Acquisitions of other business or investment in subsidiaries should be shown under IA. If such Investments are made by issue of shares or convertible debentures, it should be excluded for the purpose of cash flow

FUNDAMENTAL ANALYSIS

NOTES ON HOW CASH FLOW STATEMENT (CFS) IS CALCULATED	
What is Direct & Indirect method?	CFS may be calculated in two ways. One method is by taking Profit before Tax that has already been arrived by the Co., as the base figure from which adjustments need to be made to arrive exact CFS. This is called Indirect method. This method is easy to arrive as only few adjustments are necessary. Another method is to account each and every transaction on it's real cash flow in or out. This method is called direct method. The indicative CFS shown above is on Indirect method.
What are adjustment entries and why they are adjusted with "Add back"?	As PBT is arrived by with accrued expenses, adjustments are necessary. For example, the following entries are non cash expenses that have been debited earlier in P&L a/c to reduce Profit. So, by adding back to PBT, we are nullifying the reduction done earlier and restore PBT on true cash **Depreciation (No real Cash involved-add back)** **Goodwill (No real Cash involved-add back)** **Amortization of expenses (No real Cash involved-add back)** **Loss on sale of asset written off (Book entry-No real Cash involved-add back)** **Bad debts written off-(Book entry-No real Cash involved-add back)** **Provisions for diminution in value of asset-(Book entry-No real Cash involved-add back)** **Provision for taxes (Book entry-No real Cash involved-add back)** **Proposed dividend-(Provision only and not yet paid-No real Cash involved-add back)** **All new provisions-(Book entry-No real Cash involved-add back)** **Net Increase in existing provisions (Book entry-No real Cash involved-add back)** **Please note that whenever any loss including on sale of Fixed assets and/or Investment assets are written off, they are shown under OA and not under respective IA or FA This practice may vary from Co to Co. Secondly, all provisions for Current or non Current assets are Liability accounts (Credit balances) created by reducing Profit or Reserves. So, these are non cash expenses. Hence any net increase that has reduced the profit earlier needs to be added back to PBT and net decrease in provision or provision written back that has been added to profit earlier by way of adjusting provision need to be reduced to PBT**

Why adjustment entries are done with "LESS" ?	As PBT is arrived by with accrued incomes, adjustments are necessary. For example, the following entries are non cash incomes that have been recognized as income on accrual basis and that have been credited earlier in P&L a/c to increase the Profit. So, by reducing them now from PBT, we are nullifying the increases done earlier and restore PBT on true cash. Net Decrease in existing Provision Provision & Credit balance written back Any other income taken on accrual basis
Why there is no adjustment in FA & IA?	CFS is calculated in OA by using PBT, as base figure. As this PBT was arrived earlier on accrual basis, few adjustment entries need to be made. So an earlier entry of cash out in PBT will appear as cash in and vice versa. This is an indirect method in OA. But in IA, & FA we calculate cash in & cash equivalent directly, not deriving from any base figure. Another reason is that FA & IA relate to non-current assets & liabilities which are Capital accounts appearing as Balance sheet accounts

FUNDAMENTAL ANALYSIS

Why working capital changes are made in CFS?	1. An investor must note that working capital is an important component of cash flow from operations. Basic metrics of buy/sell is that when one buys asset by cash payment, his cash balance is reduced and when one raises liability by availing loan, his cash balance is increased. 2. Current assets are running accounts. They are brought forward from previous year, purchases during the year added and consumption during the year deducted and the net is arrived which is the outstanding asset for the current year. Similarly Current Liability is arrived. For CFS purpose, changes viz increase/ decrease is taken to calculate the net cash in-flow or out-flow, instead of the amount outstanding as at the year end, because of it`s accounting that have a brought forward effect from the previous year meaning it has earlier been included or excluded for it`s cash flow. To illustrate further:-

(Rs in crores)

Inventory-CA –Year 2018		Inventory-CA –Year 2019	
B/f from pr. Year	100	B/f from pr. Year	70
Add Purchases in 2018	150	Add Purchases in 2019	160
Less consumed in 2018	180	Less consumed in 2019	120
Closing Balance	70	Closing Balance	110

Inventory being current asset, Increase between 2018 & 2019 is 40 which mean, from the available cash flow, Rs 40 crores cash has been used and hence it is to be reduced. Besides, cash flow calculation on outstanding in Inventory will lead to accounting twice. Using the above reasoning, we make changes in WC as under:-

	Add:-Increase in Accounts Payable (CL) & Decrease in Accounts Receivable (CA) & Decrease Inventories (CA)
	Less:-Decrease in Accounts Payable (CL) & Increase in Accounts Receivable (CA) & Increase Inventories (CA)
Why changes in few current assets & liabilities and not in non-current assets?	1. Business cycle is length of time, a Co., takes to convert its` raw materials to finished goods and from finished goods to sales and from sales back to cash. Based on this cycle, the Co.`s working capital needs are assessed. But, non-current assets are not primary part of the operational activity,though, of course, they are associated assets in generating revenue either in IA or FA 2. Current assets & liabilities are running or evolving accounts from previous years and hence their changes between previous and year under report are factored into whereas non-current assets & liabilities are non evolving accounts from the previous year meaning they are specific for the year under report. 3. In Current assets, Inventory & Accounts receivable (Debtors) are the prime revenue generating assets in operational activity, part or whole of which are purchased from suppliers on cash and/or on credit terms as evidenced by outstanding Accounts payable (Creditors) for expenses. Accounts payable are, thus, expenses for which actual cash payment is yet to be made. So, the available cash flow is either added or reduced by the amount of increase or decrease in current liability respectively. 4. Keep in mind: Increase in liability increases cash flow & Decrease in liability decreases cash flow while Increase in asset decreases cash flow & Decrease in asset increases cash flow

FUNDAMENTAL ANALYSIS

RATIO ANALYSIS AND ITS` BENEFITS
The Co., reports it`s yearly performance to all general public, including share holders, by publishing audited P&L, Balance sheet, CFS, Auditors` report, Directors` report. Ratio analysis, on the other hand, is a set of ratios that are calculated from these various audited figures for the purpose of analyzing and easy understanding on whether the Co., is progressing or regressing over a period of time. By comparing set of financial data of the previous years and the year under report, an investor can forecast it`s future performance, besides, evaluating it with the Company`s own history of past performance. With ratio analysis, an investor can compare the Company`s performance with that of it`s peers / rivals/other companies in the same industry and take an informed assessment on the Company`s standing with reference to it`s rivals. An investor can also reach an holistic view on the Company`s performance on stand alone and performance of the sector in which it operates.

IMPORTANT RATIOS	
Profitability ratio	Analyses it`s profit generating capacity in terms of it`s capital structure viz Equity fund, Debt fund of long term& short term etc
Leverage ratio	Analyses it`s leverage with debt funds or otherwise, it`s ability to service it`s debt funds etc

Operational efficiency ratio	Analyses it`s performance in turning over working capital assets and liabilities in tune with various targets it set to achieve viz sales, inventory norm, purchase policy etc.
Valuation ratio	Analyses valuation of equity share in terms of it`s book value, earning value per share, return value to investors etc

WHY RATIO ANALYSIS IS IMPORTANT

Investor must know that it is the ratio analysis that reveals the true health of a Co., based on which it`s stocks are valued and appropriate investment decisions are taken by all stake holders in the stock market. Ignorance of these ratios is, therefore, risky from investors` /traders` point of action.

FUNDAMENTAL ANALYSIS

PROFITABILITY RATIOS	
EBITDA	EBITDA stands for Earnings Before Interest, Tax, Depreciation and Amortization. Interest is Finance cost, Tax is applicable corporate Tax, Depreciation is an annual non-cash expenditure that a Company charges to it`s profit with reference to cost of a physical asset till it`s assessed life expectancy. Amortization refers to the process of writing down the value of either a loan as per schedule of a loan repayment or an intangible asset. In other words EBITDA =Operating Revenue –Operating Expenses Where Operating Revenue =Total Revenue—Other Income Operating Expenses=Total Expenses—Finance Cost—(Depreciation + Amortization) Other income is income from Investments and from non operating activities
EBITDA MARGIN	$$\frac{\text{EBITDA}}{\text{(Total Revenue –Other Income)}}$$ By excluding other income like income from investment & non-operating activities, one can find how much EBITDA is earned from the Co`s operational activity alone
PROFIT BEFORE TAX (PBT)	Profit Before Tax is also referred as Pre Tax profit or EBT viz Earning before Tax.PBT is used to know profit before incurring tax obligation. This provides insight on comparable tax liability of other Companies and their performance
PAT & PAT MARGIN (PROFIT AFTER TAX)	PAT is Profit after Tax & PAT Margin =PAT/Total Revenue This is to assess how much Profit after Tax is generated with the given amount of total revenue and safety margin on it.

RETURN ON EQUITY- IN % (ROE)	$$\frac{\text{NET PROFIT}}{\text{SHARE HOLDERS EQUITY}} \times 100$$ Net Profit is before payment of dividend to shareholders. This ratio helps assessing the company`s efficiency in generating cash flow with the amount of equity it holds. This ratio is a growth indicator and a tool to compare the Co`s performance with it`s peers/competitors
RETURN ON CAPITAL EMPLOYED- IN % (ROCE)	$$\frac{\text{PROFIT AFTER TAX}}{\text{Net Worth + Loan Funds}} \times 100$$ Where Net Worth=Equity Capital + Reserves. This ratio is different from ROE above, since ROE is calculated with equity while ROCE Is calculated with Equity and Debt. This ratio tells how much profit is generated for each Rs 1/-of equity & debt capital employed
RETURN ON ASSETS (ROA)	$$\frac{\text{NET PROFIT}}{\text{TOTAL ASSETS}}$$ This analyses the earnings generated from the invested capital ie assets. Difference between ROE & ROA is that ROE is calculated with equity while ROA is assessed with equity & debt (total asset= total liability). The limitation of this ratio is that it is industry specific and can not hold good across other industries as asset base differs from industry to industry. So this a tool to compare with those in the same industry
RETURN ON SALES- IN % (ROS)	$$\frac{\text{EBIT}}{\text{NET SALES}} \times 100$$ This ratio analyses growth of profit generated with growth of sales. ROS is a tool to compare companies in the same line of business.
Performance of the Company has to be assessed by comparing all the above profitability ratios with those of the Company`s competitors/ peers / Industry and also with the company`s own historical performance.	

FUNDAMENTAL ANALYSIS

LEVERAGE RATIOS	
DEBT/ EQUITY RATIO (D/E) or NET GEARING RATIO	$$\frac{\text{TOTAL DEBT}}{\text{TOTAL EQUITY}}$$ Where Total Debt is both Short Term and Long Term Debts. D/E ratio of more than 3 signals that the Company is too leveraged and may not be able to generate enough cash to meet it`s debt obligations. This can go up depending upon the type of industry like capital intensive industry.
LONG TERM DEBT TO EQUITY RATIO	$$\frac{\text{LONG TERM DEBT}}{\text{TOTAL EQUITY}}$$ Here only long term debt is taken into to assess debt burden of the Company. Banks for appraisals purposes of long term debts consider this ratio up to 2 as safe, meaning twice their equity capital.

DEBT SERVICE COVERAGE RATIO (DSCR)	$$\frac{\text{OPERATING REVENUE/INCOME}}{\text{TOTAL DEBT SERVICE}}$$ The debt-service coverage ratio reflects the ability to service debt with the given income. Total Debt service means current debt obligations which are due within one year, including interest on short term &long term debts and, principal, sinking fund lease payments. Ratio of less than 1 is considered negative as cash generation of the Company is inadequate to meet it`s debt obligations.
DEBT/ ASSET RATIO	$$\frac{\text{TOTAL DEBT}}{\text{TOTAL ASSET}}$$ Where Total Debt is both Short Term and Long Term Debts. This ratio is to assess how much of Company`s assets have been financed by debt capital. A ratio less than 1 shows that a portion of assets is funded by debt and the remaining by own capital viz equity. A high ratio of more than 1 means that the Co., relies too much on debt funds to finance entire assets and squeezes it`s own equity funds. The Co., may be at a risk of default on its loans.
FINANCIAL LEVERAGE RATIO	$$\frac{\text{AVERAGE TOTAL ASSET}}{\text{AVERAGE TOTAL EQUITY}}$$ Where Average Total Assets is average of beginning and ending Assets of a year. Average Equity is average of beginning and ending equity of a year. This is to assess how much of assets have been funded from equity alone.
INTEREST COVERAGE RATIO	$$\frac{\text{EANING BEFORE INTERST \& TAX (EBIT)}}{\text{INTEREST PAYMENT}}$$ Ratio measures the ability of the Co., to pay interest expenses on it`s debt from it`s earnings. Higher the ratio higher the capacity of the Co to meet it`s interest obligations

FUNDAMENTAL ANALYSIS

LEVERAGE RATIOS	
LIABILITY TO EQUITY RATIO	$$\frac{\text{TOTAL LIABILITY}}{\text{TOTAL EQUITY}}$$ Total Assets=Long Term Liability + Short Term liability + shareholders equity. A high debt/equity ratio is often associated with high risk; it means that a company has been excessively relying on debt fund to finance its growth.
DEBT TO CAPITALIZATION RATIO	$$\frac{\text{SHORT TERM DEBT + LONG TERM DEBT}}{\text{SHORT TERM DEBT + LONG TERM DEBT + EQUITY}}$$ This is to measure financial leverage of the Co. and assess how much debt is used in the capital structure to finance the activity
DEGREE OF FINANCIAL LEVERAGE RATIO	$$\frac{\text{EBIT}}{\text{EBIT—INTEREST}}$$ Interest being normally fixed expense, this measures to what extent leverage helps in increasing or decreasing return/revenue

DEBT/EBITDA LEVERAGE RATIO	$\dfrac{\text{DEBT}}{\text{EBITDA}}$ Debt means both Long Term and Short term debts. Ratio assess the Co`s ability to pay off it`s total debt obligations. By comparing with the past figures, an investor can find whether it is declining or not. A declining figure tells the Co is paying off it`s debts or it`s earnings are increasing.
FIXED CHARGE COVERAGE RATIO	$\dfrac{\text{EBIT}}{\text{Interest on Long term Debts}}$ This ratio tells how much cash flow is there to service interest on Long term debts.

FUNDAMENTAL ANALYSIS

OPERATIONAL EFFICIENCY RATIOS	
ASSETS TURNOVER	$\dfrac{\text{NET SALES}}{\text{AVERAGE TOTAL ASSETS}}$ Where Average Total Assets is average of the beginning and ending Assets of a year Net sales is total sales less returns. This ratio is to assess how much of sales has contributed to build up of total assets or how many months of sales is to total assets.
FIXED ASSETS TURNOVER	$\dfrac{\text{OPERATING REVENUE}}{\text{AVERAGE TOTAL ASSET}}$ Where Operating Revenue=Total Revenue—Other Income Other income is income from Investments and from non operating activities This is useful in assessing the extent of revenue generated in comparison with it`s fixed assets viz Plant &Machinery, like Plant capacity utilization in manufacturing industry. Higher the ratio higher the efficiency of the Company
WORKING CAPITAL RATIO	$\dfrac{\text{CURRENT ASSET}}{\text{CURRENT LIABILITY}}$ Current assets are liquid assets which can be easily converted into cash or consumed or used or sold or exhausted. Current assets include cash, cash equivalents, accounts receivable, stock inventory, marketable securities, pre-paid liabilities, and other liquid assets, advances paid to receive supplies/ services within a year. Current liabilities are a company's short-term financial obligations that are due within one year which includes, short term debts,, Accounts payable, Dividends payable, Interest payable on debts, Tax due and payable, advance amount received from customers for services to be rendered within a year. WC ratio as per appraisal norms of Banks in India is 1.33 : 1, meaning for current liability of 1, current asset should be 1.33. This is not rigid and 1.25 :1 is also accepted. This ratio is to assess the Company`s ability to convert liquid assets into cash and pay off current liabilities. Current asset minus Current Liability is known as working capital surplus that the Company uses for it`s day to day business operations.

WC TURNOVER	$$\frac{\text{REVENUE}}{\text{AVERAGE WC}}$$ Average Working Capital is average of Current Assets minus Current Liabilities at the beginning and end of a year. This is to assess the company's efficiency in earning revenue with the amount of working capital it has. Higher the ratio, higher the efficiency
TOTAL ASSETS TURNOVER	$$\frac{\text{OPERATING REVENUE}}{\text{AVERAGE TOTAL ASSET}}$$ This is to assess the company's efficiency in earning revenue with the given amount of total assets
INVENTORY TURNOVER	$$\frac{\text{COST OF GOODS SOLD}}{\text{AVERAGE INVENTORY}}$$ Average Inventory is average of closing inventory at the beginning and ending of a year. Higher the inventory turnover higher the efficiency

FUNDAMENTAL ANALYSIS

OPERATIONAL EFFICIENCY RATIOS	
ACCOUNTS RECEIVABLE	$$\frac{\text{REVENUE}}{\text{AVERAGE RECEIVABLES}}$$ Average receivable is average of closing Trade receivables at the beginning and end of a year. Ratio is useful to assess how much of revenue is accounted from Receivables, with the given amount of revenue. Receivables are credit sales and by comparing it's number of days sales it represents, one may check whether profit on sale/revenue has been accounted from over aged Receivables
INVENTORY TO DAYS	$$\frac{\text{INVENTORY}}{\text{NO.OF DAYS SALES}}$$ Divide annual sales, less return, if any, by 365 to arrive daily sales and divide closing inventory by daily sale to arrive how many days' sale is held as inventory. This is to assess how fast the company sells it's inventory. Inventory being finished goods, this ratio is useful to know the extent of demand and brand value that the Co.,'s product enjoys in the market as high brand products normally need very few days stocking.
SALES TO DAYS	$$\frac{\text{TRADE RECEIVABLE}}{\text{NO.OF DAYS SALES}}$$ Divide annual sales, less return, if any, by 365 to arrive daily sales and divide trade receivables (which represent credit sales) by daily sale to arrive how many days' sale is held as Trade receivables. This is to assess how quickly the company collects cash from its' trade receivables. This ratio is also useful to know the Co's willingness to extend sales on credit and time norms it prescribes to collect it. Giving higher collection period may signal push through approach.

PBT TO SALES	$\dfrac{\text{PROFIT BEFORETAX (PBT)}}{\text{Net Sales}} \times 100$
	Profit before tax is the value used to calculate a company's tax obligation. PBT is also referred as Pre Tax Profit or EBT. This helps to assess profit before consideration of tax with reference to it's net sales.
CASH FLOW TO CAPITAL EXPENDITURE RATIO	$\dfrac{\text{CASH FLOW FROM OPERATIONS}}{\text{CAPITAL EXPENDITURE}}$ This ratio tells us how much of a Co.,'s Capital assets / new acquisitions can be funded from it's cash flow and how much from debts funds. A ratio greater than 1 means the Co, has surplus fund flow and less than 1 is an indication of the need to fund it from debts

FUNDAMENTAL ANALYSIS

VALUATION RATIOS	
PRICE TO SALES RATIO P/S	$\dfrac{\text{Current Market price of the share}}{\text{Sales (or revenue) per share}}$ Where sales per share is Total Revenue divided by Total no. of Shares. P/S ratio is a key tool that shows how much investors are willing to pay per Rs1/- of sales for a stock. A low ratio signals that the stock is undervalued while a higher ratio maybe that the stock is overvalued.
BOOK VALUE PER SHARE (BVPS)	$\dfrac{\text{Equity Share Capital + Reserves (excluding Revaluation reserve)}}{\text{Total Number of Equity Shares}}$ Book value per share indicates a firm's net asset value ie., total assets minus total external liabilities on a per-share basis. It helps to assess the valuation per share with respect to it's market price and gauge whether share is undervalued or over- valued. BV also means what remains after paying off all its' debts in the event of liquidation of the Co.
PRICE TO BOOK VALUE (P/BV)	$\dfrac{\text{Current Market price per share}}{\text{Book Value per share (BV)}}$ Book value per share indicates a firm's net asset value ie., total assets minus total external liabilities on a per-share basis. Ideally, price to book value should be higher than 1 but less than 3. A stock having book value higher than 1 is considered overvalued and conveys that the market is willing to pay more for each rupee of it's book value. In other words, market value reflects future earnings of the Co., that an investor anticipates, based on BV, a historical data. When a stock is undervalued, it will have a higher book value per share. This tool is useful in valuation of stock in relation to it's book value.

EARNING PER SHARE (EPS)	$$\dfrac{\text{Profit after Tax}}{\text{Total Number of Equity Shares}}$$ EPS indicates how much profit a company earns on per share. EPS is a widely used to estimate corporate value. Higher the EPS higher the efficiency of the Co.. This ratio is important as this is a component in assessing P/E ratio
PRICE TO EARNING RATIO (P/E)	$$\dfrac{\text{Current Market price of the share}}{\text{Earning per share (EPS)}}$$ The price-to-earnings ratio or P/E is the market price of stock divided by earning per share. For example, if a stock has a P/E ratio of 25, it means an investor is willing to pay Rs 25/- in the stock for Rs 1/- of it`s current earnings. While EPS is historical/ actual data, market price is a price that an investor is willing to pay, anticipating higher returns in it`s future earnings, based on it`s past performance on EPS. P/E is one of the most widely-used stock analysis tools used by investors for determining stock valuation. Besides helping to know it`s value viz under valued or overvalued, this ratio is also used to compare P/E with it`s peers. Though two Co.s with the same set of assets may earn different EPS, their market price depends on the investors` perception about their future earnings.

FUNDAMENTAL ANALYSIS

VALUATION RATIOS	
RETURN ON INVESTMENT (ROI) IN %	$$\dfrac{\text{Equity Capital + Long Term Debt}}{\text{Earnings (Before Interest, Tax, Dividend)}} \text{ x } 100$$ This measures the performance the Co.,viz it`s efficiency in utilizing both the equity capital and Long Term debt capital to generate the given amount of earnings. This is more relevant when it is compared with the Co.,`s own past figures.
CASH EARNING PER SHARE (CPS)	$$\dfrac{\text{Net Profit +Depreciation}}{\text{Total Number of Equity Shares}}$$ Earnings Per Share (EPS) is calculated on Net profit after Depreciation while Cash Earnings per share (CPS) is calculated on Net profit before Depreciation. Hence Depreciation, being non cash expenditure do not require any cash outflow, and is added back to calculate Cash Earnings per share. This is another measure to value per share
CASH P/E	$$\dfrac{\text{Day`s Closing Price}}{\text{Cash Earnings per Share (CPS)}}$$ Cash P/E with CPS & P/E with EPS differ as calculation of CPS factors depreciation while EPS is not. Why depreciation is considered important in accounting practices is the fact that the Co by charging depreciation, a non cash outlay, to Profit a/c enjoys Tax benefit. This ratio indicates cash earnings per share relating to it`s market price.

EARNING PRICE RATIO	$\dfrac{\text{Earnings per share}}{\text{Current Market Price of the Share}}$ x 100
	This ratio indicates how expensive is the current price of the share in relation to it`s earning per share. In the perception of an analyst, current market price is determined by investor`s anticipation in the Co`s future earnings in relation to it`s current earnings per share.
PAY OUT RATIO	$\dfrac{\text{Dividend per Share}}{\text{Earnings per Share}}$ x 100
	The dividend payout ratio indicates how much money a company is returning to shareholders as dividends and how much it is retaining to add either to cash reserves or to reinvest or any other purpose in tune with it`s business policy. An investor may know through this ratio maturing or otherwise of the Co`s dividend policy.
VOLATILITY RATIO	$\dfrac{\text{Highest Price of Share–Lowest Price of Share}}{\text{Lowest Price of Share}}$ x 100
	A stock with high swings is called a volatile stock. When a stock is Volatile, it means it`s price is unpredictable and hence considered riskier. Normally, a stock may be volatile when the Co., is expected to release it`s quarterly/ annual report or when the report having been released, has beaten the estimates of stock analysts.
YIELD IN %	$\dfrac{\text{Dividend per Share}}{\text{Current Market Price per share}}$ x 100
	The dividend yield shows how much a company pays as dividends each year relative to its current stock price. This ratio is a tool to compare the dividends pay out of other Companies in the same sector/industry and the Co`s own past pay out.

CHAPTER 3-A

TECHNICAL ANALYSIS-SINGLE & MULTIPLE CANDLESTICK PATTERN

CONTENTS

1 Various Time frames
2 Candlestick price momentum indicators-with pictures
3 Single Candlestick pattern with pictures of appearance, Prior Trend, Time Frame, Where to Fix Stop Loss, Trade signal, Price to Trade

   Marubozu-Long body, Short body, Spinning Top, Doji, Hammer, hanging Man, Shooting Star
4 Multiple Candlestick pattern with pictures of appearance, Prior Trend, Time Frame, Where to Fix Stop Loss, Trade signal, How to ensure, Validation

   Engulfing Pattern, Doji, Piercing Pattern, Dark Cloud, Harami, Morning Star, Evening Star, Gap Up, Gap Down. Dragonfly Doji, Gravestone Doji
5 Advanced Candlestick pattern with pictures-Pattern behavior, Identification, Prior Trend, Time Frame, Trade signal, Trend Reversal

   Island Reversal, San-ku Triple Gap, Kicker Pattern, 3 White Soldier, 3 Black Crows, 3 Line Strike,

   2 Black Gapping, Abandoned Baby, On Neck Pattern
6 Setting Stop loss in Single and Multiple Candlestick Patterns
7 Useful tips to identify trends

TECHNICAL ANALYSIS (TA)

Aim of any stock trader is to earn profit, as much as possible, in the shortest time. However, just like any other venture, profit earning in stock trading, too, is no easy task. It needs skill and knowledge on (i) forecasting price direction (ii) identifying trading opportunities (iii) time to enter and exit the trade (iv) choosing the right stock to trade (v) Holding period of the trade (vi) risk tolerance. Among these, choosing a stock, forecasting it`s price direction and identifying trading opportunities are the important trading skills. If you learn these, rest of them may be slightly easier for you to deploy. So, If a trader, with correct forecasting on the price direction of a chosen asset enters the trade at the right time, then his success on the trade is almost certain. However, prediction of future in terms of price movements is not as easy as one assumes. It is this vital criteria that technical analysis study and forecast how a stock is likely to behave in future with reference to it`s past price data. Technical analysis can be classified into two (i) charting pattern (ii) technical indicators with statistical data,, namely, leading and lagging indicators. TA`s concept can be applied to any class of asset. Moving forward, Charting type are of three kinds namely Line chart, Bar chart, and candlestick chart. Of all the three, candlestick chart is considered the most reliable because of it`s visibility and clarity on a chart.

JAPANESE CANSDLESTICKS & THEIR PATTERNS

A Japanese rice merchant is said to have discovered this candlestick in 18th Century. This charting was later in 1980s widely used in the western countries. Before going into detail, a trader should know how and what to study from candlestick pattern plainly and also with reference to the duration i.e., time frame taken into for such study. In a chart, candles are drawn by connecting the closing prices of an asset in day/week/month which appears as candles. So, in order to study candlestick pattern one needs to choose the time frame & look back period.

<table>
<tr><td rowspan="2">T i m e frame</td><td colspan="6">Time frame is the time duration with which a trader likes to study the candle chart and form trading view. Various time frames are given below :-</td></tr>
<tr><td>Time frame</td><td>Open</td><td>High</td><td>Low</td><td>Close</td><td>No.of candles</td></tr>
<tr><td></td><td>15 minutes-Intra day</td><td>Opening price at the beginning of the Ist minute</td><td>Highest price during 15 minutes time the stock traded</td><td>Lowest price during 15 minutes time the stock traded</td><td>Closing price as at the end of 15 minute</td><td>25 candles per day</td></tr>
<tr><td></td><td>30 minutes-Intra day</td><td>Opening price at the beginning of the Ist minute</td><td>Highest price during 30 minutes time the stock traded</td><td>Lowest price during 30 minutes time the stock traded</td><td>Closing price as at the end of 30 minute</td><td>12 candles per day</td></tr>
<tr><td></td><td>Daily</td><td>Opening price at the beginning of the day</td><td>Highest price during the day stock traded</td><td>Lowest price during the day stock traded</td><td>Closing price as at the end of the day</td><td>One candle per day/252 candles for a year</td></tr>
</table>

	Weekly	Opening price at the beginning of the week	Highest price during the entire week stock traded	lowest price during the entire week stock traded	Closing price as at the end of the week	52 candles per year
	Monthly	Opening price at the beginning of the month	Highest price at the beginning of the month	Lowest price at the beginning of the month	Closing price as at the end of month	12 candles per year

Look back period	Look back period is simply the number of candles you wish to view before taking a trading decision. For instance, look back period of 3 months means you are looking at today`s candle in the backdrop of at least the recent 3 months data. In this manner you will develop decision making on today`s price action with reference to last 3 month`s price action.
Patterns	Pattern formation is identified by single or multiple candles, depending on stocks` price behavior and the display of prior or following candles. Normally patterns are formed by multiple candles. Patterns have two types-Reversal Pattern & Continuation pattern.
Reversal pattern	Reversal patterns predict change in price direction either in up or down
Continuation pattern	Continuation patterns predict extension in the current price direction.
Reliability	Patterns can be relied for a maximum of 3 to 4 candles after completion of pattern

CANDLESTICK PRICE MOMENTUM INDICATORS

Candles can be classified as Bullish or Bearish. Bullish candles are identifiable by it`s color code in Blue/Green (Ash Grey) and Bearish candles in Red (Black) code. A description of what candles convey in Bullish and Bearish trend is given.

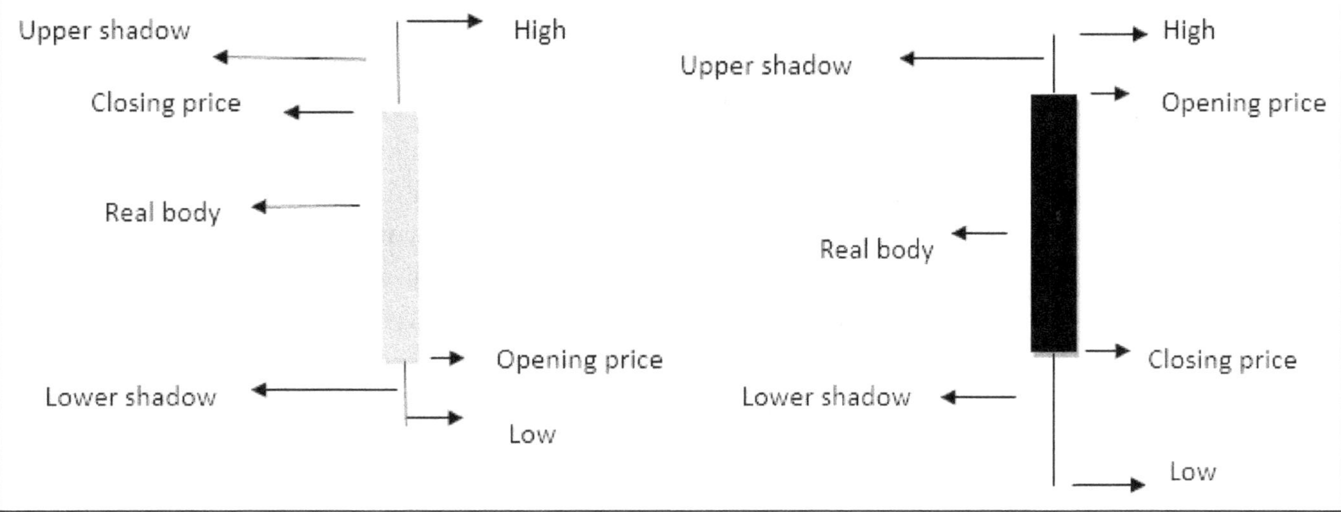

Bullish candle	When Closing price is higher than Opening price, it is bullish candle-Blue (Ash Grey) color
Bearish candle	When Closing price is lower than Opening price, it is bearish candle-Red (Black) color
Prior Trend	While looking at Bullish pattern (Blue/Ash Grey), prior trend should be Bearish (Red/Black). Similarly while looking at Bearish (Red/Black) pattern, prior trend should be Bullish (Blue/Ash Grey). Prior trend means prior candle. Looking for prior trend is confirmatory action to identify future price movement.
No Prior trend	For both Bullish & Bearish Marubozu candles, NO prior trend need to be looked to as they may appear anywhere in the chart without prior trend

Different forms of candles with their indications are described below

Size	Indication
Long body	Long body indicates heavy trading activity on the stock as shown by long length between it`s opening price & closing price. If it is bullish, long blue candle appears and signals overwhelmingly heavy buying and establishment of bullish trend, despite the pulls from sellers on the stock. If bearish, long red candle appears and signals clear edge by sellers with their heavy selling and establishment of bearish trend, despite the pressures from the buyers. For ex., if opening price is say Rs 450/- high @Rs 500/-low @Rs 440/- & closing @ Rs 480/- it indicates bullishness i.e up in price by more than 6%. If following 3/4 day candles indicate pattern with higher highs and higher lows, it is an indication of uptrend or trend reversal
Short body	Short body, on the other hand, indicates subdued or less trading activity as shown by short length between it`s opening price & closing price. For ex if opening price is say Rs 390/- high @ Rs 410/-Low @ Rs 350/-& closing price @ Rs 385/- it indicates bearishness by marginal decline in the closing price. If following 3/4 day candles indicate pattern with lower highs and lower lows, it is an indication of downtrend or trend reversal.
Shadow indication	In a bullish candle, high price indicates the peak price point at which buyers are willing to buy and their continued buying pressure entailing in ultimate success of buyers by clear lead over sellers in a given time as can be seen from the day`s closing price settling just below the high. Similarly, indication in bearish trend is that sellers` control of the trade and their clear lead over buyers in the stock in a given time is evidenced by the day`s closing price settling just above the low. In other words, in a given time, high and low are the maximum and the minimum price points at which buyers and sellers are ready to pick or sell a stock while the price range between opening & closing shows intense trade if it is long body and marginal trade if it is short body.
No upper /lower shadow	Marubozu candles will have no upper or lower shadow. Bullish Marubozu forms when buying interest is high and buyers are willing to buy the stock at any price so much so that the stock closed near it`s high price. Similarly, Bearish Marubozu forms indicating that the selling interest is so high that sellers are willing to sell at any price and in the process the stock`s closing price is close to or equals it`s low price.

SINGLE CANDLESTICK PATTERN

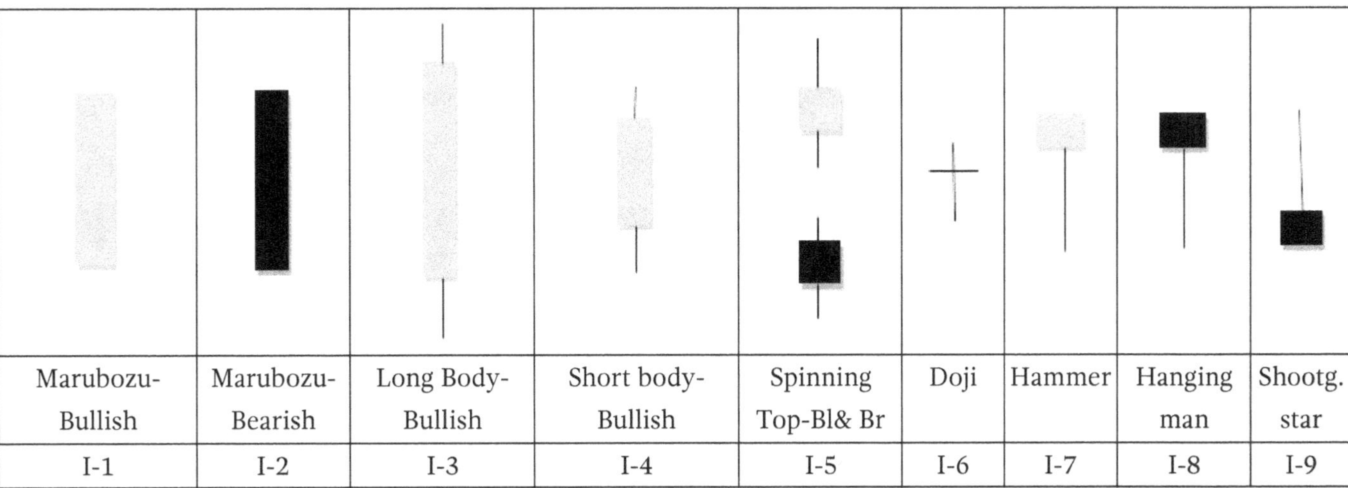

Marubozu-Bullish	Marubozu-Bearish	Long Body-Bullish	Short body-Bullish	Spinning Top-Bl& Br	Doji	Hammer	Hanging man	Shootg. star
I-1	I-2	I-3	I-4	I-5	I-6	I-7	I-8	I-9

Candlestick	Appearance	Prior Trend	Time frame	When&Where to fix SL	Trading signal	Price to Trade
BULLISH MARUBOZU Single candlestick	No upper & lower shadow See I-1	No Prior Trend	One day	Open=low & Close = High STOP LOSS (SL)@ low	Buy	@ Closing Price
BEARISH MARUBOZU Single candlestick	-do- See I-2	-do	-do-	Open=High & Close=Low SL @high of the candle	Sell/Short	@low
AVOID TRADING	Avoid trade during extremely small candle (below 1% range) OR long candle (above 10% range) as small candle indicates subdued trading activity and long candle indicates extreme trading activity.					
BOTH BULL & BEAR SPINNING TOP- Single * Pl see note next page	Small body, upper & lower shadow are equal See I-5	Look for	One day	Open & close prices are very near No SL	Market is in Indecision	Shows reversal or continuation of trends
DOJI-Single candlestick * Pl see note next page	No real body-looks like + sign See I-6	Look for	-do-	Open & close prices are equal- No SL	-do-	View Doji with other pattern
BULLISH-HAMMER-Single candlestick	Long lower shadow, NO upper shadow & small upper body & Length of lower shadow should be at least twice the length of the real body-See I-7	Preceded by Downtrend-appears at bottom of the downtrend	-do-	Open & Close should almost be the same SL @low of the candle	Downtrend is reversing and hence Buy	At hammer price
BEARISH-HANGING MAN-Single candlestick	-do- appears at top end of the uptrend-See I-8	Preceded by Uptrend	-do-	-do- SL @ high of the candle	Uptrend is reversing. Hence Short/Sell	At Hanging man price

Candlestick	Appearance	Prior Trend	Time frame	When&Where to fix SL	Trading signal	Price to Trade
BEARISH-THE SHOOTING STAR-Single candlestick	Long upper shadow, NO lower shadow & small lower body & length of upper shadow should be at least twice the length of the real body-See I-9	Preceded by Uptrend-appears at top end of the trend	-do-	Current price is more or less equal to Low price Looks like upside down of paper umbrella SL @ high of the candle	Trade same day, As uptrend is reversing, Short/Sell	At close of the price

MULTIPLE CANDLESTICK PATTERN-1

Bullish Engulfing Pattern	Bearish Engulfing Pattern	Bearish Doji
Prior trend-Down trend	Prior trend-Up trend	Prior trend-Up trend
Buy after ensuring 3rd day candle is Blue	Sell after ensuring 3rd day candle is Red	Ensure 3rd-4th day candle is Red-Indecision-Watch
I-10	I-11	I-12

Bullish Piercing Pattern	Bearish Dark Cloud
Prior trend- Down trend	Prior trend-Up trend
Buy after ensuring 3rd day candle is Blue	Sell after ensuring 3rd day candle is Red
I-13	I-14

MULTIPLE CANDLESTICK PATTERN-1

Candlestick	Appearance	Prior Trend	Time Frame	Trade signal*	Ensure that	Validation
BULLISH-ENGULFING PATTERN-Two candle formation	Small Red candle on Day1 & Long Blue Candle on Day 2. Long Blue candle of Day 2 engulfs **completely** small Red candle of Day 1 –Appears at bottom of Down trend- See I-10	Downtrend Prior candle is RED	2 Trading Sessions	Signals Uptrend - Buy SL @ lowest low in D1 & D2	The 3 rd day candle is Blue	1. Current Market price at close of Day 2 should be higher than Day 1`s open. 2. Open on Day 2 should be equal to or lower than Day1 ` close
BEARISH-ENGULFING PATTERN-Two candle formation	Small Blue candle on Day1 & Long Red Candle on Day 2. Long Red candle of Day 2 engulfs **completely** small Blue candle of Day 1 –Appears at top end of uptrend See I-11	Uptrend-Prior candle is BLUE	2 Trading Sessions	Signals Downtrend - Short/Sell- SL @ highest high of D1&D2	The 3 rd day candle is Red	1. Current Market price at close of Day 2 should be lower than Day 1`s open 2. Open on Day 2 should be higher than Day 1`` close
BEARISH-DOJI-Two candle formation	No real body-Looks like + sign, appears on 3 rd Day-Doji is followed by Long Red candle See I-12	Uptrend	2/3 Trading sessions	Market indecision No SL	3rd/4th day candle is Red	Whenever Doji follows Bearish engulfing pattern, huge opportunity may be there for Trade
BULLISH-PIERCING PATTERN-Two candle formation	Day 2 `s Blue candle **partially** engulfs Day 1 `s Red candle-appears at bottom. See I- 13	Downtrend-Prior candle is RED	2 Trading session	Signals Uptrend-Buy SL@ Lowest low in D1&D2	3rd candle is Blue	D2`s blue engulfs partially i.e.,50% to less than 100% of D1 red
BEARISH-The Dark Cloud Cover-Two candle formation	Red candle of Day 2 engulfs **partially** Day1 ` Blue candle-appears at top end of uptrend See I -14	Uptrend Prior candle is BLUE	2 Trading session	Signals Downtrend. Sell-SL @ Highest high of D1&D2	3rd day candle is Red	D2`s red engulfs partially i.e.,50% to less than 100% of D1 blue

*SL stands for Stop-Loss

*Doji looks like a cross, inverted cross or +sign. In Doji open & close are equal and generally signals reversal pattern. When Doji/Spinning Top is alone, it is neutral pattern. Dojis are commonly seen in periods of consolidation and can help identifying potential break-out. If either a Doji or a Spinning Top is spotted, look for other indicators like Bollinger Band to determine if they are indicative of neutrality or reversal	
Foot notes	Foot notes will appear wherever required, with remarks like confirm the trend with Bollinger band, Stochastic, Moving Average, RSI etc which are all technical data indicators the lessons of which are given in next chapter.

MULTIPLE CANDLESTICK PATTERN-2

Bullish Harami Pattern	Bearish Harami Pattern	Bullish Morning Star
Prior trend-Down trend	Prior trend- Up trend	Prior trend-Down trend
Buy after ensuring 3rd day candle is Blue	Sell after ensuring 3rd day candle is Red	Buy after ensuring 3rd day candle is Blue
I-15	I-16	I-17
Bearish Evening Star	Gap Up Opening	Gap Down Opening
Prior trend-Up trend	No prior trend	No prior trend
Sell after ensuring 3rd day candle is Red	Caution-Wait & Trade	Caution-Wait & Trade
I-18	I-19	I-20

MULTIPLE CANDLESTICK PATTERN-2

Candlestick	Appearance	Prior Trend	Time Frame	Trade signal*	Ensure that	Validation
BULLISH-HARAMI PATTERN-Two candle formation	Similar to engulfing. First candle is usually long and the second candle has a small body. Day 1 is RED and Day 2 is BLUE –Appears at bottom end of downtrend See I-15	Downtrend-Prior candle is RED	2 Trading Sessions	Signals Uptrend-Buy SL@ lowest low of D1&D2	3rd Day candle is Blue	1. Current Market price at 3.20 pm on Day 2 should be less than Day 1`s opening 2. Opening on Day 2 should be higher than close of Day1
BEARISH-HARAMI PATTERN-Two candle formation	Similar to engulfing. First candle is usually long and the second candle has a small body. Day 1 is BLUE & Day 2 is RED –Appears at top end of the uptrend-See I-16	Uptrend-Prior candle is BLUE	2 Trading Sessions	Signals Downtrend. Sell. SL@ highest high of D1&D2	3rd candle is Red	1. Open price on Day 2 should be lower than close price of Day 1 2. Close price on Day 2 should be greater than open price of day 1
BULLIISH-MORNING STAR-Three candle formation	Pattern evolves over 3 days-Appears at bottom end of the downtrend. Day 1 has long RED candle, Day 2 has spinning top or Doji-Day 3 has a BLUE candle See I -17	Downtrend-Prior candle is either Spg. top or DOJI	3 Trading sessions	Signals trend Reversal-Buy. Trade on Day3 SL@ lowest low of D1,D2,D3	3rd Day candle is Blue	1. Day 1`s candle is Red 2. With a gap down, opening Day 2 should be either a Doji or Spinning Top 3. Current market price at 3.20 PM should be higher than the opening of Day 1
BEARISH-EVENING STAR-Three candle Formation	Pattern evolves over 3 days-Appears at top end of uptrend-Day 1 has BLUE candle-Day 2 has a Spinning Top or Doji-Day 3 has a RED candle-See I 18	Uptrend-Prior trend is either Spinning Top or Doji	3 Trading sessions	Signals trend reversal-Sell. Trade on Day3 SL @highest high of D1,D2,D3	3rd day candle is Red	1. Day 1 should be Blue candle 2. Day 2 should be a Doji or Spng. Top 3. Day 3 should be a Red candle with gap down. 4. Current Market price at 3.20. PM on Day 3 should be lower than the opening of Day 1
GAP UP OPENING	Shows gap in uptrend between Candlesticks of 2 trading session-occurs when opening price is higher than previous day`s closing price. See I-19	Nil	Nil	Caution	Nil	Occurs due to buyers` enthusiasm caused by any events etc
GAP DOWN OPENING	Shows gap in down trend between candlesticks of 2 trading session-occurs when opening price is lower than previous day`s closing price-See I-20	Nil	Nil	Caution	Nil	Occurs due to sellers` enthusiasm caused by any events etc

*SL –Stop loss

MULTIPLE CANDLESTICK PATTERN-3

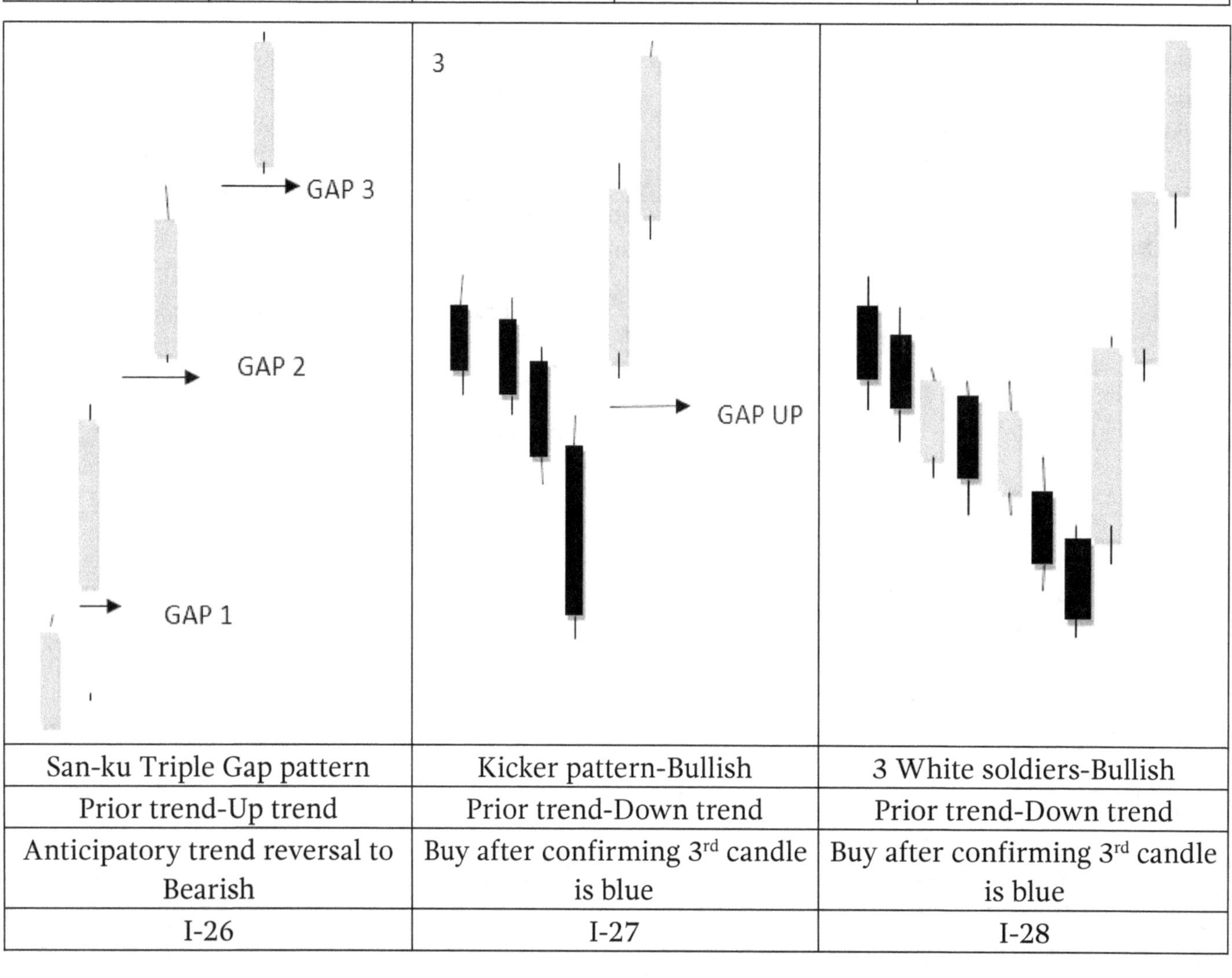

Doji	Dragonfly Doji	Gravestone Doji	Island Reversal-Bullish	Island Reversal-Bearish
Prior trend-Any	Prior trend-Any	Prior trend-Uptrend	Prior trend-Downtrend	Prior trend-Up trend
No trade signal by single	No trade signal by single	No trade signal by single	Buy after the gap up and blue candle	Sell after the gap down and red candle
I-21	I-22	I-23	I-24	I-25

San-ku Triple Gap pattern	Kicker pattern-Bullish	3 White soldiers-Bullish
Prior trend-Up trend	Prior trend-Down trend	Prior trend-Down trend
Anticipatory trend reversal to Bearish	Buy after confirming 3rd candle is blue	Buy after confirming 3rd candle is blue
I-26	I-27	I-28

CANDLESTICKS AND THEIR PATTERNS/BEHAVIOUR-3

BULLISH HARAMI CROSS WITH DOJI	BEARISH HARAMI CROSS WITH DOJI
In downtrend, If Doji (See I-21) appears which is within the real body of the prior session, reversal is likely from Down to Up.	In uptrend, If Doji (See I-21) appears which is within the real body of the prior session, reversal is likely from up to Down.

Pattern	Trend	Appearance of candlestick	Trdg Sesn	Always appears at	Prior Trend	Body/Color of prior candle			Trend reversal		Trade signal
						Day 1	Day 2	Day 3	From	To	
Single Candlestick	Bullish	Hammer, Inverted Hammer	1	Bottom	Down	NA	NA	NA	Down	Up	Buy
	Bearish	Hanging Man, Shooting Star	1	Top	Up	NA	NA	NA	Up	Down	Sell
Two Candlestick	Bullish	Engulfing (Full), Piercing (Partial)	2	Bottom	Down	Small Red	Long Blue	Blue	Down	Up	Buy
	Bearish	Engulfing (Full) Dark Cloud (Partial)	2	Top	Up	Small Blue	Long Red	Red	Up	Down	Sell
	Bullish	Bullish Harami	2	Bottom	Down	Long Red	Small Blue	Blue	Down	Up	Buy
	Bearish	Bearish Harami	2	Top	Up	Long Blue	Small Red	Red	Up	Down	Sell
Three Candlestick	Bullish	Morning Star	3	Bottom	Down	Long Red	SpgTop/ Doji	Blue	Down	Up	Buy
	Bearish	Evening Star	3	Top	Up	Long Blue	SpgTop/ Doji	Red	Up	Down	Sell
	Bull/ Bear	Dragon fly Doji, appears like `T`	3	Top/ Botto	Up/Do	Blue/ Red	Dragon Doji	Rd/ Bl	Up/ Do	Do/U	*
	Bearish	Gravestone Doji, like inverted `T`	3	Top	Up	Blue	Dragon Doji	Red	Down	Up	Sell *1

* Candle that follows Dragonfly Doji (See I-22) on 3rd day confirms the trend. If the 3rd day is Blue, it is uptrend & if 3rd Day is Red, it is down. Trade signals Buy/Sell so vary. *1 Gravestone Doji See I-23

Note:-1) Marubozu & Spinning Top excluded. 2) Long Blue or Long Red candles indicate buying/ selling pressures respectively.

Name of pattern	Trend	Pattern Identification	Signal Trend	Trdg Sesn	Prior Trend	Body/Color of prior candle			Trend reversal		Trade signal
						Day 1	Day 2	Day 3	From	To	
Island Reversal	Bullish	Identify gap between reversal candlestick Doji & 2 candles on either side of it. Price is moving down, gaps lower, then gaps up and price continues higher. For trade, enter Long after the gap and move in the opposite direction-I-24	Short term	2/3	Down	Red	Gap & Doji	Gap & Blue	Down	Up	Buy
	Bearish	Identify gap between reversal candlestick Doji & 2 candles on either side of it. Price is moving up, gaps up, then gaps down and price continues lower. For trade, enter short after the gap and move in the opposite direction-See I-25	Short term	2/3	Up	Blue	Gap & Doji	Gap & Red	Up	Down	Sell
	Exit	When price thrust is weakened and price moves back to fill the gap, reversal is invalidated									

Note: Traders need to identify the trend carefully and confirm the same by deploying technical analysis, RSI, Stochastic, Bollinger Band, Moving Averages, before entering the trade.

ADVANCED CANDLESTICK PATTERNS-4

Name of pattern	Trend	Pattern Identification	Signal Trend	Trdg Sesn	Prior Trend	Body/Color of prior candle			Trend reversal		Trade signal
						Day 1	Day 2	Day 3	From	To	
San-ku Triple gap Pattern	Bearish	It is created in 3 trading sessions in a row with gaps in between in up trending candles. Usually, at least, 2 or 3 of such up trending candles are long. There are 3 gaps higher in a row. Pattern is an anticipatory trend reversal signal that reversal is likely in the near future. See I-26	Short term	3	Up trend	Blue	Blue With gap from Day 1	Blue With gap from Day 2	Up	Down	Sell

Note; Before entering the trade look for additional evidence through RSI, Cross over of MA.

Name of pattern	Trend	Pattern Identification	Signal Trend	Trdg Sesn	Prior Trend	Body/Color of prior candle			Trend reversal		Trade signal
						Day 1	Day 2	Day 3	From	To	
Kicker pattern 2 candle	Bullish	It is characterized by a very sharp reversal in price during a span of 2 candlesticks. Lower move Is reversed by a **gap up** and a large candle in the opposite direction ie from Down to top. First large blue candle is kicker candle. Second large candle shows follow through the first, confirming the reversal. Kicker pattern is considered the most reliable & strongest pattern See I-27	Short term	3	Down trend	Red candle and then a gap	Long Blue indicating reversal	Long Blue confirming the reversal	Down	Up	Buy

Name of pattern	Trend	Pattern Identification	Signal Trend	Trdg Sesn	Prior Trend	Body/Color of prior candle			Trend reversal		Trade signal
						Day 1	Day 2	Day 3	From	To	
3 White Soldiers	Bullish	Appears at the end of downtrend, consisting 3 large Bullish candles, each closing higher than the last. There should be NO gaps between candles, each candle opens within the body of the one preceding it, upper wicks are short & non-existent- See I-28	Uptrend	3	Downtrend- Red	Large Blue Without gap	Large Blue Without gap	Large Blue Without gap	Down	Up	Buy

Note:-Expansion of volume accompanying 3 white soldiers will lend additional strength to the signal. Look for additional chart confirmation.

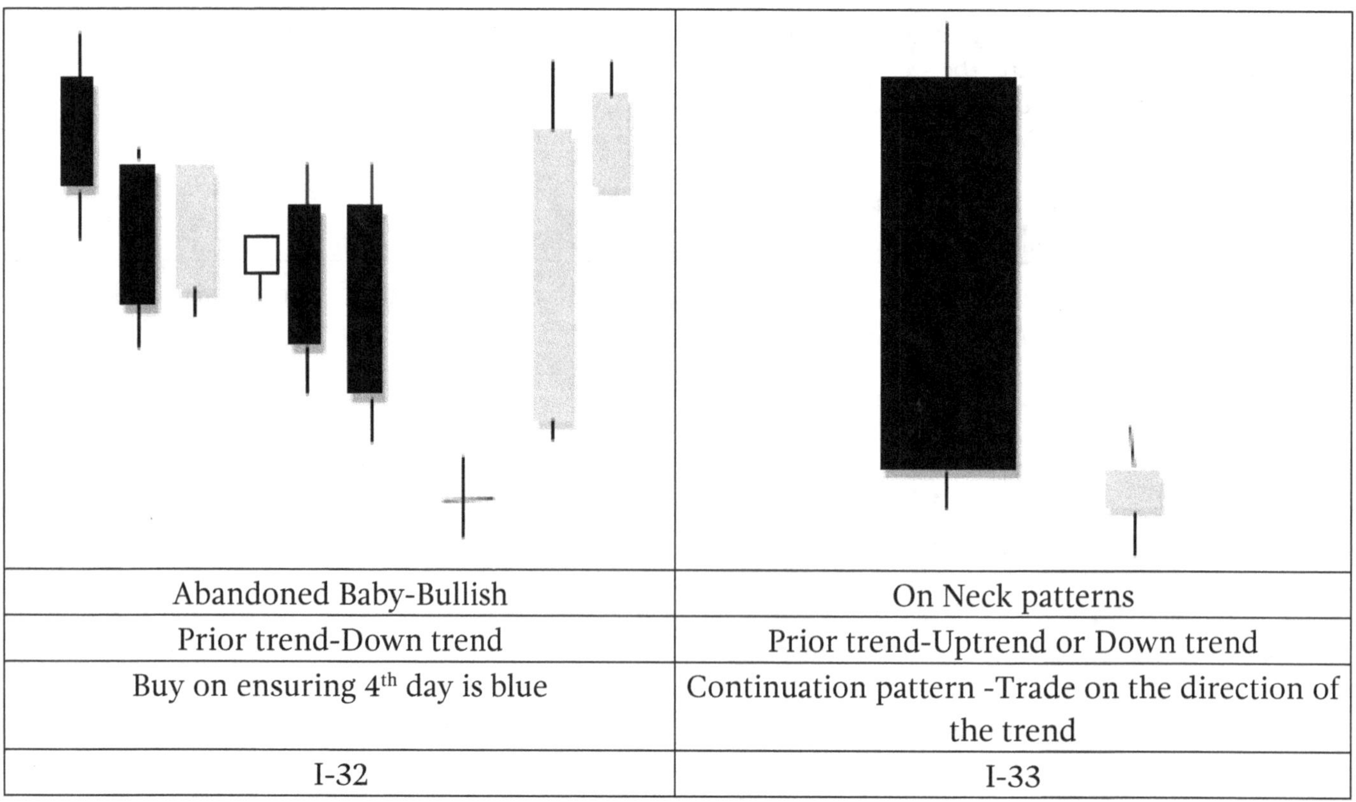

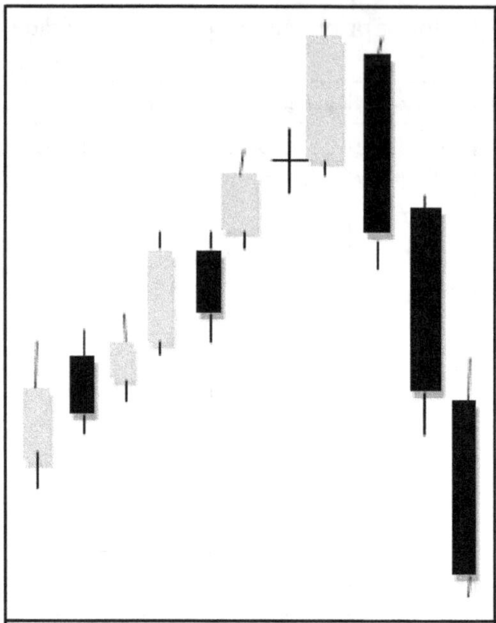 3 Black Crows-Bearish	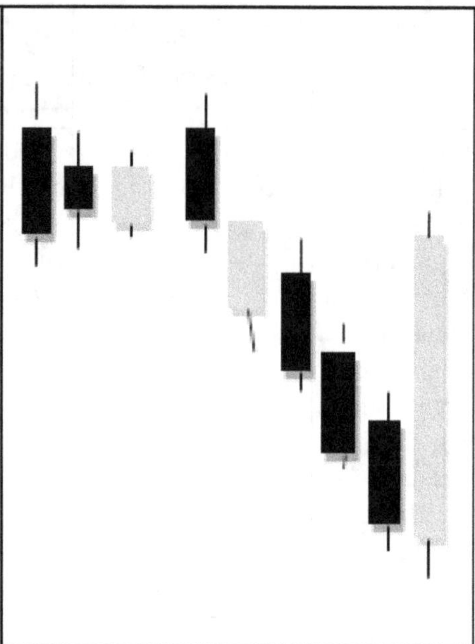 3 line strike- Bullish	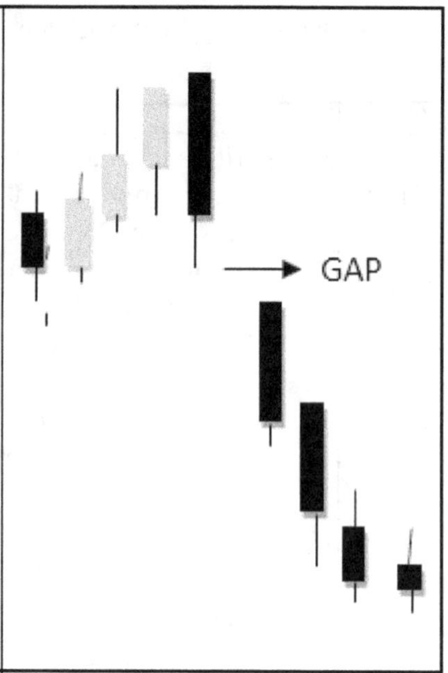 2 Black gapping-Bearish
Prior trend-Up trend	Prior trend-Down trend	Prior trend-Up trend
Sell	Buy after ensuring 4th candle is blue	Sell-Continuation of decline
I-29	I-30	I-31

Abandoned Baby-Bullish	On Neck patterns
Prior trend-Down trend	Prior trend-Uptrend or Down trend
Buy on ensuring 4th day is blue	Continuation pattern -Trade on the direction of the trend
I-32	I-33

ADVANCED CANDLESTICK PATTERNS-5

Name of pattern	Trend	Pattern Identification	Trad sessn	Prior Trend	Body/color of prior trend				Trend reversal		Trade signal
					Day 1	Day 2	Day 3	Day 4	From	To	
Unique Three river pattern	Bullish/ Bearish	Formation should meet the following:-1) The market is in a bearish trend. 2) **Day 1** candle is a bearish long real body in red 3) **Day 2** candle is a hammer with a lower shadow that sets a new low (any color) 4) **Day 3** candle has a short green Body that is below the real body of the day 2 candle and it does not exceed the high or low of the day 2 candle.	4	Down trend	Long body in Red	Hammer, any color	Short green	Confirmatio candle Red/ Blue	Up/ Down	Down/ Up	*

*Confirmation candle on Day 4 determines whether trend is reversed to bullish OR bearish trend continues. Trade may be initiated accordingly

Name of pattern	Trend	Pattern Identification	Trdg Sesn	Prior Trend	Body/Color of prior candle			Trend reversal		Trade signal
					Day 1	Day 2	Day 3	From	To	
3 black crows	Bearish	Consists 3 consecutive long bodied bearish candlesticks with short, or no shadow or wicks. These 3 candlesticks form within the real body of the previous candles and close lower than the previous candle. Downward pressure should sustain over 3 trading sessions, indicating start of the bearish downtrend. This pattern is opposite of 3 white soldiers. See I-29	3	Uptrend-Blue candle	Large Red Body with short or no shadow	Large Red Body with short or no shadow	Large Red Body with short or no shadow	Up	Down	Sell
Volume		Volume during uptrend leading up to the pattern formation is relatively low & 3 crows pattern comes with relatively high volume								
Other Technicals		Other technical indicators like RSI should be used to confirm the reversal and ascertain oversold position								

ADVANCED CANDLESTICK PATTERNS-6

Candlestick patterns signal either reversal in price direction or continuation in current price direction. Accuracy of few patterns is as under:-

Pattern	Pattern Identification	Used for Predicting	Accuracy of prediction
3 Line Strike	Prediction with 3 Red candles in sequence. Each Red candle posts a lower low and closes near the intra bar low. 4th bar opens even lower, but reverses with Bullish green that closes above the high of Ist candle. See I-30	Reversal from Bearish to Bullish that occurs in 4 candles	Predicts higher prices with accuracy rate of 83%
2 Black Gapping	2 Bearish Red candles appear at the top of the uptrend with gaps downwards posting lower lows. See I-31	Continuation of Downtrend in 3 candles	Predicts continuation of decline in prices with accuracy rate of 68%
3 Black Crows	3 Bearish Red candles starts near the high of an uptrend with each Red candles posting lower lows and closing near the intra bar lows See I-29	Continuation of lower prices in 3 candles	Predicts continuation of lower prices with accuracy rate of 78%
Evening Star	A tall Green candle appearing at the top of the uptrend. Market gaps on the next candle with a narrow range. A gap down on the 3rd bar completes the pattern. See I-18	Reversal from up to Down in 3 candles	Predicts continuation of decline will accuracy rate of 72%
Abandoned Baby	After a series of Red candles, abandoned Baby (Doji) appears at the low of the downtrend. With gaps preceding Doji and in Uptrend after Doji, bullish green candle appears predicting Uptrend-See I-32	Reversal from Down to Up on 3 candles	Predicts reversal with higher prices with accuracy rate of 49.73%

COUNTER ATTACK LINES PATTERN
Counter attack lines pattern Is a two candle reversal pattern that appears on a candlestick chart. It can occur during an uptrend or downtrend signaling a potential reversal. The pattern is composed of two candles in opposite color/direction

BULLISH COUNTER ATTACK LINE- Conditions to be met	BEARISH COUNTER ATTACK LINE- Conditions to be met
1. Market is in DOWNTREND	1. Market is in UPTREND
2. The first candle is RED with a long real body	2. The first candle is GREEN with a long real body
3. The second candle is GREEN with GAP DOWN on the open and with a real body that is similar in size to the first candle and closes near the first candle`s close	3. The second candle is RED with GAP HIGHER on the open and with a real body that is similar in size to the first candle and closes near the first candle`s close
4. Reversal should be confirmed by formation of 3 rd or 4 th candle as possibility of reversal is 50% only	4. Reversal should be confirmed by formation of 3 rd or 4 th candle as possibility of reversal is 50% only
5. If confirmation is occurred, a stop loss should be placed BELOW the LOW of the pattern FOR LONG trade	5. If confirmation is occurred, a stop loss should be placed ABOVE the HIGH of the pattern FOR SHORT trade

Limitations	Formation of these patterns is not frequent and hence trading opportunities are limited and short lived. So NO target price can be fixed

Difference between Engulfing and Counter attack line pattern is (i) in engulfing pattern, candles are side by side and (ii) 2nd candle`s real body fully engulfing the real body of the 1st candle, while in Counter attack line pattern, both Up and Down candles have real bodies of similar size

ADVANCED CANDLESTICK PATTERNS-7

ON NECK PATTERN	
CONDITIONS OF FORMATION	1. On neck is a pattern that occurs during a downtrend or a pullback within an uptrend. 2. The 1st candle should be a long real bodied RED/Bearish down candle. 3. The 1st candle is followed by a 2nd candle which is small GREEN/Bullish up candle that gaps down on the open but then closes near the prior candle`s close. The small bullish 2nd candle could be of any form like Doji or any small bodied bull candle than the previous one. 4. Closing price of BOTH candles should be equal or nearly equal. See I-33
TRADE SIGNAL	On neck pattern is considered a continuation pattern during downtrend or a pullback within an uptrend.
CAUTION	This should be used in conjunction with other technical analysis/follow-up candles for confirmation.
DIFFERENCE	Difference between On neck pattern and Counterattack line pattern:- (i) in Counter attack line pattern, both Up and Down candles have real bodies of similar size while in the On Neck pattern, 2nd candle has smaller body (ii) On neck pattern is a continuation pattern while Counter attack line pattern is a reversal pattern.

ADVANCED CANDLESTICK PATTERNS-8

USEFUL TIPS ON HOW TO IDENTIFY TRENDS IN CANDLESTICK PATTERNS AND INITIATE POTENTIAL BUY & SELL								
Cand	Ist	2nd	3rd	When Bullish trend	Cand	Ist	2nd	When Bearish trend
2	Red	Green	–	When close of both candles is equal	2	Green	Red	When close of both candles is equal
2	Red	Red	–	When 2nd candle is fully contained in Ist candl				LEFT BLANK
2	Red	Green	–	When Ist is engulfed by 2nd candle and & also when 9 Day crosses from below 21 Day EMA	2	Green	Red	When Ist is engulfed by 2nd candle and & also when 9 Day crosses from above 21 Day EMA
3	Red	Green	Green	When 2nd is within Ist Red, 3rd is squeezed within 2 nd & both 2nd & 3rd within Ist Red				LEFT BLANK
1	Green	–	–	When Green is Marubozu & also when 9 Day crosses from below 21 Day EMA	1	Red	–	When Red is Marubozu & also when 9 Day crosses from above 21 Day EMA
2	Red	Green	–	When both are Marubozu & 2nd is gap up from Ist	2	Green	Red	When both are Marubozu & 2nd is gap down from Ist
2	Red	Green	–	When High & Low of 2nd candle is lesser than Open & close of Ist candle	2	Green	Red	When High & Low of 2nd candle is lesser than Open & close of Ist candle
2	Red	Red	–	When Low AND close of both match & also when 9 Day crosses from below 21 Day EMA	2	Green	Green	When High AND close of both match & also when 9 Day crosses from above 21 Day EMA

NOTES NO.1	The above are other than patterns like Shooting Star, Morning/Evening Star, Harami, Engulfing, Piercing, Dogi, which are described elsewhere.
2	Shooting Star is like an inverted paper umbrella that appears at top end of a rally. Shooting Star always signals Bearish
3	Hanging Man is a paper umbrella, appearing at top end of the rally.
4	Color of the paper umbrella does not matter What matters is open & close of paper umbrella is quite close to each other.
5	It is Hammer if paper umbrella appears at bottom & Hanging Man if it appears at top end
6	Signals of candlestick patterns should be confirmed with technical analysis of Moving averages, Oscillators etc

SETTING STOP LOSS ON CANDLESTICK PATTERNS	
Single candle-When Bullish	**Single candle-When Bearish**
Set stop loss at low of the candle	Set stop loss at high of the candle
Multiple candlestick pattern-When Bullish	**Multiple candlestick pattern-When Bearish**
Set stop loss at lowest low of of the candles involved	Set stop loss at highest high of the candles involved

KEY POINTS TO REMEMBER WHILE IDENTIFYING CANDLES FOR TRADING

Very few traders will be patient enough to make the right prediction especially with the validation points like measuring length of candles with opening & closing prices etc. But trader may find that candlestick pattern is easy to identify than those with 1 or 2 candle solo formation. For ex. It is easy to identify patterns like 3 white soldiers, 3 black crow, Abandoned baby, Pattern formation with Doji, dragonfly etc.

As a precautionary approach and check point before entering into a trade, it is always good for a trader to ensure that trading signals that are identified from the candlestick charting pattern are confirmed by technical analysis with statistical data like Moving averages, Bollinger Bands, etc

Long term Investors normally do not bother market swings and market risks, as their investment outlook is long term growth unlike swing traders. So for them, candlestick charting pattern and technical analysis are less important.

Patterns can be relied for a maximum of 3 to 4 candles after completion of pattern

Please learn more on pattern trading in technical analysis with statistical data in the next chapter

CHAPTER 3-B

TECHNICAL ANALYSIS TOOLS FOR TRADING (1)

CONTENTS

1 Momentum Indicators

2 Various Terminology and their meaning in Technical Analysis

3 Volume and Volume linked Technical Analysis
Volume Weighted Average Price (VWAP),On Balance Volume (OBV), Money Flow Index (MFI)
Accumulation/Distribution Indicator (A/D), Volume Oscillator

4 Support & Resistance (S&R)

5 Relative Strength Index (RSI)

6 Moving Average (MA)

7 Cross over of Moving Average- Golden Cross & Death Cross

8 Exponential Moving Average (EMA)

9 Double Exponential Moving Average (DEMA)

10 Triple Exponential Moving Average (TRIX)

11 Moving Average Convergence Divergence (MACD)

12 Bollinger Band

13 Stochastic Oscillator

14 Fibonacci Retracement

15 Dow Theory-Double Top & Double Bottom

16 Triple Top & Triple Bottom

17 Head & Shoulder Pattern

18 Pennant, Ascending Triangle, Descending Triangle, Symmetrical Triangle

19 Rising Wedge, Falling Wedge

20 Pivot Points

21 Average Directional Index (ADX)

22 Aroon Indicator,

23 Aroon Oscillator

24 Risk, Risk Perception & Risk Mitigation, Risk to Reward- Calculation

25 Beta and how Beta indicators work

26 Know the difference between Retracement and Reversal

27 Know the difference between Reversal and Pull back

28 Know the difference between Consolidation and Continuation

29 Know the difference between Trending Market and Sideway Market

30 Know the difference between Noisy market and Normal Market

31 FAQ on Technical Analysis

Earlier in the previous chapter, we studied technical analysis on candlestick charting patterns and their trade signals. In this chapter, we will move on to study technical indicators that interpret various price movements and volumes to analyze how a stock or asset will behave in near future and predict their price direction. While, in fundamental analysis, analysis is done on revenue, profit margin, P/E Ratio etc., in Technical section, analysis is done on technical indicators. Technical analysis can be used on any asset with historical trading data. There are few types of technical indicators.

Momentum indicators	Momentum is a relative term to price change. When stock's price changes more rapidly, momentum is said to be high & vice versa. Momentum indicators are of 2 types, viz Leading Indicator & lagging indicator
Leading indicators	Leads the price, means, signaling the occurrence of reversal or a new trend **in advance.** Not all leading indicators are accurate. Few of them may give false signal too. Majority of leading indicators is Oscillators which oscillates between two ranges viz 0 to 100
Lagging indicators	Lags the price, means, signaling the occurrence of a reversal or a new trend **after it has occurred.** In other words, lagging indicators confirm the trend and changes in trend. Popular among the lagging indicators is Moving Averages. Lagging indicators are based on past prices.
VARIOUS TERMINOLOGY AND THEIR MEANING IN TECHNICAL ANALYSIS	
Strategy	Strategy is a knack of deployment of one or the other statistical indicators to achieve objectives and desired goals- goal being to predict as far as possible, accurate price direction of a stock or an asset, factoring into it's historical data in a given term.
Volume	In stock trading volume refers to number of shares that have changed hands in the course of a day's trading. If one sells 100 shares to another who buys 100 shares, volume of that trade is 100 and NOT 200.
Momentum	Momentum is the rate of change in an asset's/ stock's price for a particular period of time. A stock's price will move up or down in a short term in accelerated way, normally, regardless of it's fundamental value. Simply put, it is the speed at which price is changing.
Look back	Look back period is simply viewing today's price action of a stock with reference to that on it's past data. For instance, look back period of 3 months means you are looking at today's price in the backdrop of recent 3 months data. For beginners, it needs to be 6 months to 1 year & for scalpers (day-trading) it could be 5 minutes.
Trend	Trend is general direction of the market or the price of a stock or an asset.
Pattern	Pattern is a formation identifiable by stocks' price behavior in a predictable way. Patterns have two types-Reversal Pattern & Continuation pattern.
Reversal pattern	Reversal is a change in price direction. Directional changes happen to upside after downtrend OR downside after uptrend
Continuation pattern	Continuation patterns suggest that price will continue in the current price direction.

Consolidation	A stock is said to be under consolidation when it trades within a limited price ranges. Consolidation is generally regarded as a period of indecision which ends when the price of the stock moves above or below the price in the trading range. The consolidation pattern in the price movement may also be broken upon a major news release or on any high volume.
Sideway	Price direction of a stock move neither upward nor downward, instead move horizontally meaning the market is indecisive on price behavior of that stock. In other words, forces of demand and supply are neutral in sideway market
Retracement	Retracement is a temporary price reversal that takes place within a large trend, usually characterized by abundant indecision.
Pull back	A pullback is a temporary reversal in the price action of an asset or security with it`s duration remaining usually only for a few consecutive sessions.
Overbought	Overbought is a term to describe a level when a stock is believed to be currently trading above it`s fair value with reference to it`s fundamental value like Price to Earnings ratio (P/E Ratio) etc. Overbought indicates likely reversal to downtrend
Oversold	Oversold is opposite to overbought. It refers to a level when a stock is believed to be trading currently at below it`s fair value with reference to it`s fundamental value like P/E Ratio etc. Oversold indicates likely reversal to uptrend.
Cross-over	Crossover is a point in a trading chart in which a security`s price and a technical indicator line intersect OR when two indicators themselves cross. Cross-over is used to estimate the performance of a stock and predict forthcoming changes in trends such as reversals or break-outs. Please see below what break-out is and when it occurs
Gap	Gap is a price gap found in price charts of an asset. Gap is said to occur when it`s price rises or falls from it`s previous day`s closing price even when there is no trading taking place in between, caused by any news impacting the asset.
Oscillator	Oscillator is a tool in analysis to construct a range with high and low of a stock`s price and identify price fluctuations that happen within this range for trading opportunities. Over bought and oversold positions are predicted based on the price reaching the high or low in the range
Standard Deviation	Standard deviation is a way of measuring a stock`s variability or volatility i.e deviation from a centre point.
Relative strength	Relative strength is identifying or selecting stocks which outperform their benchmark or market, for ex., if a stock in a financial services sector is performing well surpassing their peers in the same sector or the overall market level, the stock is said to be relatively stronger
Accumulation	Accumulation is a term used when quiet and implicit buying of stocks by institutional investors happen in a market characterized by sideway price movements. Normally sideway market indicates buying opportunities as the price of a stock is stable, trading with average volume. For investors, this period is considered a good entry point to buy before the price rises.

Distribution	Distribution is opposite to accumulation phase. Distribution refers to sell off by Institutional buyers in small quantity gradually throughout the day so that their sudden selling in one bulk do not result in drop in prices. A trader can watch for abnormal increase in a day`s volume traded on that day and he may sell the stock before price drops.
Convergence	Convergence is when price of a stock moves in tandem with it`s technical indicators.
Divergence	Divergence is when price of a stock and it`s technical indicators move in opposite direction. When price rises and indicator falls, it is an indication of weakening trend and hence fall in price in the near term.
Support	Support or support level is a price point below which a stock`s price is not expected to fall till a time period market forces move to play and change the trend. Support level is a line drawn by connecting price points of lowest lows in a period. Since at the lowest price buyers will flow in to buy stocks at lower prices and thereby increasing demand, reversal in trend is anticipated from down to up
Resistance	Resistance or resistance level is a price point above which a stock`s price is not expected to rise till a time period market forces move in to play and change the trend. Resistance level is a line drawn by connecting price points of highest highs in a period. Since at the highest price sellers will flow in to sell stocks at higher prices and book profits and thereby increasing supply, reversal in trend is anticipated from up to down.
Range	Range is the difference between the highest and lowest price point of a stock in a given period. For ex., if a stock is trading at it`s lowest price say @Rs 825/- in March and highest price say @ Rs 1028/- in June, we may define the stock is trading in a range between Rs 825/- & Rs 1028/-in period of four months. Here lowest price is it`s support level and highest price is it`s resistance level for that period. This range may break out at times of new corporate announcements or restructuring in holding pattern like buying or selling by Foreign Institutional investors/domestic institutional investors, policy announcements from Govt., etc
Break-out	Break out refers to price direction when price of a stock moves above it`s defined resistance level or below it`s defined support level on increasing volumes. When a stock breaks out with high volume, it`s price is likely to move further in the same direction.
Channel	Channel is a stock`s trading range within it`s support and resistance level
Price action	Price action is general movement of price of a stock or asset over a period. It is a range of prices at which stock or asset is traded over a period of time-Daily, weekly, monthly etc. For example, price action of a day refers to the highest and lowest price of a stock at which it was traded on a day. Price action is important as technical analysis and charts are calculated from the price action in the past.

Target Price	Target price is an analyst`s or an investor`s projected future price of a stock or an asset based on it`s fundamental analysis and/or technical analysis. Usually, target price is quoted by analyst in their research report along with buy, sell and hold recommendations. Hold refers to neutral position meaning neither buy nor sell
Hold	Hold normally appears in research reports of analysts. When they recommend a stock to hold, it means the company is expected to perform at the same pace as it`s peers in the market meaning they recommend neither buy nor sell but neutral
Volatility	Volatility occurs when a stock`s price moves with big swings either up or down over a sustained period.
Trend line	Trend lines are tools to analysts which are drawn by connecting highs of price points or connecting lows of price points in a time frame. It shows uptrend when highs are connected and downtrend when lows are connected. Thus trend lines can also be applied to draw support or resistance or create a channel.
Rally	Rally is a period of sustained **increase** in prices of a stock or indexes which can happen in bull or bear market. It`s important feature is that rally will follow a period of flat or declining prices.
Noise	In financial markets, noise refers to any activity that confuses or misrepresents genuine underlying trends. Noise includes short term price correction or volatility that a trader feels difficult to discern what genuine price movement is and what is caused by mere rumors.
Exhaustion	Exhaustion is perhaps rare in India, but still it is better to know. Exhaustion refers to a situation where there will be no more buyers when selling a stock since everyone have already bought it, thereby causing the price to fall.
Histogram	Histogram is a graphical representation of grouped data points into user specific requirement for easy visual interpretation with X axis representing grouped data and Y axis representing percentage of such data.

UNDERSTANDING TECHNICAL ANALYSIS CONCEPT AND DEVELOPING SKILL

Before learning technical analysis, a word of advice. A trader needs to understand that investing his hard earned money blindly will end up in disaster and therefore, acquiring fundamental knowledge and skill are essential for successful trading in stock/asset. So, it is imperative to know on how to deploy technical tools to get indicators or signals for opportunity in trading, when to enter a trade, how to analyze various price points and volume traded, thrown open by technical analysis charts, indicators etc, how to predict or forecast future price movements with evolving risk perception on the trade and ways to mitigate risks by exiting the trade or otherwise, either with minimal or no loss. Note not to miss the key points and tips that are given at the end of this chapter.

VOLUME & VOLUME LINKED TECHNICAL ANALYSIS

Volume plays a very important role in creation of market forces-demand & supply. A stock`s trending strength or weakness and divergence can be interpreted by increase or decrease in the volumes traded on the stock. We give below general trend in volumes and their impact on price points like signals they send to initiate trade and other technical analysis which combine volume with price to predict future trends.

Stock`s Price	It`s volume	Trend indicator	Interpretation	Trade signal
Increase	Increase	Bullish	A rising market - caused by heavy bulk buying by Institutional investors	Go with trend and Buy
Decrease	Increase	Bearish	A falling market - caused by heavy bulk selling by institutional investors	Go with trend and sell
Increase	Decrease	Retailers` play	Indicates no bulk buying. Price rise on decreasing volume may signal weakening trend and warn of divergence or potential reversal shortly from it`s prior trend.	Watch for potential resistance. If yes, sell
Decrease	Decrease	Retailers` play	Indicates no bulk selling. Price fall on decreasing volume may signal trend has weakened and warns of potential bottom end before accumulation	Watch for a false break out. If not a false one, buy

Note:-

1. Increase in volume and increase in price can be attributed to continuing uptrend when a stock breaches past it`s resistance level or it`s range

2. Increase in volume and decrease in prices can be attributed to continuing downtrend when a stock breaches down it`s support level or it`s range

3. Attributes of false break out are:- Stock will open beyond resistance or support price and later in the day, it will move back to it`s prior price range.

4. Trader should wait for confirmation that the stock does not move back as in 3 above before trading break outs.

5. Trade signal for the last two (Retailers` play) is only suggestive and trader may take trading decision on his own assessment of the market.

6. Break-out occurs when the price of a stock moves above the defined resistance level or below the defined support level, both happening always with increase in volume. Proper Identification of support & resistance is important to confirm break-out.

VOLUME WEIGHTED AVERAGE PRICE (VWAP)

VWAP is an average price of a stock that is arrived based on both the price and it`s volume traded. It gives confirmation on the trend and value of a security. VWAP being an intraday tool, is calculated on time frame like 1 min, 5min, 10 min etc with it`s price and volume traded in each minute to arrive VWAP as under. It cannot be applied on EOD (End of day) data and therefore, VWAP calculated on multiple day data will give wrong indicator. VWAP is different from Simple moving average as the latter do not factor volume

HOW IT IS CALCULATED
1. Record average of high, low & close = Typical Price (TP) 2. Multiply TP with volume = Volume Price (VP) 3. Get cumulative by adding current VP to previous VP = Total VP 4. Get cumulative by adding current volume to previous volume = Total Volume 5. Divide Total VP by Total Volume i.e.3/4 = VWAP

TRADE SIGNAL	
If current price is lower than VWAP	Stock is trending down
If current price is higher than VWAP	Stock is trending up
If current price is in between high & low	Stock will remain volatile
BUY	At a price lower than VWAP
SELL/Short	At a price higher than VWAP

ON BALANCE VOLUEME (OBV)

OBV is a technical indicator of momentum that predicts change in stock`s price by using flow of volume. So, even if volume spikes sharply without much change in price for now, eventually price will move upward or downward. OBV theory says large investors buy when retailers start selling. As a result of such selling volume increases pushing the price up when large investors start selling. Divergence is said to occur when trend is higher and volume is decreasing that signals potential reversal. Likewise, higher volume and lower trend signal potential reversal. OBV indicator may be relied after confirmation from moving averages as OBV may produce false signal too..

HOW OBV IS CALCULATED

OBV is a cumulative total of assets` trading volume. For ex, in 10 day OBV calculation, closing price (CP) of a stock and it`s traded volume is taken. If a day`s CP is higher than previous day`s CP, it`s volume is taken as flown in and added. If a day`s CP is less than previous day`s CP, it`s volume is taken as flown out and subtracted. There are three rules when calculating the OBV. They are:-

If today`s closing price is > yesterday`s closing price, then,	current OBV = Previous OBV + Today`s volume
If today`s closing price is < yesterday`s closing price, then,	current OBV = Previous OBV - Today`s volume
If today`s closing price is = yesterday`s closing price, then	current OBV = Previous OBV

TRADE SIGNAL	
When OBV is rising	Indication is buyers tend the prices higher
When OBV is falling	Indication is sellers tend the price lower
When Price & OBV is rising	Indication is the continuation of the trend
When Price is rising & OBV is falling OR price is falling & OBV is rising it means Divergence	Trend is not backed by strong buyers and could soon reverse

MONEY FLOW INDEX (MFI)	
MFI is a technical oscillator that uses both price and volume data for identifying overbought and oversold signals in an asset, with readings between 0 to 100. It can also be used to spot divergence which warns of a trend change in price. Difference between MFI & RSI (Relative strength Index which is another momentum indicator) is that MFI incorporates both price & volume while RSI incorporates just price alone. MFI is considered a leading indicator as they indicate possible reversals. Learn more on RSI below in this chapter.	
DIVERGENCE	
One of the primary uses of MFI is to identify divergence. Divergence is when price is moving up while oscillator is moving down in the opposite direction. When MFI is falling below 80 while price continues to rise, then, it is a signal for reversal of price to fall. Similarly when MFI is climbing above 20 while the price continues to fall, it is signal for reversal of price to rise.	
TRADE SIGNAL	
Buy	when oscillator is reading **below** 20 which is considered oversold. When an asset is in uptrend, a drop below 20 or 30 and then a rally back above it, could indicate that the pullback is over & price uptrend is resuming.
Sell	when oscillator is reading **above** 80 which is considered overbought. A short term rally could push MFI up to 70 or 80, but when it drops back below it, that could be the time to enter a short trade in preparation for another drop.
Alert	False signal	As MFI is likely to send false signal, the trader should confirm the signal by using other technical indicators.

ACCUMULATION/DISTRIBUTION INDICATOR (A/D)	
A/D is a cumulative indicator that uses volume & price to assess whether the stock is accumulated or distributed. It seeks to identify the divergence between stock price & volume flow and how strong trending is. It helps to know how demand and supply factors are influencing the price in a given period and to determine whether price closed in the upper or lower in it`s range. AD line is drawn with multiplier effect and money flow volume. Convergence and Divergence between price of the stock and AD line signals the trend.	
Trade signal on Divergence	If the price is rising but A/D is falling, it signals underlying`s weakness and potential decline in price.
	If the price is falling & A/D is rising, it signals underlying`s strength and price may start to rise.
Trade signal on Convergence	If both A/D & price is rising, it confirms the trend will continue to rise.
	If both A/D & price is falling, it confirms the trend will continue to decline.
Difference	Though both On Balance volume (OBV) and A/D use price and volume, difference between them lies on their calculations. OBV is calculated on whether price is higher or lower from it`s previous close and if higher, volume is added and if lower, volume is subtracted. A/D, on the other hand, is calculated based on a multiplier, factoring whether the price closed within a range.

Confirmation	As A/D is likely to give false signal, use A/D in conjunction with other analysis for confirmation.

VOLUME OSCILLATOR
A volume oscillator measures volume by measuring the relationship between two moving averages. Volume oscillator helps confirm price movements of a stock.
WHY VOLUME IS IMPORTANT
Market move is based on the principle that without strong volume, market move or a stock`s price move is not valid because volume is an indicator of enthusiasm or lack of it. Volume, thus, plays an important role on indicating reversal or momentum.

Reversal	In reversal, a trader must determine whether stock`s price momentum and volume momentum go along with each other. If not, trend is likely to be weak and reversal is likely to happen. Volume momentum also shows the level of enthusiasm in buying and selling activity

HOW VOLUME OSCILLATOR IS CALCUATED
To calculate, add the number of shares traded on a day on a stock or an asset. Fix fast moving and slow moving averages. Fast moving average is usually 14 days or weeks of volumes traded and the slow volume moving average is 28 days or weeks of volumes traded. Difference between these two is plotted as a histogram. Histogram becomes an oscillator and fluctuates above or below a zero line indicating positive or negative values respectively.
HOW VOLUME OSCILLATOR IS INTERPRETED

When histogram is above zero line	it is +ve and suggests that enough market support exists to continue the drive in the direction of the current trend
When histogram is below zero line	it is −ve and suggests lack of support indicating that prices may become stagnant or reverse.
Bearish	Rising volume and declining prices OR increasing price with declining volume are display of bearish trend.

MONEYFLOW
Money flow is indicator of trading interest in a stock through money flown between days. It is calculated by averaging high. Low and closing price of a stock and multiplying it with the volume traded on the day. By comparing the data arrived similarly for the previous day, a trader can identify positive or negative money flow. For ex. if a high, low & closing price of a stock is say Rs 200/-,Rs 180/-& 190/-, & the volume traded is say 25000, then money flow for the day is 25000X (200+180+190/3) i.e.,25000x190=47,50,000. If the data for the previous day is say 45,00,000, today`s money flow is +ve, while the previous day is −ve. Positive money flow indicates price is likely to rise and negative money flow indicates price is likely to fall.

SUPPORT & RESISTANCE (S&R)
Support & Resistance level is the most important tool in technical analysis. They are upper and lower price barriers within which a stock oscillates. When a stock`s price reaches a high or low price point, forces of demand and supply set in in the form of buyers or sellers interest as a result of which, the price is resisted from moving further up or down. If the price moves up or down breaching the barrier, it continues in that direction until it creates another new support or resistance level. S&R is the fundamentals for drawing Trend lines trading, Channel trading, Range trading, rectangle trading. Understanding the concept is, therefore, the most important pre-requisite for successful trading.

SUPPORT
Support is a price level in a downtrend below which prices do not fall further owing to increased demand for buying caused by lower prices. Support is where traders expect maximum demand in terms of buying. The likelihood of prices falling up to Support level and then rising is high. Support level can also be identified by drawing trend line or Simple Moving average.

RESISTANCE
Resistance is a price level in an uptrend above which prices do not rise further owing to increased supply by selling caused by higher prices. Resistance is where traders expect the maximum supply in terms of selling. The likelihood of price rising up to Resistance level and then declining is higher. Resistance level can also be identified by drawing trend line or Simple Moving average.

Trend line method	Side way trend	Up trending	Down trending
To draw Support	Connect all low prices in a sideway trend chart in which case it will appear as flat line	Connect all low prices in an up trending chart in which case it will appear as sloping up line	Connect all low prices in a downtrend chart in which case it will appear as sloping down line.
To draw Resistance	Connect all high prices in a sideway trend chart in which case it will appear as flat line	Connect all high prices in an up trending chart in which case it will appear as sloping up line	Connect all high prices in a downtrend chart in which case it will appear as sloping down line.
Trend line method	Trend lines can be drawn in a chart to view support & resistance for any time period a trader wants.		
Moving Average (MA) method	In an uptrend,50,100,200 day MA may act as Support level & in a downtrend, 50,100,200 day MA may act as a Resistance level. In Moving average method, Resistance level is always above the current market price and Support level is always below the current market price.		

TRADE SIGNAL

Buy	As floor/bottom price has been reached at support level, Uptrend is expected. Hence Buy
Sell	As ceiling has been reached at resistance level, Downtrend is expected. Hence Short/Sell
Confirmation	Confirm Support & Resistance formation in conjunction with Candlesticks, Volumes, Moving Average, Trending etc

RELATIVE STRENGTH INDEX (RSI)

RSI is a "leading" momentum indicator that measures degree of recent price changes to evaluate overbought and oversold conditions. It is a momentum oscillator between 0 to 100 which helps identifying early sign of trend reversal/ correction with overbought & oversold price area. It is plotted below the graph of a stock`s price with a look back period of 14 days data points. Look back period may be changed according to a trader`s choice. Uptrend/downtrend may continue from a few days to few years. Hence RSI may remain in the overbought/oversold position for a long time too.

HOW IT IS CALCULATED

RSI is calculated by using average price gains and price lost over a given period of time. Record price changes in a stock over a period of 14 days. Take a base closing price. (1) Add all increase (gain) in price and average it by look back period viz 14 days. Similarly, (2) add all decrease (lost) in prices and average it by look back period. (3) Divide result of 1 by result of 2. (4) Apply formula 100—100/(1+(3)) (Here 3 is the result of ½) Result tells you overbought or oversold area.

OVERBOUGHT AND OVERSOLD

Reading between 70 to100 indicates overbought position that implies that the positive momentum in the stock is high and it cannot sustain in the overbought position for long, signaling possible correction to downward. Similarly, reading between 0 to 30 means oversold position which indicates that the negative momentum is high, signaling possible correction to upward.

FALSE SIGNALS OF RSI

As RSI is a momentum indicator with recent price changes in price, it may give false signals too when changes in stock`s price happen swiftly with substantial impact. With such moves RSI can stay in the overbought area for extended period while the stock is in an uptrend. The indicator may also remain in oversold territory for a long time when the stock is in a down trend. Therefore, it is necessary to get confirmation from other technical analysis before initiating trade on signals of RSI alone.

COMPLEMENTARY SOURCES FOR CONFIRMATION

MACD	Moving average convergence divergence (MACD) is a technical analysis that a trader may get confirmation as MACD is also a momentum indicator though MACD compares momentum by short term and long term moving averages as against RSI that compares momentum based on recent price change. In MACD, MACD line is drawn by subtracting 26 day EMA from 12 day EMA. A signal line is drawn using 9 day EMA. Cross over between these lines signal trading opportunities. When both RSI & MACD display buy or sell signal, a trader gets confirmation. Learn more on MACD below in this chapter
Moving average Cross overs	Short term moving average 5 EMA crossing over 10 EMA is taken for confirmation. 5 EMA crossing from above to below the 10 EMA confirms the RSI's indication of overbought conditions and possible trend reversal. Conversely, an upside crossover provides an additional indication that a market might be oversold. For detailed study on SMA, EMA, please see below in this chapter

Doji formation	Formation of Doji may also confirm trend reversal depending on the candle that follows Doji. If the following candle is red, it signals downtrend confirming overbought. If it is blue candle, it signals confirmation of uptrend and oversold.

TRADE SIGNAL	
Buy	If RSI moves **ABOVE** 30 or if RSI stays in oversold position for prolonged period
Sell	if RSI moves **BELOW** 70 or if RSI stays in the overbought position for prolonged period

MOVING AVERAGES

Moving average (MA) is a method of calculating and averaging closing price points of a stock mathematically for a given period time with constant up-date of input price data. For EX., to calculate MA of 10 days price data, add all the closing prices of a stock for the last 10 days and average it by 10. By constantly updating it with inclusion of new data and discarding old data, trader can get an updated average price When 10 day price points are connected on a chart, a curve forms which is 10 day MA. It is a lagging indicator as it relies on the past price data. It indicates trend direction and also helps determining support and resistance level. There are few types of MAs known as simple moving average (SMA), exponential moving average (EMA), double exponential moving average

(DEMA) and triple exponential moving average (TEMA). In SMA, price data are assigned equal weight-age while in EMA recent price data is given more weight-age and old price data are given less weight-age, thus making EMA more reactive to recent price changes.

TIME FRAME

Time frame means the number of price data that have been taken for calculating MA. It can be 5 day, 9 day, 21 day, 25 day, 50 day, 100 day & 200 day. Choosing the right time frame depends on the choice of a trader and his comfort with it. Longer the time frame means more number of data points and hence less sensitive to price changes. Shorter time frame gives, on the other hand, more response to price changes and more trade signals. Generally 20 SMA is taken for analytical purposes. MA`s signal strength depends on the length of time frame one uses. For short term traders 20 day MA is more helpful and 200 day MA is helpful for long term investors.

OTHER TECHNICAL ANALYSIS BASED ON MOVING AVERAGES	
MACD	MACD is about convergence divergence of moving averages that indicate strength or weakness of trending It deploys 26 day EMA, 12 day EMA & 9 day EMA.
Cross over	Cross over is about short term moving average 5 day SMA crossing above or below long term moving average 15 day SMA
Bollinger Band	Bollinger Band measures volatility of a stock with 20 day SMA as central line and 2 standard deviation above and below the central line

TRADE SIGNAL AND OTHER DISPLAYS	
Up trend	When stock is trading above its moving average (MA) price, it indicates trend is up. Buy low and book profit on short term up movements
Down trend	When the stock is trading below it`s MA, it indicates trend is down. Sell high and book profit on short term down trend.

Flat	When MA is moving horizontally for a sustained period of time, it means price is not trending, rather it is ranging
Angled up	If MA is angled up, it shows an up trend is underway, though it is not predicting up trend. Note MA is the average price of the past period.
Caution	MA works well in a trending market meaning when the price is making sustained moves in one direction or the other. Confirm the trend with cross overs.

CROSS OVER OF MOVING AVERAGES

Crossover is a point in a trading chart in which a security`s price and a technical indicator line intersect OR when two indicators themselves cross. Cross-over are used to predict forthcoming changes in trends such as reversals or break-outs or break down. Cross overs are used to confirm the trends and patterns

Deployment	By deploying short term 5 day MA with long term 15 day MA or short term 9 day MA with long term 21 day MA, a trader can identify cross over between short term and long term line and confirm the trend reversal or break out or break down

TRADE SIGNAL

Buy	If upward momentum is confirmed with cross over when Short term MA crosses above a long term term MA
Sell	If downward momentum is confirmed with cross over when Short term MA crosses below a long term term MA

GOLDEN CROSS AND DEATH CROSS

Golden cross and Death cross are cross over pattern. Golden cross indicates a long-term bull market, while a death cross signals a long-term bear market. Both refer to the confirmation of a long-term trend by the occurrence of a short-term moving average crossing over a long-term moving average. Both are considered very reliable confirmation in trend changes.

HOW GOLDEN CROSS AND DEATH CROSS RESPOND TO TRENDS

Signal	Golden Cross	Death cross
Trending	Indicates long term bull market	Indicates long term bear market
Confirmation	Confirms trend change in bullish trend that has already taken place	Confirms trend change in bearish trend that has already taken place
Significance	Confirmation is more significant when accompanied with high volume	Confirmation is more significant when accompanied with high volume
Support & Resistance	On occurrence of cross over, long term moving average is considered support level from the cross over point	On occurrence of cross over, long term moving average is considered resistance level from the cross over point
Trade signal	Is predictor of Uptrend which appears on a chart when a short term 50 day MA crosses **ABOVE** it` 200 day MA	Is predictor of downtrend which appears on a chart when a short term 50 day MA crosses **BELOW** it` 200 day MA

EXPONENTIAL MOVING AVERAGE (EMA)		
EMA is an improvisation of SMA with a difference in calculating method. In EMA, each price data is given weight-age according to their new or old entry in calculation. Thus, recent entry data is given maximum weight-age and the oldest one is given the minimum weight-age, based on a typical formula. In contrast, in SMA all data points are assigned equally. As EMA is weighted average, it`s response to price changes is quicker than SMA. Unlike SMA, EMA indicates trading opportunities both in trending market and sideway market. To identify more accurate trading opportunities, trader can use crossover, instead of relying EMA alone,		
Cross over	By combining two EMAs, one short term 9 day with long term 21 day or one short term 12 day with long term 26 day, a trader can identify trading opportunities.	
Trade signal	Buy	When short term EMA crosses above long term EMA.
	Sell	When short term EMA crosses below long term EMA.
	Signals	Both SMA & EMA work in trending and sideway market.

DOUBLE EXPONENTIAL MOVING AVERAGE (DEMA)		
DEMA is extension of EMA which reacts to price changes more sharply than EMA. DEMA is used in the same way as MAs are used. It helps confirm uptrend or downtrend. A trader may also identify trading opportunities by crossover of two different DEMA by choosing 20 DEMA & 50 DEMA. Trader can choose any look back period like 5,15,100 period		
Trade signal	Buy	If the price moves above DEMA from below, that could be a signal that the downtrend is over & the price is going to rise/
	Sell	If the price drops below DEMA from above, that could be a signal that the uptrend is over and the price is going to fall.
Trade signal by cross over	Buy	when 20 DEMA crosses above 50 DEMA.
	Sell	when 20 DEMA crosses below 50 DEMA.

TRIPLE EXPONENTIAL MOVING AVERAGE (TRIX)	
TRIX is a calculation of triple exponential moving averages. Trix is used (i) as an oscillator to identify overbought and oversold market (ii) as a momentum indicator for increasing or decreasing momentum (iii) as a cross over to signal buy or sell and (iv) as divergence indicator between price and TRIX. Main advantage of TRIX is filtration of market and it`s tendency to be a "leading" indicator. TRIX is considered one of the best trend reversal and momentum indicator.	
TRADE SIGNAL	
When TRIX is used as an oscillator	+ve value indicates overbought market and −ve value indicates oversold market
When TRIX is used as a cross over	When TRIX crosses **above** zero line, it gives buy signal and when it crosses **below** zero lien it gives sell signal
When TRIX is used as a momentum indicator	+ve value suggests momentum is increasing and −ve value suggests momentum is decreasing

Divergence between TRIX and price	Signals the trend reversal. If TRIX is rising & price is falling, it signals trend reversal to up trend while TRIX is falling & price is rising, it signals trend reversal to down trend.

MOVING AVERAGE CONVERGENCE DIVERGENCE (MACD)

MACD is a trend following momentum indicator. It deploys two Exponential moving averages- 12 day EMA & 26 day EMA. By subtracting 26 day EMA from 12 day EMA, a line is plotted called MACD line. In order to give visible and easy identification of buy or sell signals, a 9 day EMA is plotted alongside, called signal line. When MACD line crosses above or below signal line, it signals buy or sell trading opportunities. Second, by calculating positive or negative values between 12 day EMA & 26 day EMA, MACD measures strength or weakness in momentum build up. Third, it predicts trend reversals using convergence and divergence between rise or fall of MACD corresponding to rise or fall on price. Do note here.1.) All EMA s are calculated on the closing price of the stock 2) Among two moving averages, one must be short term and another one long term.3) MACD is used normally with 12 day EMA & 26 day EMA. A trader can use any time frame of his choice. MACD works better in trending market.

FORMULA FOR MACD AND IT`S DIFFERENT INDICATIONS

Formula **for MACD=12 EMA—26 day EMA**	Assumed propositions on different EMAs and their indications without signal line

When 12 day EMA is	When 26 day EMA is	MACD	Indicates what
500	500	0	Means both MA intersect. You draw a vertical line from this intersection point in the chart down to hit MACD line; Draw a horizontal line at the hitting point parallel to Y axis. That is base line. Base line is the central line. Up from central line is bullish and down from central line is bearish
300	500	−200	Down. Momentum is negative.
400	700	−300	Down momentum is getting stronger. Bearish trend is confirmed
600	300	+300	Up. Momentum is positive
650	250	+400	Up momentum is getting stronger. Bullish trend is confirmed.

HISTOGRAM

Histogram is a visual presentation of trend changes above or below base line in color codes. Up trend appears above base line in blue or green. Down trend appears below base line in red color. Base line trend changes exactly where MACD line crosses above or below 9 day EMA to indicate trend changes. MACD staying above or below base line for a sustained period indicates likely up trending or down trending respectively.

DISPLAY OF CONVERGENCE DIVERGENCE		
In MACD	In Price chart	Indicates what
Connect two lows by a line	Connect corresponding two lows by a line	If MACD line is slope up and Price line is slop down, it is bullish divergence. When both are rising, it is convergence and up momentum is likely to continue
Connect two highs by a line	Connect corresponding two highs by a line	If MACD line is slope down and Price line is slope up, it is bearish divergence. When both are falling, it is convergence and down momentum is likely to continue

TRADE SIGNAL							
Between MACD& 9 day EMA Signal line			When cross over between short & long term EMA			When divergence between MACD & Price	
Bullish			Bullish momentum confirmation			Bullish divergence*1	
Buy	when MACD line is above signal line	Buy	When 12 day crosses 26 day to above from below	Buy	When MACD slopes up & price falls		
Bearish			Bearish momentum confirmation			Bearish divergence*2	
Sell	when MACD line is below signal line	Sell	When 12 day crosses 26 day to below from above	Sell	When MACD slopes down & price rises		

*1 A bullish divergence that appears during a long-term bullish trend is considered confirmation that the trend is likely to continue.

*2 A bearish divergence that appears during a long-term bearish trend is considered confirmation that the trend is likely to continue.

BOLLINGER BAND (BB)
Bollinger Band is a technical analysis tool used to measure overbought and oversold of a stock with 20 day SMA as middle band and +2 standard deviation & –2 standard deviation as upper & lower band respectively from the middle band. 20 day SMA is the average of the first 20 day`s closing price. Standard deviation is a statistical measure of variance from it`s average price and is used to measure volatility of a stock. BB is one of the most useful tool for traders.
HOW IT ISCALCULATED
If 20 day SMA is say 1000,Standard deviation is say 50, then, +2 SD is 2x50 & upper band price is 1000+100=1100 Similarly lower band is 1000–100=900. Normally, price will oscillate between these two bands, here between 1100 to 900.
WHAT BB TELLS US
If Current market price is around upper band or lower band, trader can expect that the price will scale back to it`s average price by small reversal. When the price penetrates above it`s upper band or below it``s lower band, a change in direction also may occur after a small reversal i.e., change to continue in the penetrated direction. Bollinger Band works well in sideway market and fails in trending market.

VOLATILITY INDICATIONS	
When a stock is volatile, upper and lower bands widen and when the stock is less volatile, bands contract.	
When upper & lower band contracts	it indicates contraction of volume and stock`s future volatility is about to increase and possible surge in price.
When upper & lower band widens	It indicates volatility in the stock and exit point for the trader.

SQUEEZE STRATEGY
Squeeze occurs when the price has been moving aggressively and then starts moving sideways in a tight consolidation. Consolidation can be visually identified when the upper bands and lower bands get closer together and squeezed which means the volatility of the asset has decreased. After a period of consolidation, the price makes a larger move in either direction, ideally on high volume. A break out with expanding volume is a sign that the price will continue to move in the break out direction.

TRADE SIGNAL		
Buy	Oversold	when current market price is around lower band, signal is oversold position
Sell	Overbought	when current market price is around upper band, signal is overbought position
Confirmation	BB is to be used for trade signals along with RSI, MACD, On Balance Volume. BB works better in side way market	
Caution	BB works well in a sideway market as price oscillates between two bands. In a trending market, it`s signals of overbought or oversold may flop.	

STOCHASTIC OSCILLATOR
This is a momentum indicator and compares a stock`s closing price with a range of it`s price pattern over a given period of time, usually 14 days. It is used to generate overbought & oversold signals using a band between 0 to100. Readings over 80 are considered overbought and readings below 20 oversold. It relies on a stock`s price history of 14 days. The theory is based on the principle that the price of a stock will close near the 14 day high in the uptrend and near the 14 day low in the downtrend. If a 3 day simple moving average line is drawn to smoother and allowed to intersect 14 day price trend, convergence or divergence between oscillator and trending will signal trend reversal too. Stochastic Oscillator is considered to be accurate Buy & Sell indicator. When the trend is up, the price should be making a new high and in a downtrend the price tends to make a new low. Stochastic tracks whether this is happening.

HOW IT IS CALCULATED
If a stock has a price history, with the highest and the lowest price in 14 day`s period and the most recent closing price is Rs 520/-(H) Rs 480/-(L) & Rs 510/-(CL) respectively, oscillator for the current session is (CL—L/H—L)*100 i.e., (510—480/520—480)*100=75. It compares closing price Rs 510/- with 14 day`s price range and reads it`s consistency to the recent high/low

Difference between RSI & Stochastic	Though both measures overbought & oversold, RSI is useful during Trending markets while Stochastic is useful in sideway market			
Trade signal	Buy	when oversold	Sell	when overbought
For more accurate signal	A trader may get more accurate signal if he uses Stochastic Oscillator in conjunction with RSI			

FIBONACCI RETRACEMENTS

Fibonacci is a technique to identify the possible price reversal trend. When there is up move or down move in the price, then the price is likely to retrace back to the extent of 23.6%,38.2% & 61.8% in this order. Retracement can be at any level between 23.6 % to 61.8%. After retracement, it resumes it`s initial move up or down.

BASIS OF FIBONACCI SEQUENCE

In the Fibonacci sequence, after 0 and 1, each number is the sum of the two prior numbers. The sequence so arrived is: 0, 1, 1, 2, 3, 5, 8, 13, 21, 34, 55, 89, 144, 233, 377, 610 and so on, extending to infinity. By dividing, a number in the series by the number that follows it, a ratio of 61.8% is arrived which is called Golden ratio. For example, 89/144 = 0.6180. The 38.2% ratio is derived from dividing a number in the series by the number two places to the right. For example: 89/233 = 0.3819. The 23.6% ratio is derived from dividing a number in the series by the number three places to the right. For example: 89/377 = 0.2360.

HOW FIBONACCI RETRACEMENT IS CALCULATED

First identify 100% Fibonacci move which can be upward or downward **Rally.** To mark 100% move, pick the most recent peak price & trough price. Once identified, use the Software that will indicate the levels. For Ex. in uptrend move, if peak is say 420 & trough is say 300, up move is 420—300=120. Calculate Fibonacci, @23.6%, (23.6%*120)=28.32. For uptrend deduct 28.32 from peak price viz 420–28.32=391.68, similarly calculating @ 38.2% is 374.16, @61.8% is 345.84. Peak price 420 will first retrace to 391.68, second to 374.16 and third 345.84, retracement not necessarily occurring up to 61.8%. Similarly for down move. For uptrend, retracement point to be deducted from peak (to fall). For downtrend, retracement point to be added to low (to rise)

TRADE INITIATION

Caution	Fibonacci need not retrace till 61.8%. It may reverse back to the prior trend at 23.6% or 38.2% also. Hence it may be difficult to identify retracement/ reversal or gauge to what extent retraced.
Confirmation	Trader may enter the trade after confirmation of trade signals from candlestick formation, volume trend and support or resistance

DOW THEORY AND PATTERNS

Dow theory prescribes three market trends.(i) primary trend- (ii) secondary trend-(iii) minor trend. Besides, Dow refers to three distinct phases of markets-(i) accumulation phase, (ii) mark up phase, (iii) distribution phase. Dow theory is important for it`s pattern formations.

DOUBLE TOP AND DOUBLE BOTTOM		
	Double top	Double bottom
Formation	1. Looks like "M" and need not be exact resemblance to "M". Stock attempts to hit the same high price twice, each time falling & moving up again to form double top. This has two peaks with pullback in between.	1. Looks like "W"- and need not be exact resemblance to "W". Stock hits two consecutive lows and rebounds back with recovery and move up. This has two troughs with rallies in the middle.
Duration	2. Duration to form between two top is approx. 1-2 months	2. Duration to form between two bottom is approx. 3 months
S&R	3. It is confirmed when the price is breaking below the support level.	3.. Two troughs that it has touched forms support level
Signal	4. It indicates reversal in existing up trend and signals beginning of down trend	4. It indicates reversal in existing down trend and signals beginning of up trend
Volume	5. Volume may spike at the two recovery price points.	5. Volume expands at the two upward price movements
Trade signal	6. Trader takes short position at the price point that breaks below the support level	6. When the 2nd rebound is approaching the high of first rebound and when volume also spikes, trader takes long position.
False signal	7. Mere formation of tops is false signal. Identify and wait till confirmation that support level is breached.	7. Mere formation of bottom is false signal. Proper identification is essential.
Caution	8. If formation is not identified properly, it may lead to loss. Trading strategy is more suitable for advanced and experienced professional traders than retail new traders	8. If formation is not identified properly, it may lead to loss. Trading strategy is more suitable for advanced and experienced professional traders than retail new traders
Chart	9. Longer time frame- week/month is more reliable than minutes chart	9. Longer time frame- week/month is more reliable than minutes chart
Occurrence	10.. Both Double top and double bottom rarely occur.	10. Both Double top and double bottom rarely occur.
Confirm	11. Confirm with other technical indicators.	11. Confirm with other technical indicators.

TRIPLE TOP AND TRIPLE BOTTOM		
	Triple top	Triple bottom
Formation	1. Same as double top, but this has three peaks with pullback in between.	1. Same as double bottom, but this has three troughs with rallies in the middle.

S&R	2. Price hits resistance level thrice and fails. After third pull back, it breaches support and reverses to down trend from existing up trend.	2. Price hits support level thrice and fails. The third rally breaches resistance and reverses to uptrend from existing down trend.
Trade Signal	Sell at breaching point of support	3. Buy at breaching point of resistance
Volume	Factor volume trend to assess the strength of the signal	Factor volume trend to assess the strength of the signal
For all other factors viz caution, confirmation etc same as double top and double bottom		

HEAD AND SHOULDER PATTERN		
	Head & Shoulder Top	Head & Shoulder Bottom
Existing trend	1. Prolonged up trend	1. Prolonged down trend
Formation	2. Price rises to peak and falls thrice. The first and third peak price is almost equal while the second peak is higher than the other two. The first and the third peak forming as shoulders and the middle one forming as head is figuratively called as head & shoulder pattern. Formation happens at up trend	2. Price declines to a low and pulls back thrice. The first and third low price is almost equal while the second low is lower than the other two lows. The first and the third low forming as shoulders and the middle one forming as head is figuratively called as head & shoulder pattern. Formation happens at down trend. This is inverse of Head & shoulder top
Draw Neckline	3. Connect low after the left shoulder with low after head is formed	3. Connect high after the left shoulder with high formed after the head
Completion	4. Wait for full completion of Head& shoulder formation	4. Wait for full completion of Head& shoulder formation
Price action	5. Wait for price action to move lower than the neckline after the peak of the right shoulder	5. Wait for price action to move above the neckline after the right shoulder
Trade	6. Enter when break out of neck line occurs.	6. Enter when break out of neck line occurs.
Stop loss	7. Place stop loss just above the right shoulder after the neckline is breached	7. Place stop loss just below the right shoulder after the neckline is breached
Caution	Wait for full completion of the pattern as pattern may not be completed or trader may have to wait for too long period for completion. Strategy is not always workable. Hence this strategy is suitable only for advanced professional traders	Wait for full completion of the pattern as pattern may not be completed or trader may have to wait for too long period for completion. Strategy is not always workable. Hence this strategy is suitable only for advanced professional traders

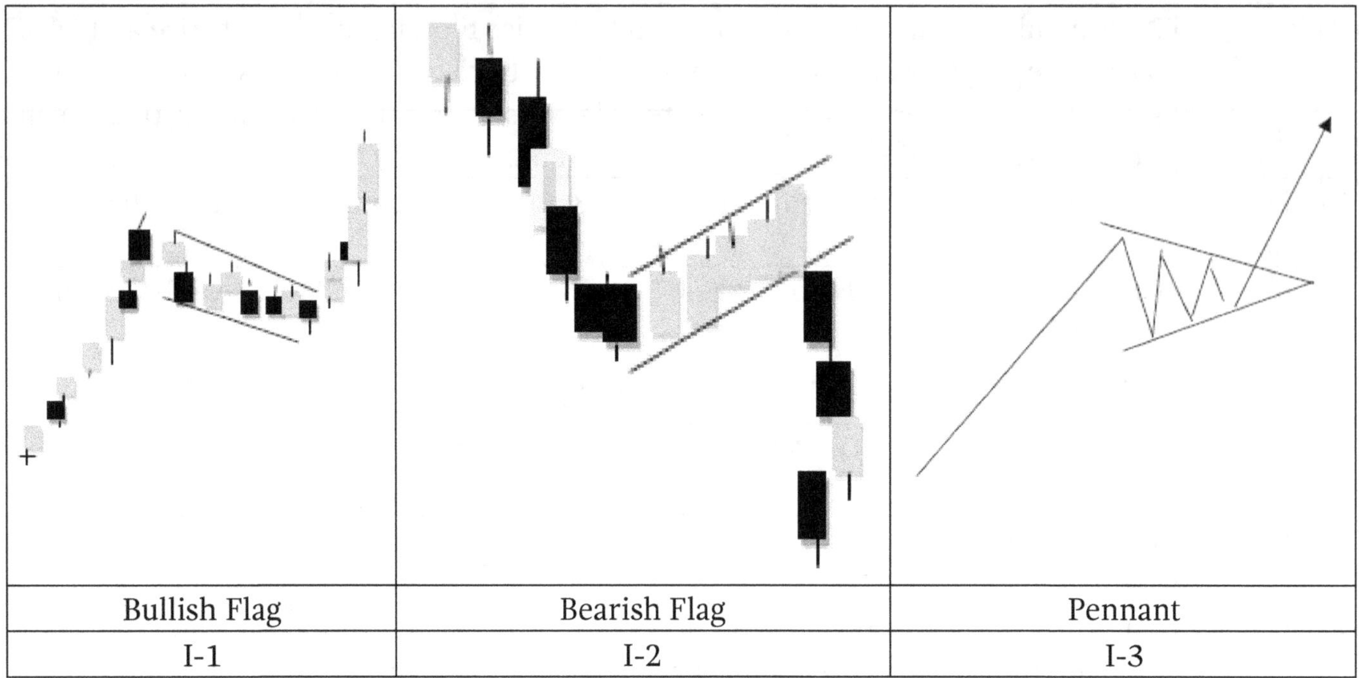

Bullish Flag	Bearish Flag	Pennant
I-1	I-2	I-3

FLAGS	
Formation in uptrend	Preceding trend is either uptrend or down trend. In uptrend flag formation happens when the price drift downward for short term, consolidates, then breaks out the range and moves up steeply in the direction of the prior trend i.e. upward trending. See I-1
Formation in downtrend	In Down trend flag forms when price moves up for a short term, consolidates, breaks down the range and moves down in the direction of the prior trend i.e downward trending. See I-2
Identification	As flag formation is counter trend, in uptrend price dips and oscillates within a range called consolidation. When trend line is drawn, trend line appears slightly slope down. Similarly, in down trend price rallies and oscillates within a range forming consolidation. Trend line drawn will appear slightly slope up. Price will move within two parallel lines forming a flag with a shape of parallelogram or rectangle. Flags are continuation pattern followed by a consolidation and break out in the direction of prior trend
Volume	In both flags, volume increases in the prior trend and dips in consolidation. Confirmation of breaching is essential before initiating trades.

Trade signal	Buy	at the point of breaching that moves up
	Sell	at the point of breaching that moves down

Target price	Difference between the price at upper trend line and lower trend line PLUS the price at the break out point.
Stop loss	Just below the price at the lower trend line
Confirmation	Enter the trade after confirmation that the price moves in the same direction as the break out.
Suited for	Advanced and experienced trade professionals than new retail traders

PENNANT	
Prior trend	Prior trend is up wards. It is a continuation pattern followed by consolidation and break out in the direction of the prior trend.
Formation	Formation is similar to Flag. From the prior large trend, price dips and rises for a few sessions which is similar to whipsaw (and need not be exactly whipsaw) and then breaks out to move in the same direction as the break out. However, Pennant differs from Flag in the formation that in Pennant trend lines converge during consolidation whereas in Flag trend lines form parallel lines. See I-3
Volume	Volume is large in the prior trend, dips in the consolidation and increases when breaking out
Break out	Wait till break out and initiate trade
Trade signal	Buy at the point of break out
Target price	Difference between the price at rally and dip PLUS the price at the break out point.
Stop loss	At the lowest point of pennant pattern
Confirmation	Confirm to check oversold with RSI and Support or Resistance
Suited for	Advanced and experienced trade professionals than new retail traders

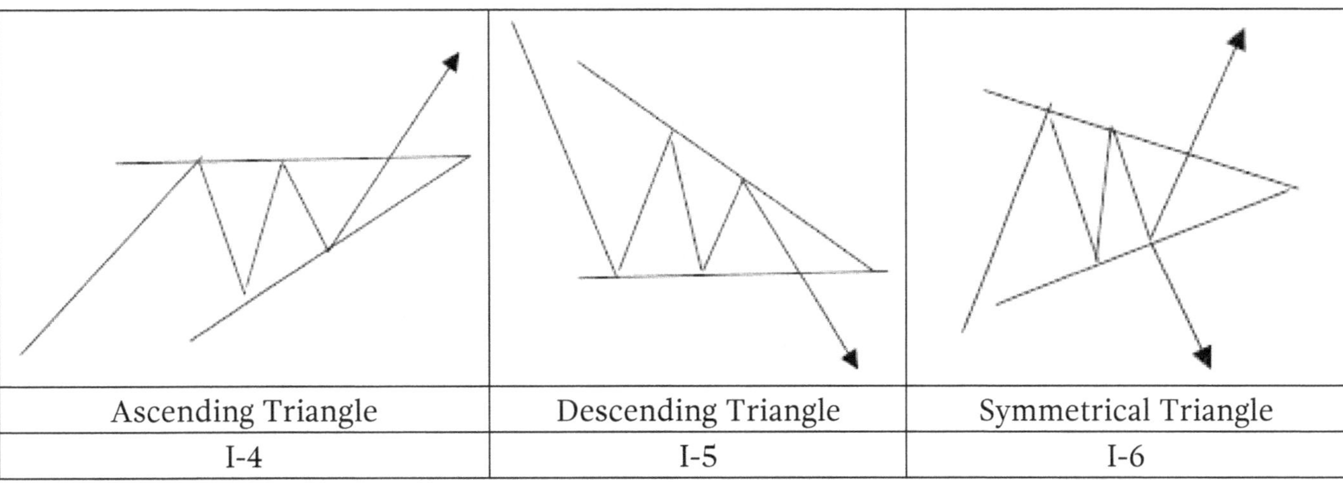

Ascending Triangle	Descending Triangle	Symmetrical Triangle
I-4	I-5	I-6

TRIANGLE PATTERNS			
	Ascending Triangle	Descending Triangle	Symmetrical Triangle
Trend line	Upper trend line is drawn connecting highs. Lower trend line is drawn connecting lows. Drawing trend line is similar to all triangles.		
Formation	Upper trend line is horizontal and lower trend line converges with upper trend line forming a corner at the right end. See I-4	Lower trend line is horizontal and upper trend line converges with lower trend line forming a corner at the right end. See I-5	Two diagonal lines- one rising as upper trend line and another falling as lower trend line- converge forming a corner at the right end. See I-6
Trend	Bullish	Bearish	Bullish/Bearish

Volume	Price breaches the upper horizontal trend line with rising volume	Price breaches the lower horizontal trend line with rising volume	Price breaches the higher or lower diagonal trend line. Volume rises after two sessions
Break out & S&R	Price breaks out the upper trend line which was, till then, resistance level. After breaching, upper trend line now becomes it`s support level	Price breaks out the lower trend line which was, till then, support level. After breaching, lower trend line now becomes it`s resistance level	Price breaks out either direction- upper trend line or lower trend line. There is no support or resistance level here.
Resumption	Price moves up in the same direction of the break out i.e. upwards	Price moves up in the same direction of the break out i.e. downwards	Prices may resume in either direction
Reversal & False signal	Failure or false signal may cause reversal i.e., to down trend	Failure or false signal may cause reversal i.e., to up trend	No false signal here as direction does not presuppose a trader.
Wait	Wait till, at least, two closing prices beyond the trend line to confirm it is not false signal	Wait till, at least, two closing prices beyond the trend line to confirm it is not false signal	Wait till, at least, two closing prices beyond the trend linel & watch for right signal
Trade signal	Buy at the price point of break out on resumption of uptrend.	Short at the price point of break out on resumption of down trend.	Watch for symmetrical triangle formation and initiate trade depending on the move.
Confirmation	Confirm the trend with RSI	Confirm the trend with RSI	Confirm the trend with RSI
Caution	Triangles are continuation pattern. So, price tends to break out in the initial direction of it`s movement. False signal can also happen. New traders may stay away from triangle pattern trading as it needs patience, identification of pattern and false signal.		

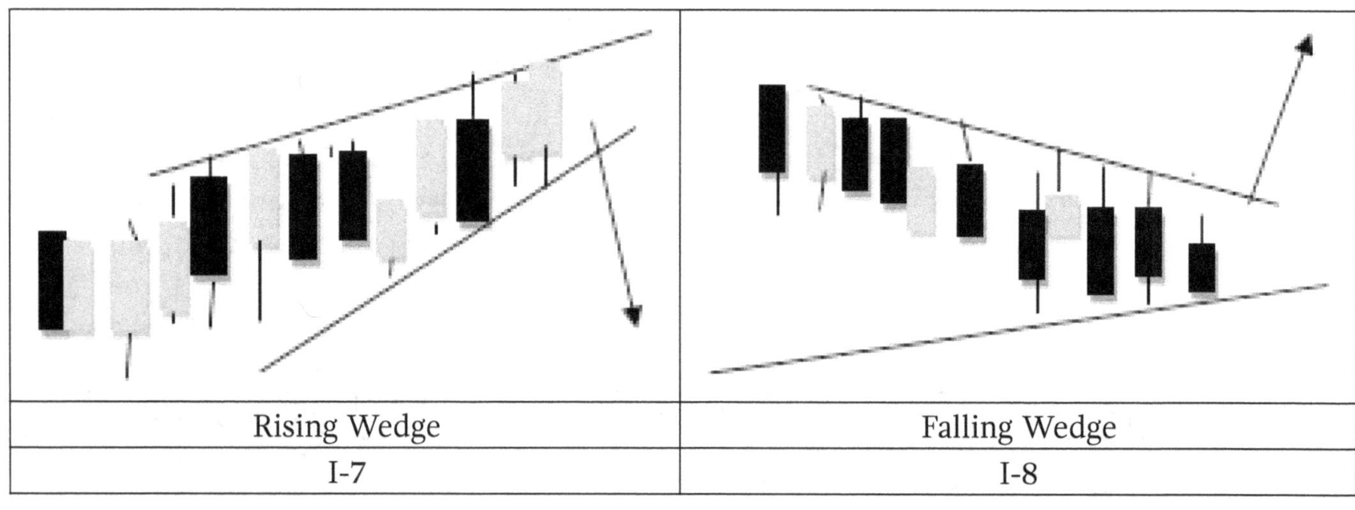

Rising Wedge	Falling Wedge
I-7	I-8

WEDGE	
Common characteristics for rising and falling wedges: 1. Converging trend lines 2. Declining volume through the pattern 3. Break out from one of the trend lines	

	Rising Wedge	Falling Wedge
Trend line	Draw two trend lines- one connecting all highs and another connecting all lows of price action during a period of 10 to 30 days. Two trend lines so drawn will appear like converging in both wedges and disclose the pattern. Note that trend lines do not converge and break out happens before convergence.	
Formation	It is rising wedge when converging trend lines appear rising-See I-7	It is falling wedge when converging trend lines appear falling-See I-8
Prior trend	Rising	Falling
Trend reversal	Reversal to bearish trend	Reversal to bullish trend
Break out	Price breaks out the lower trend line and reverses to falling prices	Price breaks out the upper trend line and reverses to rising prices
Trade signal	Short at the price of break out point	Buy at the price of break out point
Target price	Difference between the price at rally and dip which is small PLUS the price at the break out point.	Difference between the price at rally and dip which is small PLUS the price at the break out point.
Stop loss	At the lowest point of the pattern	At the lowest point of the pattern
Confirmation	Wait till two closing prices after break out is confirmed	Wait till two closing prices after break out is confirmed
Caution	New traders may stay away from trading as it needs patience and identification of pattern.	

PIVOT POINTS				
Pivot point is a technical analysis calculation and is used to determine the overall trend of the market over different time frames. Besides indicating trading signals, it also displays support & resistance level based on the calculation of pivot point. It is mostly helpful for intra-day traders.				

HOW PIVOT POINT IS CALCULATED				
Pivot point –P	Resistance 1 (R1)	Resistance 2 (R2)	Support 1 (S1)	Support 2 (S2)
P= High+ Low+ Closing price /3 where H,L,CP are prices of prior trading day	R1=(Px2)— LOW	R2=P+(HIGH-LOW)	S1=(PX2)-HIGH	S2=P-(HIGH-LOW)

SUPPORT & RESISTANCE		
	Support 1 & 2	Resistance 1 & 2
Reversal	When the price reaches S1, price may reverse and move up	When the price reaches R1, price may reverse and move down

Confirmation	When the price breaches S1 and moves further below towards S2, down trend is confirmed	When the price breaches R1 and moves further above towards R2, up trend is confirmed
Range trading	When the price moves between SI & R1, it lets the trader know the direction in which price is trending, with signal for range trading opportunities.	
TRADE SIGNAL		
Bullish Trend	If the current market price is trading above Pivot point, it is bullish and positive	
Bearish Trend	If the current market price is trading below Pivot point, it is bearish and negative	
Advantage	By calculating the pivot point based on the close of the previous day`s trading session, trader can plan his **trading the next day in advance**	
Buy	If price is ABOVE pivot point, go long in the early session	
Short	If price is BELOW pivot point, short in the early session	
Target price Exit Entry	For buying set targt price @R1 level of price. If price breaks out R1 and moves further up, fix@ R2 level only after confirmation. Alternately, trader may exit at S1-R1 level after completing the trade and enter new trade at S2 –R2 level depending on the price movement	
	For selling set target price @S1 level of price. If price breaks down S1 and moves further down, fix @S2 level only after confirmation. Alternately, trader may exit at S1-R1 level after completing the trade and enter new trade at S2 –R2 level depending on the price movement	
Stop loss	As per the direction of the trend	
Alert Retracement	When price breaks up at resistance level or breaks down at the support level, do not rush with trades. Wait till a day as the price, after breaching, may retrace to support or resistance level before or at the end of the day`s closing session.	
Difference	Pivot point differs from Fibonacci retracement. Pivot point is based on the average of high, low, closing price of the previous trading day while in Fibonacci retracement level is at percentage terms. Besides, Fibonacci can be created with high and trough price, drawn on a chart at any point.	
Application of Pivot chart	For Intra-day traders	Pivot point is useful when OHLC data points are calculated on the prior day`s trading session to apply on the next day
	For Swing traders	Pivot point is useful when OHLC data points are calculated on the prior week`s data to apply for the next week
Confirming trend Direction	Success rate of trading is high, if trend direction by Pivot point is confirmed by other technical analysis like MACD, Candle sticks, Moving Averages.	

AVERAGE DIRECTIONAL INDEX (ADX)
Average directional Index, also called Direction Movement Index (DMI) is a collection of three lines (1) ADX line to measure trend strength (2) +DI positive directional Index and (3) –DI negative Direction Index. Latter two lines indicate current price direction. So trader can determine trend strength & it`s direction by using BOTH.

MEASURING TREND STRENGTH		
Strong Trend	Weak Trend	Reversal
When ADX is above 25 or 30	When ADX is below 25 or 30	ADX may show trend is strong in reversal too, as it measures trend strength and not price direction

MEASURING PRICE DIRECTION & TRADE SIGNAL			
Uptrend &Buy	When ADX is above 25 and +DI is above –DI OR when +DI crosses above –DI	stop loss	at current day`s low
Down trend &Sell	When ADX is above 25 and –DI is above +DI OR when –DI crosses above +DI	stop loss	at current day`s high
Volatility increases	When +DI & –DI move apart, intra-day traders or short term traders can trade on increasing volatility		
Volatility decreases	When +DI & –DI contract, trader may anticipate surge in price with increase in volume		
Look back period	Normally 14 days		
False signal	ADX may still show strong trend even when reversal has occurred. Price may not move in the direction as cross over indicates.		
Caution	Use ADX analysis in combination with other technical indicators to confirm the trend.		

AROON INDICATOR
Aroon is a technical analysis that measures trend changes in price and strength of that trend. Difference between others and Aroon indicator is that Aroon indicators focus on price changes of a stock relative to time. The concept of the indicator is that an up trending stock will move with higher highs and down trending stock will move with lower lows.

HOW AROON INDICATOR WORKS
It is by plotting two lines –A line called Aroon up is calculated based on the length of time since a stock has reached a recent high in a period of 25 days. Similarly, another line called Aroon down is calculated based on the length of time since a stock has reached a recent low in a period of 25 days. In 25 days period, 50 reading of Aroon low means lowest low occurred 13 days ago. Similarly, Aroon Up reading 50 means highest high occurred 12 days ago. These two lines fluctuate between zero to 100 indicating strength or weakness of the trend.

	TREND STRENGTH AND TRADE SIGNAL	
	Aroon Up	Aroon Down
Strength of trend	Trend is strong up trend when it is close to 100	Trend is strong down trend when it is close to zero
Above 50	Indicates that within the last 12 days, Aroon Up has highest highs	Within the last 13 days, Aroon Down has highest lows
Below 50	Indicates that there is no new high and price is consolidating	Indicates that there is no new low and price is consolidating
At 50	Indicates that Aroon Up has highest high 12 days ago	Indicates that Aroon Down has lowest lows 13 days ago
Bullish/ Bearish	It is bullish when Aroon up is above Aroon Down	It is bearish when Aroon Down is above Aroon Up.
Cross over	Buy	When Aroon Up crosses above Aroon Down AND/OR when Aroon Up is above 50
	Sell	When Aroon Down crosses above Aroon Up AND/OR when Aroon Down is above 50
Confirmation	Trade signal is to be in confirmation with similar signals from other technical analysis like Candle stick, MACD, Moving Averages	

AROON OSCILLATOR
Aroon oscillator is an extension of Aroon indicator. After calculating Aroon Up and Aroon Down as is being done for the Aroon Indicator, difference between them is plotted in the form of oscillator called Aroon Oscillator. The oscillator swings between -100 to + 100 with 0 level as the centre point and indicates current trend direction of the asset.

TRADE SIGNAL	
Start of Up trend	When the oscillator moves above zero line, it means Aroon Up is crossing above Aroon Down
Start of Down trend	When the oscillator moves below zero line, it means the Aroon Down is crossing below the Aroon Up.
Confirmation	Confirm the trend reversal with other technical analysis like Candle stick, MACD, Moving Averages

RISK, RISK PERCEPTION AND RISK MITIGATON
Risk is everywhere and everyone is exposed to some sort of risk on day to day life. Risk occurs in a trade when price moves against you. Risk, in financial sector, refers to the possibility or outcome of difference in an investment`s expected return and actual return, When an investor buys stock with anticipation that it would give a return of say 18% in a year and receives return only at a rate of 15%, an element of risk might be attributed to have caused loss of 3% on which an investor has neither control nor can he perceive such risks beforehand because risks can occur at any time or form. Returns are high when risk is high. Bank deposit offers low interest but have no or less risk while a Company may offer high interest, but the risk of bankruptcy of the company and losing investment is high. In stock investment, there are two risk factors called systematic risk and unsystematic risk.

Unsystematic Risk	Unsystematic risk refers to risk of losing an investment due to a company's own misdeeds, actions, hazards etc or specific industry's likely fall in a new environment. Unsystematic risk is, therefore, company specific or industry specific risks, which may arise say when the company is involved in unlawful activities like a scam, fraud, money laundering, insider trading, etc or an industry falling through discovery of new technology etc,.
Risk Mitigation	A trader can mitigate unsystematic risk by diversification of stocks/sector in portfolio investment and avoid investment on the stock or sector that a trader feels risky. Secondly, market itself adjusts to such risk with investors dragging the price of such stocks or sectors to bottom.
Systematic risk	Systematic risk is known as market risk that affects overall market known as macroeconomic risk like, reduced GDP, new controlling measures on financial sector, inflation, Interest policy, fiscal deficit, etc and political risks like unstable Govt, new policy aberrations by Govt., that tend to retard growth etc
Risk Mitigation	Controlling market risk is relatively difficult. However, a trader can mitigate it (1) by hedging his portfolio investments (2) by periodically doing regular risk assessment and (3) by placing stop loss orders to minimize his losses.
Understand risk	Trader must understand that risk is always on downside risk and not otherwise.

RISK TO REWARD
Risk to reward is a measure of prospective reward/gain a trader earns for each rupee he risks on a trade. It is also used by a trader or investor, before investment, to assess the expected return and risk of a given trade. A good risk reward ratio is anything greater than 1 in 3 ie, risking Rs 1/- for a return of Rs 3/- Risk is assessed with stop loss as core point.

How it is calculated	If a trader buys 50 stock say at Rs 800/- and fixes target price for sale say at Rs 840/- with a stop loss of Rs 790/-meaning his loss should not exceed Rs 500/-, then his reward is Rs 2500/- (840—790)*50 while risk is Rs 500/-i.e., (800—790)*50. Here risk to reward is 500/2500 i.e 1:5. If the same trader puts stop loss at Rs 780/-, then, risk is Rs 1000/-& reward is Rs 3000/-(840-780)*50. Risk to reward is 1:3

BETA
Beta is a greek symbol that measures the volatility of an individual stock in relation to the market. In other words, beta describes approximately the effective change in return of a stock in response to swings in the entire market. It provides insight on how much risky or volatile a stock is, relative to the rest of the market. It is used as a tool while hedging portfolio of an investment. Hedging is a strategy to insulate an investment from losing it's value and return from market swings. It is calculated on a statistical formula using relationship between two assets called co-variance and mean deviation between them called variance.

WHAT BETA INDICATES	
When Beta is equal to 1	Stock has neutral risk with the overall market. In other words, stock's volatility is in line with the overall marker

When Beta is greater than 1	Stock is more volatile than the overall market
When beta is less than 1	Stock is less volatile than the overall market

<table>
<tr><td colspan="4" align="center">HOW BETA`S INDICATORS WORK</td></tr>
<tr><td colspan="4">Beta of market indices BSE & NSE is always +1.0. So, volatility of a stock is measured either up or down from market indices i.e. +1.0</td></tr>
<tr><td>Beta value less than 0</td><td>Beta value greater than 0& less than 1</td><td>Beta value equal to 1</td><td>Beta value greater than 1</td></tr>
<tr><td>Assuming market moves UP by 1%</td><td>Assuming market moves UP by 1%</td><td>Assuming market moves UP by 1%</td><td>Assuming market moves UP by 1%</td></tr>
<tr><td>Assuming beta of the stock is −0.6</td><td>Assuming beta of the stock is +0.7</td><td>Assuming beta of the stock is +1.0</td><td>Assuming beta of the stock is +1.2</td></tr>
<tr><td>Beta less than 0 means it is negative. It indicates the stock is inversely related or market and stock move in opposite direction. If a beta of a stock is say −0.6 and if market rises by 1.0%, then negative beta is expected to decline by 0.6%. If the market moves down by 1%, stock`s price volatility is expected to move up by 0.6%</td><td>Stock and market move in the same direction, but with different proportion. Market move up by 1% is expected to impact stock`s price activity to move up by +0.7%. A move down by 1% in the market influences stock`s volatility down by 0.7%. Stock is called low beta stock and less risky by 30 %</td><td>It indicates that there will be no impact on the price volatility of the stock relative to market swing. It also indicates that adding the stock to portfolio does not add any risk. Normally, a stock with beta of 1.0 is rarely found.</td><td>It indicates that stock`s price volatility will move up by 1.2% when the market moves up by 1%. Similarly, if the market moves down by 1% the stock`s price volatility will move down by 1.2% meaning more risky by 20%</td></tr>
<tr><td colspan="4" align="center">NOTES:-</td></tr>
<tr><td colspan="4">1. Return from a high beta stock should be greater as risk is higher in that stock compared to a low beta stock where risk is lower</td></tr>
<tr><td colspan="4">2. Beta is useful in determining short term risk since beta, in long term, may change depending upon the fundamentals and other factors of the company.</td></tr>
<tr><td colspan="4">3. Beta is based on historical data. Hence it may not be correct to predict a stock`s future price movements.</td></tr>
<tr><td colspan="4">4. While evaluating a stock on beta`s indicator, an investor should also evaluate it from the perspective of it`s fundamentals</td></tr>
</table>

DIFFERENCE BETWEEN VARIOUS INDICATORS	
DIFFERECNE BETWEEN RETRACEMENT AND REVERSAL	
Retracements	Reversal
1. Are temporary price reversal that take place within a large trend	1. Reversal is when trend changes direction
2. Are characterized in uptrend by higher lows & higher highs	2. Price is likely to continue in that reversal direction for an extended period
3. Long term up trend or down trend is intact	3. In reversal, directional changes happen to upside after downtrend OR downside after uptrend
4. In retracement, a stock does not breach support or resistance nor does it violate uptrend or down trend. If it does, it is reversal and not retracement	4. In reversal, price may also breach support or resistance
5. Have abundant indecision.	5. Reversals display authoritative action
DIFFERENCE BETWEEN REVERSAL AND PULL BACK	
Reversal	Pull back
1. Reversal is long term	1. Pull back is for temporary duration and it will last for a few trading sessions.
2. Reversal is when trend changes direction-to upside after downtrend OR downside after uptrend	2. Pull back happens with a moderate drop in price within a continuing uptrend. After a pause, uptrend resumes
3. Price is likely to continue in that reversal direction for an extended period	3. In pull back, price drops temporarily,offering opportunity to traders entry point to buy
4. Reversals display authoritative action	4. Pull back may signal reversal also. So, traders should keep watch on Support & Resistance level to confirm the trend.
DIFFERENCE BETWEEN CONSOLIDATION AND CONTINUATION	
Consolidation	Continuation
1. Consolidation is when price oscillates within a defined trading pattern or two horizontal trend lines	1. Continuation is notable for pattern formation in the middle of a trend
2. It is generally regarded as indecision	2. Pattern formations like Triangle, flag, Pennant occur during the middle of the trend and after completion of pattern formation, price will move in the prior direction
3. Price may move in the same direction when it breaches up or down, ending indecision.	3. Trend reversal is also likely after completion of pattern formation

DIFFERENCE BERWEEN TRENDING MARKET AND SIDEWAY MARKET	
rending market	Sideway market
1. It shows general trend-up or down in price direction	1. Market moves neither upward nor downward, instead move horizontally or sideway. It shows forces of demand and supply are neutral
2. It is up trending market when it closes high and down trending market when it closes low	2. Market is regarded indecisive
3. Usually, trades take place with fluctuations in prices, with high volumes or above average volumes.	3. Prices of stocks are relatively stable with average volumes

HOW TO DISCERN NOISY MARKET FROM NORMAL MARKET	
Noisy market	Normal market
1. In noisy market, traders are reactionary relying on rumors or news spread by word of mouth which has no relevance to an assets` or stock`s fundamental value	1. Traders rely on fundamental analysis and its` changes on genuine trading
2. Dividend pay out may cause noise with price volatility	2. Dividend payout is overall market sentiment and volatility may not sustain for long in such scenarios.
3. Price changes rapidly, making a trader feel it difficult as to which one is genuine and which one is not. Corrections take place when the noise is over.	3. In a genuine trending market, trending is evidence based which can be discerned by comparing a stock`s historical prices over a period of time
4. Noisy traders including intra-day traders may congregate to target a single company or industry with buying and selling and create noise. This subsides later in one or two session.	4. Corrections take place to adjust overvaluation of a stock which is attributable to overall regular market cycle.

KEY POINTS TO REMEMBER ON TECHNICAL ANALYSIS TOOLS
Question 1. Is it necessary to know and follow the trade signals of all the above technical analysis (TA) tools to initiate a trade?
No. There are tens of technical analysis all of which cannot be mastered. Only handful of analysis is enough to study. Most important and useful among TA are (i) Oscillators which are useful in identifying overbought and oversold level like Stochastic oscillator, RSI, Money Flow Index (ii) lagging indicators which are useful in identifying price movements based on historical data like Moving Averages, MACD, Bollinger Band.
Question 2. How could a trader develop confident trading?
A trader should find an opportunity to trade preferably with three trading behavior, at least.. (i) Based upon a positive signal emanating from a TA that uses both price move and volume data (ii) By getting a confirmatory signal emanating from candlestick pattern & MACD, to substantiate the trading opinion formed by the trader earlier through TA (iii) By getting a confirmatory signal on overbought or oversold level through RSI. Note that this is only suggestive and not to be strictly

followed upon, since developing trading skill depends on traders` individual perception of risk, capital deployment in trade, formation of his opinion on market /stock`s momentum and ability to analyze indicators to his advantage.

Question 3. Is it necessary on the part of a trader to plot data points for visualizing a trade ?

No. Trading platforms of Depository Participants offer software that are programmed to draw graphics, Moving Averages, MACD, RSI etc using input data specification of the trader. Trader is just to identify the signals that are thrown open by TA and take trading decision. However, note that software will not discern pattern formations like Triangle pattern, Pennant, Flag formation patters, Head & Shoulder patterns etc which need to be identified by trader himself.

Question 4. Why pattern formations are not for new traders?

Patterns are formed during the price action point or price zone of a stock over a period of say one or more months, the identification of which needs patient waiting and accuracy or near-accuracy. Failure of this may lead to loss of trade for a new trader. For instance, Triangle pattern, Pennant, Flag formation patters, Head & Shoulder patterns are all patterns. Opportunity to trade may be identified after gaining reasonable experience in such trades by new traders.

Question 5. What is one of the important signals that a trader needs to identify from TA tools

TA interprets price data and volume to predict change in price direction of an asset/stock. So, a trader`s skill lay on identifying the change in direction. Reversal, Retracement, Pull back, Continuation, Consolidation, Sideway trending, Break out & Identifying Support & Resistance level and formation of new S&R on break-out are few important directional changes. Trader may familiarize the differences between various price action moves/trends/pause etc., detailed earlier.

Question 6. How volume assumes importance in trading strategy?

1. Price rise or fall with little volume is not a strong signal while the same with high volume is a strong signal that goes to suggest that stock has changed fundamentally

2. Assume Price of a stock declines on increasing volume and moves back higher. If the stock`s price declines again but it is not lower than the earlier low and the second decline is with diminished volume, it is interpreted as bullish sign.

3. Assume a stock`s price moves higher or lower for long time. After that, if it moves within a range with little price change and heavy volume, it is interpreted as likely reversal for change in price direction.

4. If a stock breaches past it`s support or resistance level, known as breakout, with increase in volume, it`s price move is considered strong while the same with decreasing volume may indicate false breakout.

5. A market with Increasing or high volume indicates rallying market, beginning of new trend/ market tops, whereas a market with decreasing or low volume indicates declining/ horizontal market/sideway market/market bottom.

6. Pull back with lower than average volume is temporary drop and insignificant. If the pull back is with higher volume, it is potential signal for reversal in trend.

7. It is always good to form trading decision analyzing price data along with change in volumes data. Ignoring volume data is an incomplete proposition.

Question 7. How to identify downtrend from Uptrend and vice versa

Downtrend from uptrend in price action of a stock is characterized by lower highs and lower lows from the recent candlesticks in a time frame of minutes, days or weeks. Similarly uptrend from down trend is characterized by higher highs and higher lows from the recent candlesticks. Lower highs and lower lows signal slow-setting less interest among traders to take long positions which in turn trigger selling interest. Opposite is true in case of downtrend to uptrend. Normally change in price action from downtrend to uptrend and vice versa do not happen in a single or sudden swing except in situations like market crash. Rather, it happens after considerable time or period of strain in it`s price move.

CHAPTER 4

INTRA DAY TRADING

CONTENTS

1 Characteristic of Intraday trade

2 Buy Today Sell Tomorrow

3 Buy Today Sell Today

4 Charting for different types of traders

5 Hints for successful Intraday trading

6 How to choose right stock for Intraday trade

7 Check List for entry and exit points

8 Strategy for Intraday Trade

9 Swing Trading

10 Short term trading

11 52 weeks high & 52 weeks low

12 Trade signal on Break out, SMA, Trending Market, Sideway Market

13 Spotting Reversal Trend

14 Market correction and its` benefits

15 Volatility

16 Risk to Reward and Stop loss

17 Volatility based Stop loss

INTRA-DAY TRADING
If a trader "shorts" (sells) first, to capitalize on high–low price fluctuations of a stock /asset in a day and closes his position by square off within a day in spot market, it is called intra-day trade.
CHARACTERISTICS OF INTRA DAY TRADE
Intra-day trade is one when trader sells the stock first, (I) i.e, before owning the stock (ii) to take advantage of it's fluctuation in price on a day and (iii) buys it back with the same quantity (iv) to square off (closing) his position within the day (v) in spot market. Obviously such trades are initiated to gain from declining prices, i.e., selling first at higher prices and buying it back at lower prices.
FEATURES OF INTRA DAY TRADE
1. Distinctive feature of the Intra-day trade is since the stock which the trader does not own and hold in his Demat a/c is sold first, as opposed to buying first and selling it later, he cannot deliver it to the buyer on T+2 Day as per SEBI norms and hence he has to close or settle his short position by buy back within the trading session of the day.
2. If intra-day trader fails to square off his position before the close of the trading session of the day, SEBI, will step into as a regulator of the trade under penal provisions and ensure that required stock is delivered to buyer after buying it in auction or otherwise, by SEBI, at the prevailing market rate on T+1 day, on behalf of the seller, at latter's risk and responsibility with attendant penalty amount, if any, arising out of such action, to be borne by the seller.
3. Few DPs offer leverage margin on intra-day trades with margin ranging from 10 to 25% under which trader, upon certain terms and conditions stipulated by DPs, can buy stocks worth the eligible amount after margin. For Ex., trader enjoying 25% margin can buy stocks worth Rs 100/- with his capital amount of Rs 25/-
BUY TODAY SELL TOMORROW (BTST)
BTST trade is said to happen when, a trader having bought a stock today, sells the same very next day to book profit from rising price of the stock that he has bought the previous day. Even though the trade looks normal, trader violates the norms of delivery trade T+2 as per which the stock can be sold only after it's delivery in his Demat a/c, i.e., he can sell it only on the fourth trading day. Note "T" refers to day of trade. By selling on T+1Day, trader has initiated sale of stock on which he has not yet acquired ownership. In these types of trades, seller of T+1 day may get trapped and penalized by SEBI, if the seller of the stock on the previous day, i.e, T day seller defaults on delivery for any reason. Note that only few DPs offer BTST trade.
BUY TODAY SELL TODAY
A trader, after buying stock as delivery based, may square it off by selling the stock on the same day, if the price moves in his favor later in the day. These types of trades will be treated as intra day trade with applicable brokerage charges and SEBI norms.
VARIOUS TYPES OF TRADERS

SCALPER	A trader who initiates fairly a large trade with an intention of holding the trade for a few minutes
SWING TRADER	A trader who holds the position for longer than a day. For successful swing trading one needs to pick large cap stocks

DAY TRADER	A trader who holds a stock anywhere from a few seconds to a few hours but NEVER more than a day
TREND TRADER	A trader who holds stocks for weeks or months

SUGGESTED CHARTING FOR DIFFERENT TYPE OF TRADERS		
Types of traders	**Time frame**	**Look back period**
Swing Trader	End of Day	6 months to one year*
Scalper	1 minute to 5 minutes	5 Days
Positional trader/Long term investor	Weekly or monthly	5 Years or more

*For plotting S&R level, increase look back period to, at least, 2 years

HINTS FOR SUCCESSFUL INTRADAY TRADING-INDICATIVE	
ESSENTIAL KNOWLEDGE BACKGROUND	**DESIRABLE ACTIONS**
1) Assess the market trend. Also know trend in Hong Kong/Singapore Stock Exchanges as that will have impact on local market. More on this below.	1) Set aside funds and more time.2) Start small 3) Avoid trading on cheap and penny stocks
2) Have knowledge of Technical Analysis like SMA, MACD,S&R, Volatility, Price actions, Bollinger Bands	4) Beginners need to watch the market without making any move for the first 15-20 minutes of the opening of the market as middle of the market is less volatile
3) Prepare Strategy set up in advance to follow & avoid deviation of set up	5) Cut loss with limit orders 6) Try Options & hedging if necessary
4) Have Knowledge on price movements of a stock	7) Concentrate only on one or two stocks daily 8) Set aside emotions
5) Know techniques to enter and exit point	
ENTRY AND EXIT POINTS	**HOW TO CHOOSE RIGHT STOCKS TO TRADE-INTRA DAY**
1) Liquidity allows you to enter or exit a stock at good price. Indications are tight spread (Difference between Bid & ask price), low slippage	1) liquidity of stock-liquid stocks tend to have high volume
	2) Medium to high Volatility of stock may be a choice.
2) Volatility measures the expected price range. More volatility means more gain or loss	3) Trade only with current intraday trend. If uptrend take LONG and if downtrend take SHORT.
3) A high degree of volume indicates lot of interest in stock. Increase in volume may be a signal of price up or down	4) Trade strong stock during uptrend and weak stock during downtrend as strong stock may move up by 2% if Index move up by 1%

4) For entry or exit, also know real time news on stock, Intraday Candlestick pattern, Doji, Engulfing Pattern for price action & Volume-whether decreasing or increasing.	5) There is more opportunity in stocks to trade that move more. Similarly, when stock drops more than the drop of the market Index, opportunity arises to trade.
5) Shorting intra-day is risky if market is bullish	6) Market depth can also help indentify it as it displays how much liquidity a stock has at various price points-above or below the current market bid and offer.

STRATEGY FOR INTRADAY
1) Set time frame for charts 5 to 15 minutes or more depending upon the trend
2) Ascertain candlestick formations, confirm MACD, SMA, Bollinger Band, Doji formation
3) Doji (resembling cross, +VE sign) is the most reliable candlestick pattern to predict reversal trend
4) Daily Pivot points –Buy at low of the day and sell at high of the day OR buy high and sell higher
5) For Long position, place STOP LOSS below a recent low and for short position place STOP LOSS above a recent high

SHORTING FUTURES TRADE
Shorting futures requires the same amount of margin and MTM as applicable to long on futures. In shorting, trader gets profit only if the price declines.

LOOK BACK PERIOD
Look back period is simply the number of candles you wish to view before taking a trading decision. For instance look back period of 3 months means you are looking at today`s candle in the backdrop of at least the recent 3 months data. In this manner you will develop decision making on today`s price action with reference to last 3 month`s price action. For beginners, it needs to be 6 months to 1 year and for scalpers (day trading) it could be 5 minutes.

FOR MORE ON INTRADAY TRADING TOOLS-SEE TECHNICAL ANALYSIS PART III

HINTS FOR SUCCESSFUL TRADE (2)

SWING TRADING	
Swing trading is a style of trading that attempts to capture gain in a security over a period of few days to several weeks based on changes in the momentum. The first and foremost requirement in swing trading is accurately determining both trend direction and trend strength, to take advantage of trading on short term price movement This can be done through the use of oscillators volume analysis and candlestick patterns.	
STARATEGY	Using oscillator and candlestick formation either independently or combining both, which is more powerful, a trader can identify the right condition for reversal
OSCILLATOR	Oscillator highlights potential reversal via Divergence. If a stock`s price is moving higher, while it`s RSI Oscillator is moving down, it shows the momentum is getting weaker and price decline is shortly to occur

CANDLESTICK	Candlestick formation can occur in two forms (i) Appearance of Bullish/Bearish engulfing or formation of 2 or 3 indecision candlesticks like spinning top together, it indicates reversal of direction, either bullish or bearish. One can trade in the direction of trend
STOP LOSS	For short trading, put a stop loss above the most recent swing high For long trading, put a stop loss below the most recent swing low
SWING CHARTING	Swing trader usually buys stock and sell it after a few days or weeks when it's price moves up. 1. For successful swing trade, one needs to pick right stock. Such stock should be from large/mid cap with high volatility and high liquidity. 2. Start watching these stocks before trading. 3. Take into account market condition and corporate events/announcements from companies of these stocks 4. Look at the stock chart. Line up the low points below which the stocks have not moved down. Draw line across these low points. This line is bottom line. Make sure that the chart shows 50 days Moving Average. Similarly draw a trend line across the high points that the stocks have hit 5. Now that the bottom line and trend line have been drawn, you can be sure of the stock trending between these two lines
ALERT	Change in market conditions be closely watched for any announcement from corporate/Govt etc that may impact your trend lines/stock

SHORT TERM TRADING		
Short term trade can last for a few minute to several days. Success lies on spotting good opportunities and also protecting one from loss. Recognize the potential trade generally following the steps as under		
Moving Average	Right stock will have a moving average that is sloping upwards. For Short, moving average is flattening out or declining	
Overall cycle of pattern	Market normally gains during Nov to April & relatively static during May to October. This may change	
Sensing market trend	If the trend is −ve, Consider shorting trade and do very little buying. If the trend is +ve, Consider buying and do very little shorting	
Controlling risk	By placing Stop loss, control the risk	
Technical Analysis	**RSI**	compares the relative strength or weakness of a stock compared to other stocks. Reading 70 indicates overbought & reading 30 oversold. Keep it in mind that prices may remain in overbought/oversold position for a considerable period
	Stochastic Oscillator	Is used to decide whether a stock is expensive or cheap, based on the stock's closing price range over a period of time. Reading of 80 signals overbought & expensive while 20 signals oversold and inexpensive

Pattern	Find good trading opportunities in patterns of stock charts like Head & Shoulder, Double Top, Double Bottom, Triangle etc.
Time frame For Charts, Analysis	1. Time frame refers to the amount of time that a trend lasts in a market which can be identified and used by traders. 2. Higher the time frame, the more reliable Trading signal is 3. Beginners should avoid Day-Trading (Intra-day), Instead try positional trading (holding the trade for a few weeks to multiple days) till one gets experienced 4. Best time frame for beginners is weekly or monthly For scalper, chart could be 5 minutes
For Scalpers/ Day Traders	1. Scalping means holding the trade only for a few minutes 2. Scalpers usually utilize a highly precise intra-day charts with I minute & 5 minutes time frame to take trading decisions 3. Besides the other things, Scalpers need to look at Global markets 4. Day Traders use simply Trend lines and volume indicators

CHECK LIST TO ENTER AND EXIT A TRADE	
Liquidity	1. Ensure that the stock has adequate liquidity 2. Look at Bid & Ask spread. Lesser the spread, more liquid the stock is 3. Keep Nifty 50 as opportunity to Trade
Volume	Look for minimum volume. Ideal minimum is 5,00,000 per day Other signals:-1. Rising market see rising volumes 2. Increasing price & decreasing volume suggest lack of interest. This is a warning of potential reversal 3. Price drop or rise on small volume is NOT strong signal while price drop or rise on large volume is a strong signal that something has changed in the stock fundamentally
Trading- Initial Process	1. In Nifty 50, scout for opportunities, looking back the recent 3 or 4 candlesticks per stock, using EOD (End of day) Charts 2. Check for recognizable candlestick pattern 3. Shortlist a few, say maximum of 5 candlesticks with recognizable pattern
Trading- Evaluation process	1. Look how strong the candlestick pattern is 2. Look for prior trend 3. Look for Volumes-whether it is equal to or > 10 days average volume 4. If candlestick & volume conform, then, check for existence of Support (for long Trade) & Resistance (for Short Trade) 5. Look at Stop Loss as defined in candlestick pattern

	6. Look for Dow patterns-Double & Triple Top & Bottom formation, Range Break-out
	7. If above are satisfactory, have a look at Reward to Risk ratio, minimum of which should be >1.3. Find lessons on risk to reward below.
	8. Look for MACD & RSI indicators, for confirmation

CHOOSING THE RIGHT STOCK FOR SHORT TERM TRADES	
IN UPTREND	Before choosing a stock, find the market trend with different time frames in a chart to ascertain how long the trend has been in existence. While using different time frames, conflicting trends may be displayed like, one time frame displaying uptrend and another one a correction. Identify one that is strong. Choose the sector that leads the market and outperforms the other sectors and pick a stock within that sector
IN DOWNTREND	In downtrend, pick a stock that is likely to perform the worst and initiate short selling
STOCK IN SAME SECTOR	Stocks in the same sector need not move in similar direction, though price movements in percentage terms may vary. For example, If any policy announcements are made by Govt/RBI on banking sector, that announcement may impact Banking stocks, though impact may vary from Bank to Bank.
52 WEEKS HIGH & 52 WEEKS LOW	
52 week high & 52 week low are the highest and lowest prices traded in an year, based on it`s daily closing price. These high and low may also be taken as resistance and support level respectively.	
52 WEEKS HIGH	When a stock reaches it`s 52 week high Intra Day and fails to register a new high, it may not go much higher in the near term
CHECK FOR	Formation of SHOOTING STAR candlestick and expect possible trend reversal and fall in price
TRADE SIGNAL	Take Profit by selling
52 WEEKS LOW	If a stock reaches it`s 52 week low intra Day and fails to hit a new low, it may be sign of bottom line
CHECK FOR	Formation of HAMMER candlestick and expect possible trend reversal and rise in price
TRADE SIGNAL	Take Profit by buying
TRADE SIGNAL ON BREAK-OUT	
Break-out is when the price moves above the resistance level or below the support level. Break-outs with higher than average volume show conviction that the price is likely to continue moving in the break out direction. Break outs with lower than the average volume are more prone to failures. So the price is less likely to trend in the break out direction. As break outs send false signals too, break outs should be confirmed with the help of volume charts. Trade signal is sell at break-out direction i.e., above the resistance and buy at break out direction i.e., below the support level, after confirmation.	

DIFFERENCE BETWEEN 52 WEEK HIGH/LOW & BREAK-OUT	
If break outs occur near 52 week high/low, it could result in the price moving to a new high/low. It should be noted that NOT all 52 week high/low are the result of recent break outs. Break-outs move above the resistance level or below the support level	

SIMPLE MOVING AVERAGE (SMA)	
TRADE SIGNAL	1. It is BULLISH signal when 50 day SMA crosses **ABOVE** 100 day SMA
	2. It is BEARISH signal when 50 day SMA crosses **BELOW** 100 day SMA

RELATIVE STRENGTH INDEX (RSI) –USEFUL IN TRENDING MARKET	
TRADE SIGNAL	When RSI moves above 70,it is overbought. Expect possible downtrend- Signal to SELL
	When RSI moves below 30,it is oversold. Expect possible up rend- Signal to BUY

STOCHASTIC OSCILLATOR-USEFUL IN SIDEWAY MARKET	
TRADE SIGNAL	When oscillator is above 80, it is overbought. Expect possible downtrend. Signal to SELL
	When oscillator is below 20, it is oversold. Expect possible uptrend. Signal to BUY

SPOTTING REVERSAL TRENDS	
To spot reversal, use moving averages or trend line. Reversal shows the price direction of an asset that has changed from going up to going down OR from going down to going up. Swing low & swing highs are used to identify the trading strategies, trend direction & volatility ranges	
Swing low	Is the lowest price in the most recent month according to traders` time frame say with 20 days, a month or week. Multiple swing lows after a prolonged downtrend indicates it`s market bottom
Swing high	Consecutively higher swing highs indicate it`s uptrend
Uptrend	A Swing high forms when the high reached is greater than a given number of highs positioned around it. A consecutive swing high indicates Uptrend
Downtrend	A Swing low is created when low is lower than any other surrounding prices in a given period of time, usually 20 trading sessions or less.
	Swing low strategy should be confirmed by Stochastic Oscillator OR by a moving average to determine the reversal
	A series of higher highs & higher lows reverses into Downtrend by changing into series of lower highs & lower lows
Large volume	When prices fall on increasing volume, the trend is gathering strength to downside.
	When prices reach a new high on decreasing volume, watch out a reversal may be taking shape
Exit	Exit the trade if the trend is not clear to identify- whether it is reversal or pull back

MARKET / STOCK CORRECTION	
Correction is a decline of 5-10% or more in the price of a stock or asset from it`s recent peak price. Correction can happen to individual stock or group of stocks or specific industry or market as a whole. Correction may last for few days to few months from 3 to 4 months.	

WHY CORRECTION HAPPENS
External macro economic factors or Govt., policies or failed management of a corporate may create corrections. Corrections may also happen in the market itself readjusting the overvalued stocks.
WHEN CORRECTION HAPPENS
It happens normally when the economy is in down turn and also when the market is in bearish trend. A reversal or pull back may also end in market correction
HOW TO PREDICT MARKET/STOCK CORRECTION
1. By using market analysis or comparing two market trends, Trader can predict it. For instance when one market is declining slowly and steadily, another market may follow suit with forthcoming correction. For example, Indian markets may follow the fall of US market or BSE to NSE
2. Market breadth indicators tell number of advancing stocks relative to declining stocks. If advancing stocks are more than declining stocks it is an indication of positive bull market. Converse is true of bear market
3. By using support & resistance method and gauging the unexplainable logic for volatility, trader can to some extent predict it. Confusing trend reversal may also turn into correction.
4. Another indication is when stocks are over inflated or individual stocks are too strong and/or over performing just before correction due to rumors or unverifiable word of mouth in which case market itself will correct after two or three trading sessions

BENEFITS AND HARMS OF MARKET CORRECTION	
Benefits	Harms
1. It offers traders opportunity to buy high value stocks at discounted price	1. Short term /Intra-day traders and leveraged traders are put to sudden loss
2. Corrections readjust overvalued stocks to it`s fair value	2. While Correction hits all the equities, most affected are small cap stocks and high volatile stocks.

WHEN CORRECTION RECOVERS
Correction last for few days to few months only. Hence market participants need not get panicked.

VOLATILITY
Volatility is synonym to riskiness in stock market. Volatility, as a trader knows, is fluctuations in an asset`s price with big swings in either direction. It is viewed as risky because price in volatility is less predictable. Higher the volatility, higher the risk. However, volatility is a statistical measure or metric for a given security or market index to find how large prices swing from the asset`s mean or average price and give returns in a given period, by using standard deviation & variance method. Volatility can also be measured by Beta & VIX. VIX is widely used to measure volatility in option, while Beta is not as it is used to measure volatility of a specific stock compared to systematic risk of the entire market. Volatility is often associated with big swings in either direction. For Ex., when the stock market rises or falls more than 1% over a sustained period of time, it is called volatile market. Volatile assets are considered riskier than less volatile assets, because the price is expected to be less predictable

Higher volatility	Means the price of the security can change dramatically over a short term period, in either direction
Lower volatility	Means the security value does not fluctuate dramatically and tends to be more steady

RISK TO REWARD RATIO (RRR)

Risk to reward ratio refers to an investor`s willingness to undertake risk with reference to expected return from an investment or trade he proposes to make. Generally, low risk investments or trade offer low returns and vice versa. In portfolio investment, risk tolerance is an important factor that varies person to person depending upon the investor`s net worth, age, capital deployed and risk appetite in terms of their readiness to withstand risk in order to achieve the targeted return in financial planning. Risk to reward is trade or investment specific while risk tolerance is, in addition to, investor or planner specific and varies based on their risk withstanding capacity. Note that what we mean risk, here, is downside risk of loss, if the trade goes against an investor.

RISK REWARD RATIO AND STOP LOSS

Financial planners assess risk to reward before taking investment decisions in order to estimate the anticipated return from the investment, proportionate to their risk perceptions. For ex., if a trader has 10 shares long on stock A having bought each at say Rs 600/- and targets to sell at Rs 640/- within say 7 days by placing stop loss order at Rs 580/- it means trader is willing to take risk of Rs 200 (600—580)*10, to earn reward of Rs 600 (640—580)*10. Here, risk to reward ratio is 200/600 i.e.1:3 which tells us that investor is willing to risk Rs 200/- to get a return of Rs 600/- Note that RRR is assessed based on stop loss fixed by investor. If he changes stop loss, RRR also changes. So, fixing stop loss assumes core role in assessment of RRR. If stop loss is faulty or too close, it can easily be knocked down in the price action, making investor`s plan going awry. How to ensure correcting it? Generally, traders or investors fix Stop loss on percentage terms like 2% above or below the current market rate.

WHAT IF RISK OR STOP LOSS RISK IS NOT PRE SPECIFIED?

Assume that the trader is not at all bothered by risk in the above example. Well, the trader will gain if the trade goes in his favor by pocketing profit of Rs 400/- (640—600)*10, within 7 days. If the trade goes against him, price may move below Rs 600/- without trigger of stop loss and the trade may end up with substantial loss as against predetermined loss of Rs 200/-with stop loss, because with stop loss trader can exit the trade with minimum loss of Rs 200/-

VOLATITLITY BASED STOP LOSS

Generally, traders or investors fix Stop loss on percentage terms like 2% above or below the current market rate. While this seems to be right, stop loss may not work with desired result if the daily volatility of the stock is say 3 to 4%. So, how to fix volatility based stop loss? Following steps may be helpful.

Step 1: Estimate daily volatility of stock A say 2.1%

Step 2: Convert the above daily volatility to targeted holding period viz 7 days volatility in the above example 2.1%* square root of 7 is 5.55%

Step 3: To find the swing for 7 days, subtract 7 day volatility from entry price i.e.,(600—5.55%of 600)=600—33.3=566.7 say 567
Step 4: Stock will swing for 7 days between 600 to 567. So set stop loss say at 560
Step 5: Calculate RRR —Risk (600—560)*10=400, Reward is (640—560)*10=800 RRR is 400/800 i.e. 1:2 means trader takes risk of Rs 1/- to gain reward of Rs 2/-
Word of caution:- Trader may change stop loss to modify risk to reward. While doing so, keep in mind the probability of success of the trade.

CHAPTER 5

TRADING FUTURES

CONTENTS

1 Derivative, Various types of Derivative and difference between them
2 Various Terminology and their meaning in Futures Trade
3 Leverage and it`s implications
4 Comparison of Futures trade with Leverage-with example
5 Margin-Why margin is required
6 Different types of margin and their risk Coverage
7 Marked to Market (MTM)
8 How margin Call is computed-Indicative Model trade
9 Difference between Initial Margin and Maintenance Margin
10 Difference between Leverage and Margin
11 Futures Pricing
12 Roll Over
13 Cash and Carry Arbitrage-Spread Trade
14 Calendar Spread-Spread trade
15 Hedge- How Hedge works in Single stock Hedging, Portfolio Hedging
16 Know the difference between shorting on Intraday and Futures
17 Open Interest- Volume and Open Interest
18 Trading opportunities in Futures Contract
19 Futures Contract-Indicative Model Trade

What derivative and derivative contract mean	Aiming to gain financial benefits in any trade is human instinct. Trading on stocks also is fundamentally an instinct to gain from divergent views between buyer or seller on the current and future price of an asset, by trading on such asset in spot market or on contracts that derive it`s price from such asset, called underlying asset in derivatives. Common forms of derivatives are Futures, Swaps, Forwards and Options. To put more clarity, derivative is a financial security with it`s price dependent upon or derived from the underlying asset like stock, commodity or bonds while a contract set under derivatives terms is called derivatives contract which are entered into between two or more parties with obligations of each party set to fulfill and honor it.
How Underlying asset differs from asset	In a derivative contract physical delivery of the underlying asset is not required, except under certain contracts. Fulfillment and settlement of contract is validated by exchange of the value of the asset between buyer and seller and not the asset. Therefore, there is no need for Demat a/c. To explain further, an asset differs from an underlying asset in the way the trade is obligated to. For Ex., when a trade is initiated on stock or commodity in spot market, it is primarily buy & sell of the stock at a price with delivery obligations to pass on the ownership of the asset. In derivatives, on the other hand, buyer and seller are obligated to honor the contract that derives it`s value from fluctuations in the price of the asset and not the asset itself.
What Futures contract means	By securitizing their opposite views and in order to gain financial benefits out of it, they enter into a contract. As per the terms of contract, set with expiry date, buyer agrees to buy the asset at a future date, at a price agreed to between them today, while a seller with opposite directional view on the stock`s price movement agrees to sell the stock at the agreed price for delivery to the buyer on a future date. So, in Futures, one traders` gain entails loss to opposite trader.

DIFFERENCE BETWEEN VARIOUS TYPES OF DERIVATIVES

Futures	Forward*1	Swaps*2	Options
Terms are standardized	Terms are customized	Terms are customized	Terms are standardized
It is traded on Exchange	Over the counter trading*3	Over the counter trading*3	It is traded on Exchange
Parties obligated to fulfill contract	Parties obligated to fulfill commitment	Parties obligated to fulfill commitment	Buyer not obligated to buy or sell
Can be bought with margin	No margin	No margin	Can be bought with margin
Contracts are tradable and regulated	Contracts are not tradable& regulated	Contracts are not tradable & regulated	Contracts are tradable & regulated

*1. Forward contracts are popular among exporters and importers to hedge against risk in exchange rate fluctuations. Forward contracts are customized in the sense that terms of contract are set in according to requirement of merchandise. Usually, Forward contracts are encouraged by Banks to protect their clients from Exchange risks. In currency forwards, Banks, institutions, corporate are big players.

*2. Swaps are entered into between buyer-Banks and seller-Banks involving Foreign Exchange based on forward contracts entered by their clients to protect against Currency/ Foreign Exchange risks. Forward and Swap contracts of Banks and their clients are regulated (and not traded) by Foreign Exchange Dealers Association of India (FEDAI)

*3 Over the counter shortly referred as OTC trading means trading via dealer- trader network and not through Centralized Exchange System.

VARIOUS TERMINOLOGY AND THEIR MEANING IN FUTURES	
F&O	F& O is an abbreviated form of Futures and Options ike EQ for equity
F&O Contracts	Unlike forward and swap contracts, Futures and Options contracts are tradable, meaning contracts can be transferred to another party any time before expiry either on exit or square off and the transferee -party can continue the trade
Futures Price	Future price refers to the price of an asset or a stock at the futures market. Difference between Spot & Future prices arises due to variables such as Interest rates, Dividends, time to expiry etc. Spot price and futures price move along each other. So, If spot price increases, futures price also increases and spot decreases, futures price also decreases.
Premium market	If future price is higher than spot, future market is said to be at Premium
Discount market	If future price is lower than spot, future market is said to be at Discount which is also known as Backwardation
Buyer of Futures	Buyer of future contract is taking on the obligation to buy & receive the underlying asset when Future contract expires
Seller of Futures	Seller of future contract is taking on the obligation to provide & deliver the underlying asset at expiration date.
Profit & loss	In futures, a buyer`s gain or loss is seller`s loss or gain respectively.
Lot size	Lot size refers to the minimum quantity that a trader has to transact in futures contract
Contract value	Contract value is the value arrived at by multiplying the futures price with lot size
Expiry	Expiry is the last date upto which the contract is valid
Expiry date	Expiry date is the date on which the final settlement obligations are determined. In India, all derivative contracts expires on the last Thursday of the month.
Pay Off	In futures trading, pay off refers to anticipated profit or loss from the trade at various price points.

Exit	A buyer of futures can exit the trade any time he wants
Square off	Square off means extinguishing contractual obligations. For Ex. a buyer closes his position by taking opposite trade, i.e., selling the same stock & same lot.
Current month	Current month refers to the expiration of the contract in the current month
Mid month	Mid month refers to the expiration of the contract in the first month following the month in which contract was entered
Far month	Far month refers to the expiration of the contract in the second month following the month in which contract was entered
Roll over	Roll over refers to extending the expiration or maturity of a position forward by closing the initial contract and opening a new long term contract for the same underlying at the current market price
Leverage	Leverage refers to a strategy whereby using small capital as margin and availing debt, an investor enhances his buying power and gets larger exposure in stock market with the aim of increasing his returns on investment.
Leveraged trade	A leveraged trade refers to a trade that uses debt to increase buying power in stocks to invest as opposed to normal trade where own capital is deployed
Risk- Avoiding risk	Risk, in financial terms, is the possible loss of some or entire invested amount. Risk can be avoided by adopting prudent trading policies and deployment of various strategies
Margin	Both buyer and seller need to deposit a certain percentage of contract value as upfront margin to protect against the risk of default by either party. Margin is meant to cover the risk of adverse price movements
Settlement day	F& O trades in India is settled on the last Thursday of the month. If last Thursday is a holiday, previous day is settlement day
Break even	Break even is the price or the amount at which neither profit nor loss is incurred.

LEVERAGE AND IT`S IMPLICATIONS

Leverage is a source of funding, being offered by a broker as debt to a stock trader to enhance traders` active participation in the stock market with increased buying power as otherwise a trader can not engage himself in the market on large scale with his small capital. If a trader wants to increase potential return on his investments, he can leverage his purchase by buying on margin. Trader, by availing leverage, can invest in large amount of equity and earn higher return which he can pocket after repaying the debt fund at the agreed rate of interest for the period he has utilized. The stocks bought on leverage will be held as collateral till the investor repays the debt. An illustration below explains how leverage helps the investor maximize his return on investment. Note that Leverage increases your profit as well as loss also.

COMPARISON OF FUTURES TRADE WITH LEVERAGE

Assume that trader A has capital of Rs 75,000/- and his favorite stock X is currently trading at Rs 742/- and it`s future price is say Rs 750/-expiring on 26th Nov`20 His broker`s margin policy for futures on stock X is 14% and the lot size is say 100. Contract value is, therefore, futures price x lot size which is 750x100=75000.

On 18th Nov`20 trader wants to exit the trade when the stock`s spot price has gone up to Rs 760/-

Trader`s own capital	Leveraged capital
1. With the capital of Rs 75,000/- he can buy 101 stocks at spot market at a rate of Rs 742/- per share	1. At 14 % contract value, his required capital is as low as Rs 10,500/- to buy 100 shares. With Rs 75,000/- he can buy 7 lots i.e 700 shares with the same amount of capital in futures.
2. Assuming the stock`s spot price has gone up to Rs 760/-on say 18th Nov`20, trader sells 101 shares @ Rs 760/- and earns profit of Rs 760-742=18x101=Rs 1,818/-	2. By exiting the trade on 18th Nov`20,, he can sell 7 lots @ Rs 760/- taking home the profit of Rs 760-750=10x700=7000/-
3. Assuming the stock`s spot price has gone down to Rs 730/-on 26th Nov`20, his loss will be 742-730 i.e Rs 12 x 101=Rs 1,212/-	3. Assuming the stock`s spot price has gone down to Rs 730/-on 26th Nov`20, his loss will be 750-730 i.e Rs 20 x 700=Rs 14,000/-
4. Assuming the stock`s price moves down by 14%.,he will incur loss of Rs 10491.88 i.e, 14% of 742 which is 103.88x101=10491.88	4. Assuming the stock`s price moves down by 14%,he will incur loss of Rs 72,716/-i.e 103.88x700 which is 97% of his capital.

Notes: 1) If price moves down by margin of 14%, futures trader loses his entire capital. Leverage magnifies both gains and losses. If an investment bought on leverage moves against the investor, his loss is even larger than if he had purchased the stocks outright.

2) Buying on leverage is useful for short term investments. As interest and commission charges on leverage will be greater for long term investments, break even also tends to be higher on returns.

CALCULATION OF LEVERAGE RATIO

Leverage ratio helps trader assess the extent of leverage and the inherent risk involved. From the above example, a trader can understand how leverage increases his gain and loss as well. Higher the leverage, higher the risk and higher is the profit potential. Loss also multiplies as gain does with leverage.

Leverage & Leverage ratio	Contract value/margin= Leverage. In the above example, leverage is 75000/10500=7.14. Leverage ratio is 1:7.14
What leverage ratio tells	Ratio shows that with one rupee you can buy 7.14 shares on leveraged trading. In another way, if a stock`s price moves up by 14%, trader will gain by 100% i.e double his capital with leverage. If the price moves down by 14%, he can lose his entire capital with leverage vide the above example. On the contrary, a small margin will make you gain double the capital or loss the entire capital even with small moves in the price that will trap your trade into high risk.

MARGIN

A trader must know about margin and their utility value before entering into futures trading. A trader has to pay upfront initial margin at a certain percentage of contract value before entering into futures. In addition to initial margin, he has to pay maintenance margin, known as mark to market (MTM) if calls raised.

WHY MARGIN IS REQUIRED
Margin is known for risk coverage on the trade. While risk is in every trade, it is high in futures since contract is to be done in lots viz 150, 200 etc., that spikes contract value. With small capital, a retail trader cannot enter into such high value contracts. So, in order to protect from the risk as well as making him participate in the trade, brokers extend leverage and insist margin. Leverage refers to extending debt to enable a trader buy stock in lots and thereby increase his potential return while trader`s margin requirement is to protect him in the event of adverse price move against him in high value contract. Another reason for margin requirement is that in futures, back end settlement is done by Exchange daily, based on day`s closing price of the stock, to capture profit and loss pay off. By doing so, trader`s deficit in margin requirement is monitored and regularized. Thus, while minimum lot size and contract value are relevant for leveraging a trade, margin requirement as a percentage to contract value depends upon lot size. Note that a trader can also enter futures contract by bringing in his own capital to the extent of 100% of contract value.

DIFFERENT TYPES OF MARGINS AND THEIR RISK COVERAGE	
SPAN MARGIN	SPAN is abbreviation of Standard Portfolio Analysis of Risk. This is the part of initial margin that will be collected from F& O trader. Calculation of SPAN and it`s revision rests with Stock Exchanges though rate of margin is prescribed by SEBI. This margin is the mandatory minimum required margin to be collected @ 7.5% of the contract value from F&O trader upfront by brokers before allowing them to initiate the trade. Brokers can hike it but cannot reduce it. This margin is considered to cover at least 99% of the risk of the trade. Note that this SPAN margin is also maintenance margin. Hence balance in trading account of a trader, falling below 7.5% of the purchase value of stock bought on leverage will raise margin call from brokers to maintain the level.
EXPOSURE MARGIN	Exposure margin is an additional margin over and above SPAN margin that will have to be collected from F&O trader at a rate of 5% of contracted value along with SPAN margin. Exposure margin is to cover the risk of volatility and as a cushion for MTM losses.
CASH MARGIN	As per SEBI guidelines, trader has to keep 50% of SPAN + Exposure as cash margin in his trading account
COLLATERAL MARGIN	As per SEBI guidelines, trader has to keep 50% of SPAN + Exposure as collateral margin in a separate new Demat a/c designated as "TMCM"(Trading Member Clearing Member) −clients` securities margin pledge account, that should be opened by the broker. When a trader buys security on margin, he has to keep those stocks as collateral pledging them in favor of the broker, who, in turn, repledges in favor of the Clearing Corporations.

NOTE: 1) As per revised guidelines, trader has to keep pledged securities with the broker in TMCM a/c after marking for pledge from depositories CDSL or NSDL

2) Penalty will be levied if the required limit of 50% is not maintained independently in cash margin or collateral margin.

3) Penalty is levied for non maintenance of required limit in cash or collateral margin while margin call is for shortfall in SPAN margin

4) Accepting what constitutes cash for the purpose of cash margin, other than cash, may vary from brokers to brokers.

5) Trader can pledge only those securities which are approved by Stock Exchanges listing their value of SPAN & Exposure margin in percentage terms after haircut. Haircut refers to difference between an asset`s current market value and the value taken for the purpose of arriving collateral value. For ex, if a stock` current market price is Rs 800/-, it`s collateral value may be assessed as Rs 600/-, difference being the haircut. Haircut, here, is 25%

CURRENT UPFRONT & OTHER MARGIN TO BE PAID BY F&O TRADER *				
SPAN	EXPOSURE	TOTAL	TOTAL UPFRONT PAYABLE	OTHER MARGIN PAYABLE DURING THE LIFE OF HE CONTRACT
7.5%	5%	12.5%	12.5% on contract value	Margin call, if only arising, on shortfall calculated by difference between initial SPAN and revised cash balance required on the current contracted value caused by drop in price.

*Check for revision, if any, with your brokers.

MARKED TO MARKET (MTM)

MTM is a fair value accounting practice whereby current value of an investment of a company or a contract including futures is determined on daily settlement to show it`s unrealized profit or loss. It is an accounting entry to assess fair value and NOT an entry passed on actual sale. In futures, current market value is based on the day`s closing price of the asset.

HOW MARGIN CALL –MARKED TO MARKET CALL–(MTM) IS COMPUTED

Marked to market call also known as margin call is raised whenever cash balance goes down the required SPAN margin during the life of a futures contract. In futures contract settlement is done on daily basis based on the day`s closing price and P&L is computed accordingly to arrive at the margin requirement. Deficiency in margin requirement is immediately brought to the knowledge of the trader by the broker to infuse additional fund in his cash account.. On default of the trader, broker can sell part of or entire collateral security at the current price, square off the trade and recover his dues with interest including commission charges on the square off An illustration on how and when margin call arises is given below:-

Buy date	Spot	F utures	Lot	Contract. val	SPAN@ 7.5%	Exposure@ 5%	Total	Sell date	Sell price	Pay off	P&L
14/09/20	Rs 677/-	Rs 680/-	200	Rs 1,36,000/-	Rs 10,200/-	Rs 6,800/-	Rs 17,000/-	18/09/20	Rs 720/-	40	Rs 8,000/-
	14/09/20		15/09/20		16/09/20		17/09/20		18/09/20		
Cl.Price	679/-		682/-		630/-		690/-		720/-		

Date	Closing Price	Contract value	SPAN@ 7.5%	Exposure@ 5%	Total margin 12.5%	MTM	Avail. Margin	Reqd. Margin	Shortfall
11/09/20	676	1,35,200/-	10,140/-	6,760/-	16,900/-	200	–	–	–
14/09/20	679	1,35,800/-	10,185/-	6,790/-	16,975/-	(200)	16,800/-	16,975/-	–
15/09/20	682	1,36,400/-	10,230/-	6,820/-	17,050/-	600	17,400/-	17,050/-	–
16/09/20	630	1,26,000/-	9.450/-	6,300/-	15,750/-	(10,400)	7,000/-	15,750/-	2,450/-
17/09/20	690	1,38,000/-	10,350/-	6,900/-	17,250/-	12,000	19,000/-	17,250/-	–
18/09/20	720	1,44,000/-	10,800/-	7,200/-	18,000/-	6,000	25,000/-	18,000/-	–

TRADER`S PROFIT ON FUTURES- Rs 8,000/-			
Sum all MTM	600+12,000+6,000—200—10,400=8,000	Final C.V –Initial C.V	1,44,000—1,36,000=8,000
Final cash balance—Initial margin blocked	25,000—17,000=8,000	Sell price-Buy price *200	680—720*200=8,000

Note 1	Trader will get a margin call on 16th Sept`20 to infuse additional cash to meet the shortfall in margin requirement
2*	Though contract commenced only on 14th Sept, 11th Sept is reckoned for calculating the closing price & MTM on 14th Sept. Hence no margin accounting
3	Stock is shown too volatile just to drive home the scenario when margin call arises. In real market, stocks may not be that much volatile in 5 days period
4	With MTM, a trader can know the current pay off from the trade on daily basis
5	If trader defaults on margin call, broker can sell part of or entire collateral security at the current price, square off the trade and recover his dues with interest including commission charges on the square off. OR trader himself can exit the trade
6	Consecutive days from 14th to 18th Sept is shown for illustration purpose to reiterate the point that MTM is calculated on the day`s closing price
7.	Margin shortfall is calculated with reference to SPAN margin only. SPAN & Exposure margins are as per the current rate which may be changed by SEBI
8.	If the stock is not traded on any particular day, the latest available closing price of a day will be considered for MTM purpose.

*Excerpts from SEBI circular:

"Initial margin requirements are based on 99% value at risk over one day time horizon. However, in the case of futures contracts (on index or individual securities), where it may not be possible to collect mark to market settlement value, before the commencement of trading on the next day, the initial margin is computed over a two-day time horizon, applying the appropriate statistical formula. The methodology for computation of Value at Risk percentage is as per the recommendations of SEBI from time to time."

DIFFERENCE BETWEEN INITIAL MARGIN AND MAINTENANACE MARGIN CAUSED BY MTM	
Initial margin	Maintenance Margin
1. Initial margin is to be paid upfront to establish or create a position	1. Maintenance margin is payable after initial position is created, to maintain the required margin, depending on the price movement of the underlying
2. Upfront payment is calculated at certain percentage of contract value which do not vary till the completion of the contract	2. Maintenance margin arises based on the day`s closing price of a stock and the available cash balance from the trader
3. Initial margin is calculated on the initial contract value	3. Maintenance margin is calculated on daily basis on the changing contract value based on the changing price of the underlying
4. Initial margin determines the initial value of the trade	4. Maintenance margin determines the current value of the trade and pay off daily

Note:-

1) Traders need to know the difference between MTM and margin call. MTM itself is not a margin. MTM is an accounting practice to assess the current value of investment or futures trade whereas margin call is the outcome of MTM accounting, demanding additional funds to meet required margin.

2) Maintenance margin noted above refers to margin requirement caused by MTM accounting.

DIFFERENCE BETWEEN LEVERAGE AND MARGIN	
Leverage	Margin
1. Leverage refers to availing debt	1. Margin refers to debt money that an investor can use for investment in different financial instruments including derivatives trade
2. Leverage is offered by a broker to a trader to increase traders` market participation	2. Margin is used by the trader to increase potential return on his investment
3. By leverage broker lends money and earns interest	3. Margin is a cushion for any losses that a trader may incur during the life of the trade

FUTURES PRICING	
Future price and spot price in futures move in tandem, meaning they move together, with a small up in future price. So, increase or decrease in spot price increases or decreases futures price respectively. Future price and spot price differ because futures price is loaded with interest cost for different maturities and time to expiry. Thus price for current month will be cheaper than the mid month. Likewise, mid month price will be cheaper than far month. All derivative contracts expire on the last Thursday of the month.	
Dividend & price	If dividends are declared on a stock, spot price and thereby futures pricing is slightly adjusted by Exchanges

Future price on expiry date	On expiry date spot price and futures price converge meaning the price difference between them on expiry date will vanish. If both prices do not converge on expiry date, it will give opportunity for arbitrage trade and free money.
DIFFERENT EXPIRIES AND PRICING	
Current month/ Near month	When a contract is bought say on 6th July`20 for the current month, it will expire on on 30th July `20 the last Thursday of July. As the days to expire is less than a month, it`s price will be cheaper. Current month is also known as near month.
Mid month	When the same contract bought on 6th July`20 is for the mid month, it will expire on on 27th Aug`20 the last Thursday of August. As the days to expire is more than a month, it`s price will be higher than that for current month.
Far month	When the same contract bought on 6th July`20 is for the far month, it will expire on on 24th Sept`20 the last Thursday of Sept. As the days to expire is more than two month, it`s price will be expensive compared to that for the current month.
Always Three expiries	Exchanges offer always three expiries for contracts. So, if the current month expired on 30th July `20, on 31st July`20, exchange will offer new expiries viz 27th Aug, 24th Sept & 29th Oct`20.
Choice on expiry	Choosing the right expiry at the time of buying the contract depends on the directional view of the buyer and it`s anticipated occurrence. Buyer can change his view any day before expiry and opt for mid month contract by buying fresh futures for the mid month or far month contract and selling the current month contract to offset the current position.
Trade entry on expiry	If a buyer of the contracts predicts bullish view on a stock to happen in the mid month or far month, he may initially buy the current month contract and roll over it to mid month as he can expect more sellers for the current month than for mid month. In other words, the contract for current month will always have more liquidity than for mid or far month.
Square off	Buyer of futures can exit the trade at any time after entering into the contract but before it`s expiry, by square off. Square off means closing his current buy position by initiating opposite trade, i.e., by selling the contract with the same quantity on the same underlying asset. Square off effectively transfers the buyer`s position to another trader who is interested in buying. If, on expiry, a trader fails to square off his position, exchange will automatically square off his position on expiry date at the spot rate which is the same as futures rate.
Enter Exit& Expiry	By entering into a contract on current month expiry, a buyer need not wait till the date of expiry for trade pay off. If the trade moves in his favor even within a minute after it`s execution, a trader can exit the trade by squaring off his position and pocketing the profit. Note that a buyer`s gain on a trade is seller`s loss
ROLL OVER	

Roll over refers to extending settlement day of a open position. When a buyer has bought a contract expiring on say 25th June`20 and rolls over it to following month say 30Th July`20, effect of his roll over is that his commitments under the initial contract have been rather extended to 30th July and not extinguished. Roll over is suited to situations like when a buyer `s prediction of bullish view on a stock do not happen in the current month, but still he feels his prediction will happen in the following month. In such a strong view, he may offset the existing contract, before expiry date, by selling at the closing price of the day and simultaneously buying at the new rate for mid month contract on 30th July using his existing margin amount. Note that selling and fresh buying should be on the same underlying and for the same quantity i.e. similar to what he had as his bindings on the initial buy contract.

CASH & CARRY ARBITRAGE-SPREAD TRADE

Arbitrage means simultaneous purchase and sale of an asset in order to profit from it`s price difference in the market. Cash & Carry arbitrage is a form of arbitrage which derives it`s name cash from spot market and carry from Futures market. Cash & Carry Arbitrage is a market neutral strategy whereby a trader, simultaneously, buys a stock low on spot and sells high on futures on current month on the same stock. Opportunities on this type arises whenever (1) market pricing is mismatched or the underlying is inefficiently priced (2) futures price is expensive than spot price to make the trade profitable (3) adequate liquidity exists at the market for the underlying.

Find trading opportunity	For Ex., Opportunity arises for a trade when spot price of a stock is say Rs 780/- and futures price on the same is say Rs 810/-. Trader buys spot @ Rs 780/-and sells futures @ Rs 810/-. Profit on price difference is 810–780= Rs 30/-As there is no risk involved in the trade, trader can pocket the profit on price differentials
Squaring off the trade	Just before expiry of futures, he can square off meaning he will sell spot and buy futures on the same underlying to close his position.
Caution before entering the trade	Before deciding on the entry to trade, trader has to ensure that pre requisite exists- viz futures price is higher than spot with the spread being adequately enough to book profit after meeting cost of broker charges etc. Note of caution here is that price differentials do not happen often.

CALENDAR SPREAD-SPREAD TRADE

Calendar spread refers to taking new position whereby simultaneous buying/selling current month`s contract and selling/buying mid month`s contract are traded. Note that the trade deals on the same stock with two different expiries both in futures as opposed to cash & carry arbitrage that deals on price differentials, one in spot & another in futures.

Find trading opportunity- Sell high & buy low	For Ex., Opportunity arises for a trade when current month`s future price is say Rs1020/- and mid month`s futures price of the same stock is say Rs 980/-. Trader sells futures current month @ Rs 1020/- and buys futures mid month @ Rs 980/-. Profit on price difference is Rs 1020- Rs 980= Rs 40/-As there is no risk involved in the trade, trader can pocket the profit on price differentials.
Buy low &Sell high	Conversely, he can also buy low current month contract and sell high mid month`s contract simultaneously, if the price differentials offer trading on such spread.

Squaring off the trade	In the above example, before expiry of current month futures, he can square off meaning he will sell mid month and buy current month on the same underlying to close his position.
Caution before entering the trade	Before deciding on the entry to trade, trader has to ensure that the spread between two expiries is adequately enough to book profit after meeting cost of broker charges etc. Note of caution here is that price differentials do not happen often.
Margin requirement	Margin requirement is reduced in this trade as trade involves combining two expiries simultaneously.

HEDGE
Hedge refers to taking an offsetting position that is intended to reduce the risk in an asset in the event of adverse price movements. It is important for an investor to remember that hedge is a strategy to prevent losses. So, it is likened taking insurance cover. The most useful application of derivatives, especially futures contract, is for hedging. Hedging is meant to protect from downside risk. Upward movement is rather a return and not risk.

HOW HEDGE WORKS-SINGLE STOCK HEDGING
When you have bought say 300 shares of Stock X on spot @ Rs 800/- per share, total cost of investment is Rs 2,40,000/- To hedge against losses due to adverse price movements, you need to go short on futures for the same quantity at a futures price which should be close to your purchase price of your initial long position so that the contract value of futures is also close to your total cost of initial investment. When the price moves up, your value of investment increases and futures pay off decreases. When the price moves down, your investment value decreases while your futures contract increases with the same value, thus, giving neutralizing effect that tends to protect your investment value to remain the same

HOW HEDGE WORKS-PORTFOLIO HEDGING
In single stock hedging, investor needs to short at current futures price of that stock. This cannot be applied in multiple stock portfolio investment since each stock will have different price volatility to market swings and it`s volatility will also vary depending on it`s weight-age in the total value of investment. Hence, investor needs to calculate portfolio`s hedge value based on which required lots, necessary for hedging a futures contract, is arrived. To arrive hedge value investor should calculate each stock`s weight-age in the portfolio, it`s beta and weighted beta. Note that, in all, portfolio hedging is done with respect to market index and it`s impact on value of portfolio as opposed to hedging on a single stock and it`s price volatility.

Beta	Beta is a greek symbol that measures the volatility of a stock in relation to entire market. In other words, beta describes approximately the effective change in return of a stock in response to swings in the market.
Weight-age Weighted beta Portfolio beta	Weight-age refers to composition of cost of one stock in the total value of portfolio. If a stock`s cost is say Rs 1,50,000/- in the total portfolio investment of Rs 10,00,000/-, it`s weight-age in the investment is 1,50,000/10,00,000*100 which is 15%. If beta of the same stock is say 0.9, multiply 0.9 and it`s weight-age i.e.0.9*15% to arrive weighted beta of that stock which is 0.135. Calculate weighted beta in the similar

	way for the remaining 9 stocks. Adding all weighted betas of all stocks, you get portfolio beta
Hedge value	Assuming portfolio beta as say 1.18, calculate hedge value by multiplying 1.18 and total investment value i.e 1.18*10,00,000/-which is Rs 11,80,000/-
No.of lots	Arrive contract value of futures for market index by multiplying minimum lot and futures price for market index. Divide hedge value Rs 11,80,000/-by contract value that gives you number of lots required for hedging.
Short index futures	Short index futures with contract value that is arrived by futures price multiplied by portfolio beta in order to protect your portfolio investment of Rs 10,00,000/-. You may decide the expiry period depending upon your holding period of investment
Effect of hedge	Only if market moves down, effect of hedging can be realized as hedging is meant to protect downside risk. Increase or decrease in market move will neutralize your portfolio.
Extending hedge	Investor may extend hedge by calculating the weighted beta, portfolio beta and hedge value all of which may require revision based on the new portfolio value that investor wants to protect now.
Strategy by other modes	Investor may also hedge the risk (1) by option contracts (2) by diversification of investible instruments.

SHORTING ON INTRA DAY AND FUTURES

Shorting (selling) is a concept of selling first at higher price and buying later in the day at lower price. Short trading is actively done by traders when they are certain that price will decline later in the day and the trade must be squared off within the day`s trading session regardless of their profit or loss on the day. However, a trader can short a stock in futures and carry forward overnight either till expiry date or till the price declines as expected by him.

DIFFERENCE BETWEEN SHORTING ON INTRA DAY & FUTURES

Shorting intra day	Shorting futures
1. Trading cannot be carried forward overnight. It should be squared off within the day	1. Trade can be carried forward overnight
2. Trader can sell high first and buy low later within the day.	2. Selling high first on a day and buying low on any day till expiry can be done
3. If not squared off by 3.20 PM, broker will square off and settle the trade	3. If not squared off on expiry, Exchange will square off and settle the trade
4. Margin requirement is applicable for intra-day trade	4. Margin requirement is applicable to F& O trade

OPEN INTEREST

Open interest tells us how many F& O contracts are open and outstanding in the market. For F&O traders, open interest helps to identify and confirm trends and trend reversals. By reading open interest, a trader can get a sense of whether the market is moving strong or weaker.

HOW TO STUDY AND ANALYZE OPEN INTEREST

When a buyer and a seller enter into futures, it means just one new contract. When an existing contract is either transferred to another by exit or rolled over, it is not a new contract. It shows how many new contracts have been entered and added while deducting contracts that were closed or lapsed on maturity. It `s position reported each day represents the increase or decrease in the number of contracts for that day and it is shown as a positive or negative number.

Upward trend	An increase in open interest along with an increase in price is said to confirm an upward trend.
Downward trend	An increase in open interest along with a decrease in price confirms a downward trend.
Trend reversal	An increase or decrease in prices while open interest remains flat or declining may indicate a possible trend reversal.

VOLUME AND OPEN INTEREST

Volume indicates the number of trades executed on a day while open interest tells how many F&O contracts are outstanding on a day with new contracts and their depth with the possible volume on such contracts. Generally, a rising volume and a rising open interest are confirmation of a **trend while a** falling volume and a falling open interest depict a sideway trend.

TRADING OPPORTUNITIES IN FUTURES

If a trader`s view on price direction of a stock or index is accurate, futures contract is more suited to increase his potential returns due to leverage. Find below various options open to buyer & seller in each scenario.

When profited before maturity- Square off	If stock moves in buyer`s favor on any day before maturity, he can exit the trade by square off meaning he will sell the futures at the rate on the date of closure, on the same underlying with the same lot to offset. On the other hand, If a stock moves in favor of seller on any day before maturity, he can exit the trade by square off meaning he will buy back the futures at the rate on the date of closure, on the same underlying with the same lot to offset.
When profited on maturity- Close	Trader need not do anything. Exchange will close and settle the trade on expiry. Trader should note that on last day of expiry, buyer has to honor by buying the underlying asset at the pre set price and seller has to honor his obligation to sell at the pre set price
If incurring loss before maturity- Roll over	If the contract is likely to incur loss before maturity but if the trader expects the price will rise in the following month, buyer can roll over the contract. To roll over he has to sell the existing contract, before maturity, at the current rate and simultaneously buy a new contract for the following month at the new rate applicable for that expiry. Similarly seller can roll over, if a buyer is available in the market.

FUTURES CONTRACT- INDICATIVE SEQUENTIALS OF FUTURES TRADING

Assume that on 4th Nov`20, Stock A is trading at spot price Rs 600/- and it`s future price is Rs 604/-expiring on 26th Nov ` 20 (last Thursday of November)) Assume that trader X anticipates that Stock A`s price is likely to go up on or before 26th Nov. So, he intends to buy futures on Stock A with lot size being say 100.

1. Contract value is futures price multiplied by lot size which is Rs 604/-x 100=Rs 60,400/-

2.. Trader X is required to hold the required margin amount on Contract value normally 10% i.e Rs 10% of Rs 60,400/-= Rs 6,040/-in his trading account

3. He scouts stock exchange for counterparty i.e seller for the proposed contract who is obviously of opposite view i.e Stock A will go down on or before 26th Nov `20

4. Exchange matches a seller Y who has exactly opposite view of trader X

5. Seller Y is required to hold the same amount of margin in his trading account as Trader X i.e 10% contract value Rs 6,040/-.

6. Both buyer and seller agree and each deposit upfront, their margin amount Rs 6,040/-. As margin amount varies from stock to stock, both buyer and seller deposit margin as required viz SPAN + Exposure margin which includes upfront margin amount of Rs 6,040/-Assume this total margin is 15% of contract value i.e.

Rs 9,060/-

7. They agree and accept that margin is to protect the risk that may arise in the event of default of either party and that depending on the trade, they will deposit further amount as additional maintenance margin whenever margin call is raised by Exchange based on the daily closing price of Stock A`s price valued as per Mark to Market (MTM) accounting

8. They agree on the terms and conditions of the contract that buyer of the contract (i) can exit the contract any time he wishes either by square off before expiry of the contract viz 26th Nov `20 or (ii) hold on the contract till 26[th]Nov or (iii) roll over the contract

9. They sign futures contract agreement digitally

10. Margin amount deposited by buyer and seller is blocked that will be released on fulfillment of their obligations under the agreement.

11. Now broad outline of the contract entered on 9th Nov`20, is as under:-

Buyer of contract	Seller of contract	Underlying asset	Spot price	Futures price	Lot size	Contract value	Contract expiry
Trader X	Trader Y	Stock A	Rs 600/-	Rs 604/-	One lot-100	Rs 60,400/-	26th Nov`20

SPAN margin	Exposure margin	Total Margin	Settlement	Leverage *1	Leverage ratio	Tradable Max.lot	Actual traded lot
@10%-Rs6,040/-	@5%-Rs3.020/-	@15%-Rs 9,060/-	Cash settlement	CV/Margin=6.66	1:6.66	6 lot i.e 600	1 lot i.e 100

Trader X gains	Trader Y losses	Trader X losses	Trader Y gains
When Stock A moves above Rs 600/-	When Stock A moves above Rs 600/-	When Stock A moves below Rs 600/-	When Stock A moves below Rs 600/-

Trader X –Buyer will receive margin call from broker*2	Trader Y –Seller will receive margin call from broker*2
When Stock A falls below Rs 566/- OR down by 6% approx.	When Stock X rises above Rs 636/-OR up by 6% approx.

*1- Means with Re1/- as your capital, you can buy 6.66 worth of stock A. In other words, with 15% as your margin/capital, you are allowed to trade 100%

*2- Shortfall in margin for margin call is calculated with reference to SPAN Margin only and not SPAN+ Exposure margin

Assuming Stock A spot is @ Rs 650/- on any day before expiry		Assuming Stock A spot is @ Rs 540/- on or before expiry	
Trader X -Buyer`s pay off	Trader Y- Seller`s pay off	Trader X -Buyer`s pay off	Trader Y -Seller`s pay off
Profit Rs 5,000/-(650—600)*100	Loss Rs 5,000/-(650—600)*100	Loss Rs 6,000/-(600-540)*100	Profit Rs 6,000/-(600-540)*100

(1) Assuming Stock A spot is @ Rs 650/- on 23rd Nov`20 i.e., before expiry

Exiting the trade	Trader X-Buyer can exit the trade on 23rd Nov`20 or hold on the trade till expiry. If he anticipates that stock A will no longer move up or if he views that holding on the contract further is risky, he can exit the trade with the available profit, by squaring off. To square off, he will sell the futures of one lot i.e, 100 on Stock A at the rate of Rs 650/-and earn profit of Rs 5,000/- as calculated above. By doing so, he offsets his open position. His profit will be settled on the same day evening. Exchange releases his margin for credit to his a/c
Transferring the contract	When a contract is exited by a buyer, the contract is not closed, rather buyer winds up the trade by just transferring his obligation as a buyer to another buyer in the market. Another buyer will continue the trade as per his own views.

(2) Assuming Stock A spot is @ Rs 650/- on 26th Nov`20 i.e., on expiry

Trader X`s obligation As Buyer	As per contract terms, Trader X-Buyer is obligated to buy stock A @ Rs 600/- from seller and he will do it gladly, as he can buy it at Rs 600/- and sell it at the spot market at Rs 650/-earning profit of Rs 5,000/- on the deal.
Trader Y`s obligation As Seller	Here, seller has to fulfill his obligation under the contract i.e., to sell at Rs 600/per share as per the contract terms. Accordingly, Trader Y sells one lot @ Rs 600/-to buyer after he himself buying it at spot rate Rs 650/-, thereby incurring loss of Rs 5000/-. Regardless of the spot price, he has to fulfill his obligation to sell at the agreed price as per terms of contract.

Process of Settlement	As contract is through cash settlement, no physical delivery takes place between them. As the trade has reached the last day of it`s life, buyer need not do any squaring off Exchange will itself close the trade by end of day and settle the amount of profit Rs 5,000/-to Trader X-buyer by transfer from Trader Y-seller`s account and release the available margin amount on 27th Nov`20 to both, as above. Contract between buyer and seller has thus been completed in full. Note that Exchange just releases the blocked margin amount while settlement of Profit & loss to buyer`s and seller`s trading account is done by the concerned brokers.
Price Settlement	A contract that was squared off before maturity by a buyer will be at the rate ruling on the date of square off whereas contract maturing on expiry date will be closed at the contracted rate.

(3) Assuming Stock A spot is @ Rs 540/- on 26th Nov`20 i.e., on expiry	
Trader X`s obligation As Buyer	Here, Trader X-Buyer is bound to buy at Rs 600/- in order to fulfill his obligation as per terms of contract, even though it`s current market rate is Rs 540/- i.e, down by Rs 60/- per share. Accordingly, he buys one lot-100 stock A @Rs 600/-per stock, thereby incurring loss of Rs 6,000/- on the deal.
Trader Y`s obligation As Seller	As Trader Y-seller is bound to gain, he buys gladly one lot of stock A at spot market @ Rs 540/- per share and sells the same to Trader X-buyer @ Rs 600/-earning profit of Rs 6,000/-on the deal. Thus, he fulfills his obligation to sell at the agreed price under the contract.
Process of Settlement	As contract is through cash settlement, no physical delivery takes place between them. As the trade has reached the last day of it`s life, Exchange will itself close the trade by end of day and settle the amount of profit Rs 6,000/- to Trader Y-Seller by transfer from Trader X-Buyer`s account and release the available margin amount on 27th Nov`20 to both, as above. Contract between buyer and seller has thus been completed in full.
Price Settlement	Futures contract, unless winded by the buyer before maturity, will be settled at the contracted price on expiry.

(4) Assuming Stock A spot is @ Rs 590/- on 25th Nov`20 i.e., one day before expiry
If trader X-Buyer thinks Stock A will move up in the following month, ie., Dec`20, he may roll over the contract by selling his 9th Nov`20 contract at the spot rate on 25th Nov`20 and simultaneously buying 31st Dec`20 contract at the futures rate for 31st Dec`20 on the same Stock A with the same one lot.
SELLER OF FUTURESCAN HEDGE TO OFFSET LOSS
The details above relate to buyer of futures and choices before him in various situations. On the other side, a seller of futures can think of hedging the risk. To hedge, he has to off-set the potential loss by buying two call options with position deltas, delta of each being 0.5. Lessons on delta and position delta follow in the next chapter.

SELLER OF FUTURES CAN EXIT BY SQUARE OFF ON ANY DAY BEFORE EXPIRY
Like buyer of the futures, seller can exit the trade by squaring off, if opportunity to profit exists. To square off, seller needs to buy back the contract in the same asset, lot and in the same expiry. Assume the stock is trading at Rs 580/- on 19th Nov 20, i.e, before expiry. Here, he will close the contract by buying back at 580/- and pocket profit Rs 2000/-(600—580)*100. Note Seller has to mention Rs 580/- as his limit price in the trading terminal. Squaring off is done not only with the intention of earning profit, It is also done with a view to cut losses.
SELLER OF FUTURES CAN ROLL OVER ON 25 th Nov`20 i.e., ONE DAY BEFORE EXPIRY
If trader Y-Seller thinks Stock A will move down in the following month, ie., Dec`20, he may roll over the contract by buying his 9th Nov`20 contract at the spot rate on 25th Nov`20 and simultaneously selling 31st Dec`20 contract at the futures rate for 31st Dec`20 on the same Stock A with the same one lot, subject to availability of buyers.

NOTES
1. Futures are mostly speculative and also leveraged. Hence loss may be substantial unless exit and entry points are not planned in advance
2. Futures are better suited to trade on market index than on individual stocks as index trade has only systematic risks, i.e, market risks unlike individual stocks where both systematic and unsystematic risks may impact your trade. Besides, index has more liquidity and relatively low volatility.
3. Placing stop loss at appropriate level is one way of minimizing the risks.

CHAPTER 6

TRADING OPTIONS I

CONTENTS

1 Various Terminology and their meaning in Option contract
2 Difference between Futures and Option Contract
3 Basic concepts of Option contract-with Illustration
4 Moneyness and intrinsic value in Option Contract
5 How to identify moneyness with various Strike rates in Call & Put Option-with illustration
6 Greeks and their risks on Premium
7 Delta in Call & Put Option
8 How Delta is useful in forecasting a trade and it`s risk
9 Selecting a right Delta value to buy Call Option-with illustration
10 Position Delta and it`s purpose
11 Delta`s impact in Call & Put Option on Long and Short trades
12 Gamma- How it works
13 Gamma and it`s impact on Delta values-with illustration
14 Theta-Effect of Theta on buyers and sellers
15 Volatility
16 Difference between Nifty Market Index and Nifty Volatility Index (VIX)
17 Historical Volatility-Implied Volatility-Actual Volatility
18 Implied Volatility and Fundamentals of the underlying Asset
19 Implied Volatility and choosing the right Option, Time frame and Expiration
20 Vega and Implied Volatility
21 Option Chain and how to read it
22 Indicative Model Put Option contract-with illustration of A to Z
23 What a trader has to look into before choosing the strike rate
24 Selecting the right Strike rate, right Expiration
25 Model Put Option contract –Illustration when purpose of trade is speculative and held till expiry
26 Illustration when trade is closed before expiry

27 Model Put Option contract –Illustration when purpose of trade is hedge and held till expiry
28 Selecting the premium-as a seller and buyer
29 Summary of effect of Greeks on premium of Call & Put Option contracts
30 P&L Pay off –choices for traders if trade is held till expiry –Illustration
31 P&l Pay off –Choices for traders if trade is closed before expiry-Illustration
32 Standard Deviation and Variance-Indicative method how to calculate it

Derivatives	We have learnt Futures contract under Derivatives in previous chapter. Now we will move on to Options contract under Derivatives. We will skip what Derivatives, Derivatives Contract & underlying asset mean, since we have explained them in the earlier chapter on Trading Futures.
Key difference between Spot & Derivatives	When a trade is initiated on stock or commodity in spot market, it is primarily buy & sell of the stock at a price with delivery obligations to pass on the ownership of the asset. Consideration for the transaction between them is immediately passed on by exchange of price value of the asset. In derivatives, on the other hand, buyer and seller enter into a sort of betting that bind both obligated to honor the betting contract, the winning or losing of which is decided by it`s value, derived from fluctuations in the price of the asset, reaching a point on expiry of betting period. Here, the transaction between them is settled with reference to the betting price and the asset`s ruling price on a day it is agreed to.
Concept of option contract	An option contract is an agreement between two parties to buy or sell an asset, at a future date, at a pre set price, called strike price with validity for a specific period called duration of contract and with terms that give holder (buyer) of the contract right to buy that asset from, or sell that asset to, writer (seller), but not with obligation, while writer (seller) is obligated to sell or buy that asset on buyer`s demand to do so, at the end of the contract.
Why use options	Traders use options contract for income, speculation and hedging purposes.
Call option	In Call option, the buyer has the right to buy the asset while seller has obligation to sell the asset to him. Each Call option contract has a Bullish buyer and Bearish seller.
Put option	In Put option, the buyer has the right to sell the asset while seller has obligation to buy the asset from him. Each Put option contract has a Bearish buyer and Bullish seller.
Holder of option	Buyers of Call & Put option are also called holder of option
Writers of option	Sellers of Call & Put option are also called writer of option
Premium	An option`s price to buy is called premium which is variable and comprises option`s intrinsic value and time value.
Why premium to buy?	Buyer of both Call & Put option always pays the premium to seller. Seller of both Call & Put option always receives the premium from buyer. By paying premium, buyer buys the right to exercise the option while, seller, by receiving premium accepts his obligation to buyer.

What is right & obligation	As per contract, buyers of option have the choice, to exercise or not to exercise, their rights to buy the asset in Call option or sell in Put option, on the last day of expiry. Sellers, on the other hand, have no such choice and they are only obligated to fulfill buyers` right of exercise under the contract on the last day of expiry.
Exercise	Exercising refers to claiming the right to buy or sell, at the agreed strike price, on the last day of expiry as per the terms of contract under European option. Exercising the right is vested with holder of the contract only viz buyer of Call & Put options.
European options & exercising the right	In India, earlier, there were two versions for trading in options viz American option and European option. Under American option, a holder can exercise his right to buy or sell on or any day before expiry. As American option is banned in India, choice for a holder is only European option. Under European option, holder can exercise his right only **on the last day of expiry**.
European option & exiting the trade	Under European option, a holder can earn profit if premium ruling on a day is higher than what he has paid initially. For ex. if premium paid initially on the trade is say Rs 5/- and premium now is Say Rs 7/- on any day before expiry, he can sell the contract back to the market and make profit of Rs 2/-* lot size (Premium Received now as seller minus Premium Paid earlier as buyer) and square off his position. Note here the difference between exiting and completing the trade. Here holder is just exiting the trade from holder`s point of view and not completing the trade from Exchange point of view.

Square off in option	In Option, if a trader buys or sells an option afresh, he is said to have created fresh position. If he closes the same by opposite trade, i.e, selling option to close his earlier buy position or buying option to close his earlier sell position, it is called square off. By squaring off, he cancels the effect of his first trade.
Contract on expiry	Under options contract, holder can (i) exercise his right to buy or sell on the last day of expiry (ii) exit the trade any day before expiry by selling back the contract to the market (iii) allow the trade to expire worthless. Seller is (i) obligated to sell or buy the asset at the agreed price when holder exercises his right (ii) exit the trade by buying back the contract before expiry (iii) when worthless, seller can retain premium received on expiry
Strike price	Strike price is the pre-set, contracted rate at which options are settled when exercised on the last day of expiry
Profit & loss pay off	If stock`s spot price is above strike price on last day of expiry, Bullish view party makes profit & bearish view party loses. If stock`s spot price is below strike price, bearish view party makes profit and bullish view party loses.

Intrinsic value	Intrinsic value is a measure to assess an asset`s worth. In Options, intrinsic value refers to difference between spot price and strike price. It is a measure of profit. If the difference between spot and strike is negative, intrinsic value is zero. In other words, intrinsic value is always a positive figure.
Time value	Time value refers to the portion of the premium above Intrinsic value that an option buyer pays for the privilege of owning the contract for a certain period. Say a stock is currently trading at Rs 50/- and the strike price as agreed to between parties is Rs 46/- & option`s premium for Call buy is Rs 5/-. Here current stock`s price is more than strike price by Rs 4/-while the option`s price is Rs 5/-. This means Rs 4/ of Rs 5/- is intrinsic value and Rs 1/- is it`s time value.
Intrinsic value and time value	Option`s premium is component of Intrinsic value and time value. These two values, combined together, determine the cost of option viz premium. Intrinsic value changes when underlying`s price changes. Time value changes as each day passes on.
Unlimited profit & Limited loss	In option, buyer earns unlimited profit if the trade moves in his favor. If the trade moves against him, he incurs maximum loss to the extent of premium paid by him.
Unlimited loss & Limited profit	In option, seller incurs unlimited loss if the trade moves against him. If the trade moves in his favor, he earns maximum profit to the extent of premium received by him.
Break even	Break even is a price point at which a trade earns no profit or loss.
Three expiries	Like futures, in options too, three expiries are offered for contract. Current month, mid month and far month refer to the respective expiration of the contracts
Margin money & Mark to Market In Option	There is no margin requirement for holders of contract viz buyers of Call & Put option as their loss is limited to the extent of premium paid by them. However, for sellers of Call &Put option their potential loss is unlimited. So, in order to avoid any default from seller in the event of huge loss, Exchanges prescribe margin for Options sellers. Margin requirement for them is approximately similar to Futures contract. Unlike Futures, there is no daily settlement of notional profit or loss as NO margin is required for buyer of option and hence NO mark to market call for buyer while for seller, margin call may arise if there is increase in the premium after writing the contract.
Abbreviation	Example:-Call option of TCS at strike price of say Rs 2250/-under European option is abbreviated as TCS2250CE where C for Call & E for European option. In Put, it is abbreviated as TCS 225OPE, P for Put and E for European Option.
Option Useful for	Options contracts are used for hedging and speculative purposes.

DIFFERENCE BETWEEN FUTURES AND OPTIONS CONTRACTS	
Futures contract	Options contract
1. Futures contract requires buyer to purchase share and a seller to sell them on a specific future date unless buyer closes the trade before expiry by exit	1. In options, buyer has right to buy or sell, but not obligated, while seller is obligated to sell or buy, at agreed price as long as the contract is alive.
2. In Futures, both buyer & seller have to fulfill their obligations under the contract.	2. In options, buyer has a choice to exercise or not to exercise his right, while seller has no choice, he has to fulfill his obligation
3. In futures, for both the buyer and seller, potential return as well as loss is high due to leverage	3. Loss is limited to the extent of premium paid in case of buyer and unlimited in case of seller
4. In futures, after initial margin, margin call may be raised to keep daily margin, from both buyer and seller	4. In option, option seller and not buyer is required to keep margin as seller's loss potential is unlimited. Here, amount of premium received by seller is blocked as his collateral margin
5. In futures, Contract is valued at Lot size multiplied by futures price and both buyer and seller are bound by contract value	5. In options, Buyer's premium is calculated as per his preference of lot size to buy and trade the option. Seller need not pay any premium.
6. Trade is settled at spot price on expiry date unless buyer exits the trade before expiry	6. In options, P&L pay off is settled at contracted price called strike price and it's length from spot price, reckoning premium paid or received.
7. In Futures, futures pricing is direct and straight forward.	7. In option, option price called premium is arrived on complex math.
8. Futures price is not much impacted by any time decay or volume and the trade is simply effect of demand and supply of the asset or market trend.	8. Option's price is vulnerable to changes frequently, by interactions of Greeks* affecting the P&L pay off

*Lessons on Greeks follow

OPTIONS IN NUTSHELL TO UNDERSTAND THE BASIC CONCEPTS

FACTORS	CALL OPTION		PUT OPTION	
	BUY	SELL	BUY	SELL
Outlook	Bullish (to expect stock price to move above strike price on expiry)	Bearish-to go down or stay flat (to expect stock price to move at or below strike price on expiry)	Bearish (to expect stock price to move below strike price on expiry)	Bullish-to go up or stay flat (to expect stock price to move at or above strike price on expiry)
Right	Buyer has **Right to buy**	Seller **Obligates to sell**	Buyer has **Right to sell**	Seller **Obligates to buy**

Right means	Buyer has choice to exercise his right to buy the asset on last day of expiry at contracted price	Seller has only obligation to sell/deliver when buyer exercises his right to buy	Buyer has choice to exercise his right to sell the asset on last day of expiry at contracted price	Seller has only obligation to buy when buyer exercises his right to sell
Premium	PAY	RECEIVE	PAY	RECEIVE
Profit potential	Unlimited	Limited to the extent of premium received	Unlimited	Limited to the extent of premium received
Loss potential	Limited to the extent of premium paid	Unlimited	Limited to the extent of premium paid	Unlimited
Intrinsic value (IV)*1	Spot Price–Strike Price	Spot Price–Strike Price	Strike Price–Spot Price	Strike Price–Spot Price
Break-even (BE)	Strike price + Premium Paid	Strike price + Premium Received	Strike price – Premium Paid	Strike price – Premium Received
P&L on last day of Expiry	Max (Spot-STR)*lot–Prem. paid Or IV—Premium paid	Prm. Recd—Max (Spot-STR)*lot Or Premium Recd—IV	Max (STR-Spot)*lot—Prm.paid Or IV—Premium paid	Prm. Recd—Max (STR-Spot)*lot Or Premium Recd—IV
When Loss *2	SPOT PRICE<STRIKE PRICE	SPOT PRICE>STRIKE PRICE	SPOT PRICE>STRIKE PRICE	SPOT PRICE<STRIKE PRICE
When Profit*3	SPOT PRICE>STRIKE PRICE	SPOT PRICE<STRIKE PRICE	SPOT PRICE<STRIKE PRICE	SPOT PRICE>STRIKE PRICE
P&L before expiry	If a trader buys or sells option before expiry, P&L on square off is the difference between premium received and premium paid.			

*1If the difference between spot and strike is negative, intrinsic value is zero. In other words, intrinsic value is always a positive figure.

CALL OPTION	PUT OPTION
In Call option buyer to buy the asset	In Put option buyer to sell the asset
Each Call option has a Bullish buyer and Bearish seller	Each Put option has a Bearish buyer and a Bullish seller
When an investor is BULLISH	**When an investor is BEARISH**
Buy a CALL OPTION or Sell a PUT OPTION	Sell a CALL OPTION or Buy a Put OPTION

Note: 1) Strike price is the pre-set, contracted rate and used to settle the contract when exercised on the last day of expiry

2) Exercise price is the price at which the holder of contract exercises his right to buy or sell on the last day of expiry. Exercise price and Strike price are the same.

3) Last day of expiry, expiration, expiry- all mean the same viz the last day of validity of the contract.

ON LAST DAY OF EXPIRY-WHEN LOSS TO WHOM-EXAMPLE*2	
LOSS TO CALL OPTION BUYER & PUT OPTION SELLER	**LOSS TO PUT OPTION BUYER &CALL OPTION SELLER**
When spot price is below the strike price on the last day of expiry, Call option buyer & Put option seller incur loss.	When spot price is above the strike price on the last day of expiry, Put option buyer & Call option seller incur loss.
Call Option Buyer:IV=(Spot—Strike) P&L :-(Spot—Strike)*100—Prem.Paid	Call Option Seller: IV=(Spot—Strike) P&L:-Prem.Recd—(Spot—Strike)*100
Put Option Seller: IV=(Strike—Spot) P&L :-Prem.Recd—(Strike—Spot)*100	Put option Buyer:IV=(Strike—Spot) P&L:-(Strike—Spot)*100—Prem.Paid
Break Even: Call Buyer:-Strike+Prm.Paid For Put seller: Strike—Prm.Recd	Break Even: Call seller:-Strike+Prm.Recd For Put Buyer: Strike—Prm.Paid
If spot is Rs 100/-,strike is Rs150/-, premium is Rs 5/- and one lot is,100, IV for Call is (Rs 100—Rs 150-)*100 is –ve and hence zero. P&L for Call buyer is (0–500) Loss Rs 500/-Loss is limited to prem. Paid IV for Put is (Rs 150–Rs 100)*100 P&L for Put seller is: (500—5,000) Loss is Rs 4,500/- Break Even: For Call:-150+5=155/- For Put 150—5=145/-	If spot is Rs 200/- strike is Rs 180/-,Premium is Rs 3/-and one lot is 100, IV for Call (Rs 200/–Rs 180/-)*100 P&L for Call seller is:(300—2,000) Loss-Rs 1700/- IV for Put (Rs 180/–Rs 200/-)*100 is –ve and hence zero. P&L for Put buyer is (0—300) Loss Rs 300/- Loss is limited to prem.Paid. Break Even: For Call:-180 +3=183/- For Put 180—3=177/-
ON LAST DAY OF EXPIRY-WHEN PROFIT TO WHOM-EXAMPLE*3	
PROFIT TO CALL OPTION BUYER & PUT OPTION SELLER	**PROFIT TO PUT OPTION BUYER & CALL OPTION SELLER**
When spot price is above the strike price on the last day of expiry, both Call option buyer & Put option seller make profit.	When spot price is below the strike price on the last day of expiry, Put option buyer & Call option seller make profit.
Call Option Buyer:IV=(Spot—Strike) P&L :-(Spot—Strike)*100—Prem.Paid	Call Option Seller: IV=(Spot—Strike) P&L:-Prem.Recd—(Spot—Strike)*100
Put Option Seller: IV=(Strike—Spot) P&L :-Prem.Recd—(Strike—Spot)*100	Put option Buyer:IV=(Strike—Spot) P&L:-(Strike—Spot)*100—Prem.Paid
Break Even: Call Buyer:-Strike+Prm.Paid For Put seller: Strike—Prm.Recd	Break Even: Call seller:-Strike+Prm.Recd For Put Buyer: Strike—Prm.Paid

If spot is Rs 300/-,strike is Rs 250/-,Premium is Rs 4/-& lot is one i.e,100	If spot is Rs 400/-strike is Rs 450/-,Premium is Rs 5/-& one lot is 100
IV for Call (Rs 300/– Rs 250/-)*100 P&L pay off:(5000—400) Profit for Call buyer is Rs 4500/-	IV for Call (Rs 400/–Rs 450/-)*100 is –ve and hence zero. P&L pay off for Call seller is (500—0) Profit for Call seller is Rs 500/-
IV for Put (Rs 250/–Rs 300/-)*100 is –ve and hence zero. P&L pay off:	IV for Put (Rs 450/–Rs 400/-)*100 P&L pay off:(5000—500) Profit for Put buyer is Rs 4500/-
(400—0) Profit for Put seller is Rs 400/-	Break Even: For Call:-450+5=455/- For Put 450—5=445/-
Break Even: For Call:-250+4=254/- For Put 250—4=246/-	

PAY OF FOR SELLERS OF BOTH CALL & PUT OPTION
While loss to buyers of both call & put is limited to the extent of premium paid, **loss to sellers** of both call & put is **unlimited.** Hence selling/writing an option by a beginner is risky. Before entering into options trade as a seller/writer, exercise caution.

P&L PAY OFF IN NUTSHELL			
When Spot is above Strike		**When Spot is below Strike**	
Who earns Profit—Bullish view	Who incurs Loss–Bearish view	Who earns Profit—Bearish view	Who incurs Loss—Bullish view
Call Option buyer & Put option seller	Call Option seller & Put option buyer	Call Option seller & Put option Buyer	Call Option buyer & Put option seller
Profit of Call buyer is loss to Call seller-Profit of Put seller is loss to Put buyer*		Profit of Call seller is loss to Call Buyer-Profit of Put buyer is loss to Put seller*	

*in terms of amount gained/lost

MONEYNESS & INTRINSIC VALUE IN OPTION CONTRACT	
Intrinsic value	As you are aware, intrinsic value is the difference between spot and strike price which is non negative figure. In other words, intrinsic value is always a positive figure. If it is a negative figure, it is zero and can never be below zero. Also, remember that Intrinsic value is reckoned on the last day of expiry to arrive P&L Pay off.
Strike Rate & Intrinsic value	In Options contract, intrinsic value is very important factor, since it indicates the money a trader is likely to earn. So, selecting appropriate strike price is decisive in arriving intrinsic value and P&L Pay off on Options contract. In order to know intrinsic value of an option contract, selected strike price is classified according to it`s nearness or far away from the current price of the underlying asset. Broadly, there are three classifications of moneyness called ATM, ITM,OTM. The classification foretells the direction that you predict your trade is likely to move on with known delta value of each, to earn intrinsic value on expiration. Please find study on Delta and other greeks below

Classification	Call Option Intrinsic Value=(Spot—Strike)	Put Option Intrinsic Value=(Strike—Spot)
ATM **(At the money)**	When spot rate is equal to strike rate i.e, ATM is spot rate IV=Zero	When spot rate is equal to strike rate i.e, ATM is spot rate IV=Zero
ITM **(In the Money)**	When spot rate is above strike rate IV is +ve number or non-zero means profit to trader	When spot rate is below strike rate IV is +ve number or non-zero means profit to trader
DEEP ITM	When spot rate is above strike rate IV is high in +ve means substantial profit to trader	When spot rate is below strike rate IV is high in +ve means substantial profit to trader
OTM **(Out of Money)**	When spot rate is below strike rate IV is —ve number and taken as zero means loss to trader	When spot rate is above strike rate IV is —ve number and taken as zero means loss to trader
DEEP OTM	When spot rate is below strike rate IV is high in -ve and taken as zero means substantial loss to trader	When spot rate is above strike rate IV is high in -ve and taken as zero means substantial loss to trader

When option contract expires in OTM	
Buyer of both Call & Put option incurs Loss by losing premium Paid	Seller of both Call & Put option makes profit by retaining the premium received

When option contract expires in ITM	
Buyer of both Call & Put option makes profit as per P&L pay off	Seller of both Call & Put option incurs loss as per P&L pay off

Premium
For both Call & Put options, premiums of ITM strikes are always higher than premiums of OTM strikes because ITM strikes carry profit potential while OTM strikes carry uncertain profit or loss.

KNOW HOW TO IDENTIFY POTENTIAL MONEY WITH VARIOUS STRIKE RATES IN CALL OPTIONS

In Call options Intrinsic value=(Spot—Strike) Assuming Spot rate@ Rs 780/-, then, ATM is 780/-

Strike rate @	750	770	690	820	840	860	900
ITM	780—750=30	780—770=10					
Deep ITM			780—690=90				
OTM				780—820=0	780—840=0		
Deep OTM						780—860=0	780—900=0

KNOW HOW TO IDENTIFY POTENTIAL MONEY WITH VARIOUS STRIKE RATES IN PUT OPTIONS							
In Put options Intrinsic value=(Strike–Spot) Assuming Spot rate@ Rs 490/-, then, ATM is 490/-							
Strike rate @	520	540	580	480	470	410	400
ITM	520—490=30	540—490=50					
Deep ITM			580—490=90				
OTM				480—490=0	470—490=0		
Deep OTM						410—490=0	400—490=0

GREEKS- WHY GREEKS IN OPTIONS AND NOT IN FUTURES?
In Futures contract, underlying asset`s price fluctuation is the prime driver of the contract meaning if underlying price increases say by 100 points, future`s price also increases by 100 points. Besides, in Futures, trading requires fairly moderate capital to enter and earn profit with leveraged capital whereas in Option, premium is small but exposure to contract value is huge. For instance, for a small premium of say Rs 15/-for one lot say 100, an option buyer bets Rs 1500/- to buy stocks worth more than 20 or 30 times of value of the stock Apart from the fact that there is no leverage in option, earning is high proportionate to capital employed in option. Hence various dimensional risks are forced through Greeks.

KEY DRIVERS OF OPTION TRADE
Unlike Futures, option contract `s core trading points are (i) Strike Rate (ii) expiration date and (iii) Premium or price of option. As premium of option is the metric for valuation of unexpired contracts at any point of time, lessons on option contracts revolve mostly around the premium and it`s changing valuation. Option traders may keep this in mind.

GREEKS AND THEIR RISKS ON PREMIUM	
Delta	Delta represents rate of change in option's price in relation to one point change in the price of the underlying asset.
Gamma	Gamma represents rate of change in Option`s Delta in relation to one point change in the price of the underlying asset
Theta	Theta represents rate of change in Option`s price in relation to time decay of the contract.
Vega	Vega represents rate of change in Option`s price in relation to one percentage change in implied volatility

GREEK DELTA –HOW IT WORKS

Delta represents rate of change in an option price in relation to one point change in the price of the underlying asset.

The value of delta ranges from -1 to 0 for Puts and 0 to 1 for Calls. Delta for ATM is 0.5, for OTM between 0 to close to 0.5, for ITM is above 0.5 to 1. If you are long on option with delta say 0.5 and if one point move is worth say Rs 200/-, then, your Call option will gain in value by Rs 100/-approximately. Similarly, if delta is say 0.4,for a movement of 100 points up, options value will gain by 40 points assuming other Greeks are constant.

DELTA IN CALL OPTION

Delta for Call option is always +ve and varies between 0 to1 because call options have a positive relationship with the price of the underlying asset. Hence premium increases when spot increases & premium decreases when spot decreases. If Delta for Call option is say 0.3 it means for every one point change in the underlying, premium is expected to change by 0.3 points. For example, if Index of Nifty is up by 50 points moving from 8500 to 8550,Delta for Call option is say 0.5 and current premium is say Rs 120/-, then option premium increases due to change in Index by 50 points by +50 x 0.5=+25,. So new premium is Rs 120/-+25/- ie 145/-Similarly, if the Index in this example, moves down by 50 points, new premium is—50 x 0.5= –25. So, 120/–25/-=95/-So, when points moves up, change of premium is added to the current premium and when moves down, change of premium is subtracted from the current premium

DELTA IN PUT OPTION

Delta for Put option is always –ve and varies between -1 to 0. Hence inversely related because they have a negative relationship with the underlying security. So premium increases when spot decreases & premium decreases when spot increases. For example, if the Nifty Index moves up say from 9000 to 9100 ie up by 100 points, current premium is Rs 130/-, & Delta for Put option is –0.6, then, change in option premium decreases by +100 x–0.6=–60. So new premium is 130/–60/=70. In this example, if the index moves down from say 9100 to 9000, change in premium is –100 x –0.6= +60 So, 60 is added to the current premium ie 130/-+60/-=190/- So premium increases when underlying decreases & premium decreases when underlying increases.

HOW DELTA IS USEFUL IN FORECASTING A TRADE AND IT`S RISK

When price of the underlying changes, Delta works to change the premium of option according to it`s metric. This helps traders (i) select the right option strike rate with reference to it`s delta value (ii) predict their trade positioning in profit or loss on expiration or before expiry, assuming that other Greeks-Theta & Vega remain constant. While other Greeks like Theta & Vega also play their role simultaneously in changing valuation of unexpired option contracts, a trader can, nevertheless, forecast direction of his options trade on expiration i.e., whether ITM (profit) or OTM (no profit) with reference to his position as to long or short. Thus, delta`s role is decisive in forming opinion on profitability or otherwise of holding the contract until expiry or exiting the trade before expiry.

DELTA`S BEHAVIOUR IN CALL & PUT OPTIONS ON LONG AND SHORT TRADES					
Options	Increase in spot price	Decrease in spot price	Options	Increase in spot price	Decrease in spot price
Call option	+Premium	−Premium	Put option	−Premium	+Premium
Long Call	+Premium	−Premium	Long Put	−Premium	+Premium
Short Call	−Premium	+Premium	Short Put	+Premium	−Premium

+ indicates premium increases. − indicates premium decreases

DELTA AND CLASSIFICATION OF POTENTIAL MONEY-APPROXIMATION		
Delta for Call option ranges from 0 to 1 while delta for Put option ranges from −1 to 0. It is useful to forecast profit or loss on expiration with the options` delta and it`s potential money. By evaluating potential money a trader can gauge likely movement of current premium from OTM (no profit) to ITM (profit) on expiration, assuming that other Greeks-Theta & Vega remain constant.		
Classification	Delta for Call option ranges from 0 to 1	Delta for Put option ranges from −1 to 0
Deep OTM	0 to 0.3	0 to -0.3
OTM	0.3 to less than 0.5	−0.3 to less than −0.5
ATM	0.5	−0.5
ITM	Above 0.5 to 1	Below −0.5 to −1
Deep ITM	0.8 to 1	−0.8 to −1

Range for Call: From 0,0.1,0.2,0.3,0.4,0.5,0.6,0.7,0.8,0.9,1 Range for Put is: From −1,−0.9,−0.8,−0.7,−0.6,−0.5,−0.4,−0.3,−0.2,−0.1,0

DELTA AND SELECTING RIGHT DELTA VALUE TO BUY A CALL OPTION		
Classification	Delta (approx)	Choosing the right money with probability of options moving to ITM (profit)
Deep OTM	0.2	Trade has a 20% chance of ending ITM and 80% chance of ending OTM. Deep OTM is a small value. To move to ITM, underlying value has to make a large move. Probability of Options expiring in ITM is very less. Hence avoid buying deep OTM. Instead let trader consider shorting as it has a 80% chance of ending OTM
OTM	0.4	Trade has a 40% chance of ending ITM and 60% chance of ending OTM. Premium is slightly expensive than deep OTM. Trader may consider shorting also, if other greeks favor the shorting
ATM	0.5	Trade has a 50% chance of ending ITM and 50% chance of ending OTM. Premium is expensive than OTM
ITM	0.6	Trade has a 60% chance of ending ITM and 40% chance of ending ATM. Probability of trade ending ITM is high. As chance of ending ITM is fairly high, never consider shorting ITM options. Also note that at ATM gamma is the highest. Remember, an option with a high gamma of say, 0.75, delta value may have less chance of expiring ITM than a low gamma option with the same delta because high gamma accelerates delta very rapidly.

Deep ITM	0.9	Probability of trade ending ITM is far high. When trade is sure to ending ITM, shorting should be avoided. When delta reaches 1, it becomes one to one movement, meaning if underlying value moves 100, premium will also move by 100

<table>
<tr><td colspan="3" align="center">NOTE</td></tr>
<tr><td colspan="3">1. The above illustration is to buy CALL option and hence delta is positive. If delta is positive, it means both underlying and premium move in the same direction.</td></tr>
<tr><td colspan="3">2. If the same is to buy a PUT option, delta is NEGATIVE. It means both underlying and premium move in the opposite direction</td></tr>
<tr><td colspan="3">3. For both Call & Put options, premiums for ITM options are always higher than premiums for OTM due to ITM`s profit potential.</td></tr>
<tr><td colspan="3">4. Above delta values are approximation. In real trade, delta values are precisely measured by their gamma values.</td></tr>
</table>

<table>
<tr><td colspan="2" align="center">POSITION DELTA</td></tr>
<tr><td colspan="2">Delta is useful in hedging the risks in portfolio or commodities. Recall that In futures, hedging is done based on beta value while in option, it is done based on delta value. Position delta is a way of hedging your options on combined positions. It is calculated by adding the delta values of each Call or Put options or delta of a long Call and short Put etc., so that final single delta value of the combined options is arrived which could be either delta positive or delta negative as per preference of a trader. While delta values of Call and Put options have positive and negative effects on changes in spot price of the underlying, it further changes it`s positivity or negativity depending on long or short trades of Call or Put options. A tabular below shows the changes. With the changes, a trader can hedge the risks depending on status of his position in portfolio. Note that position delta is used (i) in portfolio investment (ii) to hedge on (iii) combined positions</td></tr>
<tr><td colspan="2" align="center">PURPOSE OF POSITIONING DELTA</td></tr>
<tr><td colspan="2">By combining deltas of two or more Call and Put or Calls long and Puts of short, or in any way a trader likes to, single delta value of combined options is found to ensure that both the underlying and combined position move in the desired direction as per the requirement of the trader.</td></tr>
<tr><td>Strategy no.1</td><td>Say delta of an ITM option you have bought is 0.6, and another one option of OTM on the same underlying is say 0.4. Adding two delta values you get positive 1 which means underlying and combined delta position move in the same direction. So, if spot of the underlying increases by 1, your value of both options moves up by 1 point. Note here the underlying is the same and both the option is Call buying.</td></tr>
<tr><td>Strategy no.2</td><td>Say delta of a OTM Call option is 0.25 for 2 lots, delta of second one on the same underlying ITM Put one lot is −0.65, third option on the same underlying ITM Call is 0.70 for 2 lots, net delta effect is:-

(i) For OTM Call buy 2 lots 2*0.25=0.50 (ii) For ITM Put 1 lot 1*−0.65=−0.65 (iii) for ITM Call 2 lots 2*0.70=1.40 Adding all,+1.25. This indicates that if increase in spot of underlying is 100 points, combined value of all options will increase by 125 points. Note Put has a negative effect</td></tr>
</table>

Strategy no.3	Say delta of a OTM short Call option is 0.40 for 3 lots, delta of second one on the same underlying ITM long Put 2 lot is −0.70, third option on the same underlying ITM long Call is 0.60 for 2 lots, net delta effect is:- (i) For OTM **short** Call lots 3*0.40=−1.20 (ii) For ITM long **Put** 2 lot 2*0.70=−1.40 (iii) for ITM long Call 2 lots 2*0.60= +1.20. (i) For short Call delta= −1.20 (ii) For long Put delta=−1.40 (iii) For long Call= +1.20 net effect is −1.40 meaning increase in spot of the underlying say 100 points will decrease options value by 140 points. Note delta sign here. Short call and long Put are negatively related while long call is positively related.

SUMMARIZING DELTA AND IT`S BEHAVIOUR ASSUMING OTHER GREEKS ARE CONSTANT

Options	Increase in spot price	Decrease in spot price	Options	Increase in spot price	Decrease in spot price
Call	+Prem	−Prem	Put	−Prem	+Prem
Long Call	+Prem	−Prem	Long Put	−Prem	+Prem
Short Call	−Prem	+Prem	Short Put	+Prem	−Prem

+ indicates premium increases while − indicates premium decreases from the current premium

GAMMA-HOW GAMMA WORKS

Gamma represents rate of change in Option`s Delta in relation to one point change in the price of the underlying asset. For this reason gamma is called $2^{nd}$ derivative to premium, Ist derivative being delta to underlying`s price. For example, if for a Call option, Gamma is 0.0030, it means for every one point change in the underlying, rate of change in delta is 0.0030. If, in the above example, change in the underlying moves up by 100 points, current delta is 0.4 & current premium is 120/-, additional premium is 100*0.4=40 So, new premium is 120/+40/- =160/- Change in delta is Gamma multiplied by change in the underlying i.e., 0.0030x100=0.3, so, new delta is 0.4+0.3=0.7. So, new money position is ITM. If change in underlying is 100 points down instead of 100 points up, the new premium is arrived by deducting from the current premium and new delta by deducting from the current delta. In the above example, new premium is 120—40=80/- New delta is 0.4—0.3=0.1. New moneyness is OTM

CHARACTERISTICS OF GAMMA

1. Higher gamma value indicates that delta could change dramatically in response to even small movement in the underlying asset

2. Gamma is highest for ATM options and lowest for deep ITM & deep OTM options

3. As expiration approaches, gamma is larger & price changes have more impact on gamma

4. Farther away from expiration, gamma is lower

5. When you buy Call or Put options you are Long gamma. When you short Call or Put options you are short gamma

6. Unlike delta, gamma is always positive number for both Call & Put options

GAMMA AND IT`S RISKS

1. If two options have the same delta value, but one option has a high gamma and other one has a low gamma, then option with high gamma has higher risk as unfavorable move in the asset will have higher impact due to high gamma.

2. An option with high gamma of say 0.0075, delta value may have less chance of expiring ITM than a low gamma option with the same delta

3. Avoid shorting ATM options because ATM is sensitive due to higher gamma, sensitive in the sense that prices change faster with rapid changing delta value.

INDICATIVE GAMMA AND IT`S IMPACT ON DELTA VALUES

Classification	Delta 1	Gamma 2	Trade	If Spot moves 100 points	Change in Prem *A (100*1)	Change in Delta*B (100*2)	Old Prem.	New Prem.
Deep OTM	+0.20	0.0004	Long Call	Up	+20	+0.04	5	5+20=25
OTM	−0.30	0.0006	Short Put	Down	+30	−0.06	60	60+30=90
ATM	+0.50	0.0020	Short Call	Up	+50	+0.20	90	90+50=140
ITM	−0.70	0.0010	Long Put	Down	+70	−0.10	90	90+70=160
Deep ITM	+0.90	0.0003	Short Call	Down	−90	−0.03	110	110-90=20
OTM	−0.25	0.0002	Long Put	Up	−25	+0.02	28	28−25=3

Change in premium*A	Change in Delta*B	Old delta	New delta	Old classification	New classification
(+0.20*100)=+20	0.0004*100=+0.04	+0.20	+0.20+0.04=0.24	Deep OTM	Deep OTM
(−0.30*−100)=+30	(0.0006*−100)=−0.06	−0.30	(−0.30)+(−0.06)= −0.36	OTM	OTM
(+0.50*100)=+50	(0.0020*100)=−+0.20	+0.50	+0.50+0.20=+0.70	ATM	ITM
(−0.70*−100)=+70	(0.0010*−100)=−0.10	−0.70	(−0.70)+(−0.10)= −0.80	ITM	Deep ITM
(+0.90*−100)=−90	(0.0003*−100)=−0.03	+0.90	−0.03+0.90=+0.87	Deep ITM	Deep ITM
(−0.25*100)=−25	(0.0002*100)=+0.02	−0.25	−0.25+0.02=−0.23	OTM	OTM

NOTES

Never trade with high gamma as high gamma accelerates change in delta rapidly. ATM will always have highest gamma. Low gamma will move delta slowly from OTM to ITM. The above results are determined by two values. (i) Up & down moves of 100 points in spot are valued with plus for up and minus for down. (ii) Sign values in change of premium are assigned based on up or down moves for 100 points in Call & Put. For instance, Up or down in Call will result in premium rise or fall respectively. For Put, up or down move will result in fall or rise respectively. To find out new classification, two steps of calculations are necessary.

1. Multiply points of moves (up or down) in Spot with delta. This will give change in premium. Based on type of option viz Call or Put and moves, up or down, add/subtract this change in premium with the old premium. Result is new premium.

2. Multiply gamma with points of moves (up or down) in Spot. This will give change in delta value. Based on sign value you get, add/subtract this change in delta with the old delta value. You get new delta value which tells you new moneyness. Note that gamma is positive number and has no effect on type of trade like buy or sell.

3. Gamma is always positive. It is the least in Deep OTM & Deep ITM, else, gamma being 2nd derivative, will accelerate Delta in Deep ITM to more than 1 and in Deep OTM less than zero, which cannot be functionally acceptable.

4. All the above changes in valuation of option and moneyness are indicative, assuming all other Greeks, Theta, Vega including implied volatility remain constant.

For delta changes see the table. Gamma is always positive. So, when it is multiplied with delta, result is delta`s sign value.

Options	Increase in spot price	Decrease in spot price	Options	Increase in spot price	Decrease in spot price
Call	+Prem	−Prem	Put	−Prem	+Prem
Long Call	+Prem	−Prem	Long Put	−Prem	+Prem
Short Call	−Prem	+Prem	Short Put	+Prem	−Prem

THETA
We have learnt that premium or price of option is comprised of two components, known as intrinsic value and time value. While Delta indicates rate of change in options value in relation to one point change in the price of underlying, theta represents rate of change in option`s value owing to time decay of the contract. Time decay refers to passage of time. Theta indicates options premium will be high if there is longer time to expiration and low if there is lesser time to expiration, all else being equal. It is expressed in points lost per day. As expiration nears, theta`s effect is up, meaning drop in premium value will be fast. Note that time decay lessens the chances of options moving from OTM to ITM.i.e, profit for a buyer since there is less time remaining to make such moves when expiration is near. On the other hand, it makes seller happy as chances of trade staying OTM and retaining premium on expiration are high.
EFFECT OF THETA ON BUYER AND SELLER
Assume that spot price of Nifty index is 11,400 on 4th Jan `21, strike rate @ 11500 CE premium @ Rs 32/- expiry on $28^{th}$ Jan`21. Intrinsic value on long Call trade on 4th Jan is zero i.e. (11400—11500) (Spot −Strike).Here, by using formula for premium viz premium = Intrinsic value + time value, intrinsic value is zero and time value is Rs 32/-that represents it`s time value for the remaining number of days i.e 25 days for expiry. This time value gets eroded as each day passes and moves closer to expiry. If theta value for the trade is say Rs −1.25, it means the trade loses it`s time value by Rs 1.25 per day making it cheaper, all other Greeks being constant.

From Buyer's position	In the above example, buyer's option will lose it's value by Rs 1.25 per day due to time decay. As time draws closer to expiry he has to take decision whether to stay on or exit the trade, in the face of losing value each day. Close to expiration, theta can severely undermine long option holder's position especially if implied volatility also declines at the same time
From Seller's position	Seller's chance of retaining the premium received by him is getting brighter on expiration. For this reason, theta is said to be good for seller and bad for buyer. In the above example, if a seller has written an option say at Rs 91/- and say, after T+8 day, the same option is trading at Rs 81/-owing to it's losing daily at the rate of Rs 1.25 and making it cheaper,, he can buy it back at Rs 81/-on the same underlying and at the same lot and earn profit of Rs 10/-, all else being equal. (Premium received earlier as a seller Rs 91 minus premium payable now as a buyer Rs 81)

CHARACTERISITICS OF THETA

1. Long Calls & long Puts will have –ve effect and Short Call & short Put will have +ve effect, due to theta, meaning buyers lose option's value daily by their theta while sellers gain the same value. Theta is expressed in points lost per day.

2. Theta increases to the highest when options are ATM & decreases when options are ITM & OTM.

3. Theta will have zero time value on expiration.

4. An option premium that has no intrinsic value will decline at an increasing rate as expiration nears.

5. Key point to keep in mind about Theta is that rate of change in premium is caused by change due to time decay of the **contract.**

THETA AND TRADING

1. Theta can also be high for OTM options if there is a lot of implied volatility

2. Theta is highest for ATM since less time is needed for transition from ATM to ITM (profit) with a price move in the underlying

3. Theta will increase sharply as time decay accelerates in the last week before expiration

4. Selling options close to expiry may favor seller as close to expiry has low premium but also drop in premium is rapid, all else being equal.

5. For beginners, contracts with longer time to expiry is suitable

VOLATILITY

Volatility is synonym to risks in stock market. Volatility, as a trader knows, is fluctuations in an asset's price with big swings in either direction. It is viewed as risky because price in volatility is less predictable. Higher the volatility, higher the risk. However, volatility, in it's true meaning, is a statistical measure or metric for a given security or market index to find how large prices swing from the asset's mean or average price and give returns in a given period, by using standard deviation & variance method. Volatility can also be measured by Beta & VIX. VIX is widely used to measure volatility in option contracts, while Beta is used to measure volatility of individual stock compared to the market as a whole. Volatility is often associated with big swings in either direction. For Ex., when the stock market rises or falls more than 1% over a sustained period of time, it is called volatile market. Volatile assets are considered riskier than less volatile assets, because the price is expected to be less predictable

Higher volatility	indicates the price of the security can change dramatically over a short term period, in either direction
Lower volatility	indicates the security value does not fluctuate dramatically and tends to be more steady
How it is measured	1) Volatility can be measured using variance and standard deviation. Learn more on standard deviation and how to calculate the volatility with standard deviation and variance, given at the end of this chapter. 2) Measuring through Beta. If beta value of an asset is 1, the price value changes 100% on every 100% move in market index. Learn more on Beta which is given at the end of this chapter. 3) ATR-Average True Range* 4) Bollinger Band* 5) VIX method, which is commonly used in option contracts. * Please find Average True Range & Bollinger Band given in Chapter 3A-Technical Tools
Volatility Index (VIX)	NIFTY`s India VIX is the official IV Index that tells investor`s perception of the market volatility over the next 30 days period. NIFTY VIX is based on the outstanding Nifty option contracts for near month and next month. (1) Higher VIX, higher the expected volatility & vice versa (2) When market is highly volatile, market moves steeply and during such time volatility index tends to rise.(3) When volatility index rises, one should become careful as the market can move in any direction (4) VIX ranges between 12 to 35. When VIX value is higher than 30, it indicates higher volatility, lower value indicates lower volatility

DIFFERENCE BETWEEN NIFTY MARKET INDEX AND NIFTY VOLAITILITY INDEX (VIX)

Market Index	Implied volatility Index (VIX)
1. Market index is computed using the price movements of stocks that indicates the direction of the market	1. VIX is computed based on the outstanding options contracts for near month and next month and useful to predict IV for option contracts.
2. Market index is a historical data on the past market	2. VIX is forecasted data on volatility
3. Market index is a number	3. VIX is denoted as an annualized percentage
4. Market index is for the overall market	4. VIX is for each and every stock on options contract.

HISTORICAL VOLATILITY - IMPLIED VOLATILITY- ACTUAL VOLATILITY

Volatility is classified into two:–historical volatility and implied volatility. Historical volatility is based on the past closing prices of stock and hence actual data.

1. Implied volatility (IV) is, rather, the projected or estimated volatility of an asset in future and embedded in option`s price.

2. IV is calculated by a pricing method by which the current market prices are estimating the future volatility of the underlying asset. Since IV is a projected data, there is bound to be gap between IV and actual future volatility. IV may, therefore, deviate from actual future volatility also.

3. IV is given as additional information to the participating option traders as a market indication.

4. IV does not indicate in which direction the price will move i.e., upward or downward movement.

5. It generally increases in Bearish market as investors tend to think prices will decline. IV decreases in Bullish market when investors tend to think price will rise over-time.

6. Change in volatility will affect both Call & Put option in the same way.

7. Like any other asset, IV is determined by supply and demand. So, when demand increases, premium rises and when supply increases, premium falls.

8. Like any other asset, IV, is also bound to play the market rule, i.e.,if it has risen extremely, it will fall later, at least to it`s mean level and bounce back.

IMPLIED VOLATILITY AND FUNDAMENTALS OF THE UNDERLYING ASSET

Implied volatility is an estimation which does not have any basis on the fundamentals of the underlying asset. It relies solely on price. Adverse news or events such as wars or natural disasters may impact the implied volatility hugely. Owing to it`s inherent strength that one cannot predict future volatility, IV is assumed to be the most important determinant of option`s price. Precisely it is because of this reason that IV is discussed more elaborately than the impact of any other greeks

IMPLIED VOLATILITY AND CHOOSING THE RIGHT OPTIONS

One of the few important steps a trader needs to do before initiating an option contract is that he should compare IV with the historical volatility of the underlying and the market`s volatility collated from VIX. If IV is higher, it will up the premium in which scenario a trader may write the option and pocket higher premium if he expects that volatility will not increase further because further increase in volatility may lead to rise in price and tend buyer of the option to exercise his right. On the contrary, if IV is lower with falling premium, a trader may buy an option with cheaper premium if he expects that further volatility will only rise to increase the premium and value of the option.

IMPLIED VOLATILITY AND CHOOSING RIGHT TIME FRAME AND EXPIRATON

Certain events impact market or stock specific. Market is impacted when RBI announces monetary policy, devaluation or depreciation of home currency to foreign currencies, economy regulations. Stock specific include release of quarterly/ annual reports, change in Corporate Board, new product launch, spin-off etc. Either prior to these events or after settling down of these events, implied volatility is likely to increase or decrease. Factoring status of IV or actual volatility is essential while deciding upon the entry and exit point of trade, strike price and expiration of contracts.

VEGA AND IMPLIED VOLATILITY

Vega represents the rate of change in premium in relation to one percentage change in underlying asset`s implied volatility. Note the difference between vega and volatility. Volatility measures fluctuations in underlying asset while Vega measures the sensitivity of the premium of an option to changes caused by implied volatility. For example, an option with a vega of 0.80 indicates the option value is expected to change by 80 paise, if implied volatility changes by 1%

CHARACTERISITICS OF VEGA

1. A change in volatility will affect both Call & Put options the same way, meaning increase in volatility will increase the value of both options and vice versa

2. Vega is at it`s maximum at ATM option that have larger time for expiration

3. Vega can increase in reaction to quick moves in the underlying asset

4. Vega is lower when the option gets closer to expiration and higher when contract is farther away from expiration.

TRADES WITH VEGA

1. Option sellers benefit from fall in volatility as chances of option ending OTM are more while option buyers benefit from rise in implied volatility as chances of option ending ITM are more. Reverse is also true when IV is high, high premiums make buying less attractive and selling more desirable. Low IV and hence low premium is more attractive for buyers and less desirable for sellers.

2. Implied volatility falls when the market shows an upward trend as investors tend to think price will rise overtime.

3. Deep OTM or deep ITM contracts are less sensitive to IV changes while ATM contracts are more sensitive to IV as time value is the highest for ATM and hence less time is needed for transition from ATM to ITM

4. When longer days are left for expiry, despite high premiums, long trades are likely to end ITM if volatility increases and longer days are there to expire.

5. Vega is expressed as a number while implied volatility is expressed in annualized percentage. Vega expresses the price change of an option for every 1% change in volatility of the underlying.

6. When IV is extremely high or low, it is also likely to revert to it`s mean.

HOW TO READ NSE`S OPTION CHAIN

WHAT IS AN OPTION CHAIN

Open Interest (OI)	Open Interest tells us how many Futures &Option active contracts are outstanding in the market. Points to be noted here is that 1. a contract between a buyer and seller is counted as 1, meaning it adds buy or sell and NOT both 2. OI increases when new contracts are added and decreases when existing contracts are squared off

	3. Transfer of contracts between one and another party are not counted as new and hence such transfers do not change OI
	4. OI is a continuous figure recorded and published by NSE
	Important points from traders' point of view :-
	OI indicates trading activity on Option contracts and the money flowing in or out on contracts. From OI, traders can gauge enhanced or muted interest in option trades in a given time.
Change in OI	tells us change in OI within expiration period, caused by closure, exercised or squared off. Traders can monitor significant changes if any to assess the market participant's interest on options contract on a particular asset or otherwise.
Volume	Tells us total number of contracts of options traded for a particular strike rate on the day. It is calculated on a daily basis. It indicates the current interest of traders on an option contract of an asset.
Implied Volatility (IV)	IV i.e., implied volatility is calculated by a pricing model formula and shown as the expected level of future volatility based on the current price of the option. Higher IV means potential higher swings and lower IV means lower or fewer swings.
LTP	Is abbreviation of last traded price of an option
Net Change	Net change in LTP indicates price changes. It is positive change if rise in price is indicated in green and negative change if fall in price is indicated in red.
Bid Quantity	It is the number of buy orders for a particular strike rate. This shows the current demand for a particular strike of an option
Bid Price	Is the price quoted in the last buy order. If the price is higher than LTP, it may suggest rising demand for option or vice versa.
Ask Price	Is the price quoted in the last sell order.
Ask Quantity	Is the number of sell orders for a particular strike price. It indicates current supply for a particular strike of an option.
Strike Price	Is the price at which an option buyer or seller wishes to contract.
Potential money	Strike rates of Call &Put option in ITM are highlighted in color while strike rates of Call & Put in OTM are shown in white shadow in order to show the traders potential money of strike rates.

INDICATIVE OPTION TRADE TO REFRESH WHAT YOU HAVE LEARNT TILL NOW

1. TYPE OF TRADER

Options trading is done for speculation and hedging purposes. If for hedging, trader with long position will buy Put or Call to hedge short position in order to protect his open position. Let us assume the trade is a speculative one.

2. VIEW-BULLISH OR BEARISH

Trader's view on bullishness or bearishness of the asset is one of the key factors for success of the trade. Let us assume the trader is bearish on the asset say X. Bearish view is due to his firm conviction that price of the asset X will fall within a specific period for the reason that judgment from High Court on Company X's appeal has been reserved on last week of Jan'21 which is believed to go against the Co and the fall is expected to sustain for a week before recovery.

3. DATE
He ensures that there is no stock or market specific events that may impact stock X`s price other than the above. He finds Q3 results are due only in Ist week of Feb. Our trader is aware of market specific events that are likely to pose threats to market like RBI`s Policy announcement etc., and early morning trends in stock markets of Hong Kong, Singapore fiscal/monetary/labor/inflation policy announcements from USA. Having satisfied himself that these events have negligible or little effect on Indian stock market, he decides to initiate option contract on 6th Jan `21
4. CALL OR PUT OPTION
Our trader anticipates increase in volatility of stock X, in the midst of prevailing calmness of the market for the past one week. His belief grows stronger that fall of stock X is imminent in view of court verdict and hence buying Put option is the right choice. So, he decides **to buy Put option** in view ofhis bearish outlook.
5. BUYING PUT OPTION –TERMS AND CONDITIONS
Our trader, having good knowledge on the options trade, is well aware of the following terms and conditions of the Put option contract that binds him as a Put option buyer. (i) As a buyer of Put option, **he has the right, but not obligated to, sell** the asset X to seller/ writer of the Put option, the right under which he can exercise on the last day of expiration to sell the number of agreed lots of shares at the agreed price known as strike price to the writer/seller who has, no choice, but only obligated to buy from him the shares as per the terms of the contract. (ii) If the trade that he is going to enter is profitable or not, he can, at his discretion, close it by exiting the trade on any day or at any time even on the same day of the contract, by selling back to the market a contract on the same asset, same lot, at the same strike and at the same expiration. (iii) If the trade is losing one, he can allow the contract to lapse worthless by not exercising his right as a result of which he losses the premium of the contract that he has to pay to seller at the time of initiating the contract.
5. (I) BUYING CALL OPTION –TERMS AND CONDITIONS
Though our trader is buying Put option, he refreshes his knowledge on buying Call options trade, the terms and conditions of which are as under:- (i) As a buyer of Call option, he has the right, but not obligated to, buy the asset X from seller/ writer of the Call option, the right under which he can exercise on the last day of expiration to buy the number of agreed lots of shares at the agreed price known as strike price from the writer/seller who has, no choice, but only obligated to sell to him the shares as per the terms of the contract. (ii) If the trade that he is going to enter is profitable or not, he can, at his discretion, close it by exiting the trade on any day or at any time even on the same day of the contract, by selling back to the market a contract on the same asset, same lot, at the same strike and at the same expiration. (iii) If the trade is losing one, he can allow the contract to lapse worthless by not exercising his right under which he losses the premium of the contract that he has to pay to seller at the time of initiating the contract.

6. SPOT PRICE

Let us assume Spot price of stock X is Rs 820/- on 6th Jan `21. Our Put options buyer knows that the intrinsic value which is the difference between the strike price he has chosen and the spot price on the last day of expiration less premium paid by him, will decide P&L of the proposed trade.

Call option buyer		Put option buyer	
Intrinsic value	Spot—Strike	Intrinsic value	Strike—Spot
P&L pay off	(Spot—Strike)*lot—premium*lot paid by buyer	P&L pay off	(Strike—Spot)*lot—premium*lot paid by buyer

7. STRIKE PRICE

Our Put option buyer expects that Stock X `s price will fall in near term on any day during the life of the contract including last day of contract. However, he is not sure about how much fall will be in percentage terms. He knows the following i.e., what strike price means to him and the importance of choosing the right strike at the time of initiating the contract.

Strike price is the contracted price between the buyer and seller of the option and it is at this price that options contract will be settled as under, when buyer of Call or Put exercises his right to buy or sell on the last day of the expiration.

	Call option Buyer	Call option Seller	Put option Buyer	Put option Seller
Profit	If spot is above strike	If spot stays flat or below strike	If spot is below strike	If spot stays flat or above strike
Loss	If spot is below strike	If spot stays flat or above strike	If spot is above strike	If spot stays flat or below strike

As he is to initiate the contract on 6th Jan`21, the remaining sessions left for expiry (28th Jan`21) is 15 days. As spot rate is Rs 820/-on 6th Jan, `21, 820/- is ATM

WHAT A TRADER HAS TO LOOK INTO BEFORE CHOOSING THE STRIKE PRICE

7 (i) FIRST KNOW ABOUT MONEYNESS OF ITM, ATM, OTM

ITM, ATM, OTM refer to position of their intrinsic value and their potential profit or loss. Intrinsic value for Call option is (Spot-Strike) while for Put option it is (Strike—Spot) Let us analyze each.

1. ITM will have intrinsic value only when strike price is below spot in Call option and above in Put option. If a trader selects ITM strike rate in Call or Put option, premium is high as the option has profit right away. So he has to pay high premium.

2. Intrinsic value for ATM option is zero as spot and strike rate are equal at ATM. But ATM options are very close to having intrinsic value. So, ATM options will have premium on time value. Premium at ATM, however, will be less costly compared to ITM options.

3. Intrinsic value for OTM options will be negative and hence zero as strike rate is higher than spot in Call and less than spot in Put option. But, OTM options will have time value. It`s premium is cheaper compared to premiums of ATM and ITM options.

4. Delta value of Call option for deep OTM is 0 to 0.3, OTM is above 0.3 to less than 0.5, ATM is 0.5, ITM is above 0.5 to 0.8, deep ITM is above 0.8 to 1.0. For delta value of Put option, it is all the same except with a negative sign. Delta value tells us the probability of earning or losing intrinsic value.Thus ATM delta says that it has only 50% chance of ending ITM. Delta of ITM 0.6 says it has a 60% chance of ending ITM while OTM 0.4 says us that it has a 40% chance of ending ITM and 60% chance of ending OTM. These delta indicators, unless massively impacted by gamma and volatility, predict the movement of premium.

5. Keep in mind that most of the traders do not wait until expiration. Instead, they do points trading meaning they profit from changes in valuation caused by movement of points backed by delta, gamma and other greeks in the near term.

(ii) SELECTING THE RIGHT STRIKE

1. Having understood classification of moneyness, our Put option buyer has to select slightly ITM strike rate. It means 1 or 2 strikes below 820 (spot) for Call option and 1 or 2 strikes above 820 (spot) for Put option. Why? If you select more than 3 or 4 strikes above or below spot, market may require more days to move to the target. Though such moves look simple, in percentage terms, it could be 4 to 5% to achieve the winning position. Note, normally, market`s rise or fall is within a range of 1% or below except under certain conditions. In our model example, let us assume our Put option buyer selects 840 as his strike rate.

2. Do not initiate contracts, lured by cheap premium of OTM or Deep OTM as transition to ITM (money) from Deep OTM/OTM (no money) may require more days to happen or may not happen at all. Remember option buyers lose time value every day.

3. Do not buy contracts, lured by high money ITM since ITM contracts are expensive to buy. It means you will have to shell out more money to buy an ITM option hoping it will remain ITM till expiration, the certainty of which depends on various factors including volatility risks.

4. Do not write ATM contracts since gamma being the maximum at ATM triggers rapid changes in delta value leading to unpredictable price moves.

5. Do not go for contracts with ATM or OTM option since both ATM and OTM have only time value and NO intrinsic value. So if you intend to hold the contract till expiration, your profit potential rests only on time value which becomes zero on expiration, transitioning your trade probably to loss.

6. Always keep in mind that if you intend to hold the trade till expiration,, then, your winning the trade do not end with spot price crossing just strike rate, rather it should cross break even i.e, break even for a Call is strike plus premium received or paid and for Put it is strike minus premium received or paid. So, if premium is Rs 100/- & strike is 9500, then for Call Break even for both buy & sell is 9500 +100=9600 while the same for Put for both buy & sell is 9500—100=9400. So, when you expect the trade to win, make it that points to move include cost of option also.

7. Let us understand that selecting appropriate moneyness of strike rate viz ATM, ITM, or OTM, is not the end in itself, because Greeks will always play their risk profile on the premium pulling it up or down, thereby casting the continual uncertainty on the trade`s profitability or valuation.

8. Why do we select slightly ITM and not ATM or OTM? In Put option, approximate delta value for slight ITM is –0.6. This means ITM put option has a 60% chance of ending ITM and 40% chance of ending ATM. Note that for a Put option buyer, decrease in underlying asset's price will increase the premium and valuation of contract.

9. If OTM strike is selected, calculate in % terms, to find the possibility of OTM to move to ITM within the remaining days for expiry, having a reference to underlying's past data and current volatility. For example, possibility is very less to expect OTM to move say 7% up or down to transit to ITM within say 20 days.

7 (iii) SELECTING THE RIGHT EXPIRATION

1. If you buy option, it is suggested to go for longer duration for expiry preferably one month because more days are available to make price moves and hence chances of trade turning in your favor is also more. If you write option, shorter duration of contract is preferable to limit your liability.

2. Monthly contracts are more suited than weekly contracts, for a trade to make larger moves

3. As a thumb rule, an option loses one third of it's value in the first half of it's life and the remaining value in the second half of it's life. Time always travels in one direction meaning time lost once cannot be regained. That is why theta is considered negative for buyer and positive for seller. Remember that seller needs to just respond to buyer exercising his right to buy or sell and if not exercised, he needs to do nothing except retaining the premium on expiration. A buyer, on the other hand, needs to observe the market and decide on holding or otherwise of the trade till expiration, if other greeks also go against him.

4. Option buyer has to be alert because while longer period gives more chances for the price of the underlying to transit to ITM, option's value also simultaneously gets declined due to time value.

5. Keep in mind that winning the trade needs to be achieved within the life of the contract.

8. PUT OPTION AND P&L PAY OFF

SCENERIO-1-WHEN THE PURPOSE OF TRADE IS SPECULATIVE

P&L PAY OFF THROUGH CASH SETTLEMENT WHEN TRADE IS HELD TILL EXPIRY

PUT BUYER

View	Option	Contract	Stock	On 6th Jan`21		Strike	Break even	Lot	Expiry
Bearish	Put Buyer	Right to Sell	X	Spot 820/-	Prem.30/-	Rs 840/–	Rs 840—30=810	2 lot=200	28th Jan`21

If trade moves in his favor on 28th Jan `21 with spot @ 800/-				If trade moves against him on 28th Jan`21 with spot @ 850/-			
When spot price is below strike, he will exercises his right to sell @840/-				When spot is above strike, contract is worthless and buyer allows it to lapse.			
Spot	Strike	**Profit- Put buyer gains**	Loss	Spot	Strike	Profit	**Loss limited to prem.paid**
800/-	840/-	{(840—800)—30}*200=2000	Zero	850/-	840/-	{(840—850)—30}*200=0	Premium paid-Rs 6000/-
Profit is unlimited to buyer.However, spot can not fall below zero, theoretically							

PUT SELLER

View	Option	Contract	Stock	On 6th Jan`21		Strike	Break Even	Lot	Expiry
Bullish	Put Seller	Obligated to Buy	X	Spot 820/-	Prem.30/-	Rs 840/-	Rs 840—30=810	2 lot=200	28th Jan`21

When trade moves in his favor on 28th Jan`21 with spot @850/-				When trade moves against him on 28th Jan`21with spot @ 800/-			
When spot price is above strike, Contract is worthless and allowed to lapse				When spot price is below strike, put seller obligated to buy @ 840/-			
Spot	Strike	**Profit-Put seller gains-limited to prem.recd.**	Loss	Spot	Strike	Profit	**Loss-Put Seller loses**
850/-	840/-	{30—(840—850)}*200=6000	Zero	800/-	840/-	{30—(840—800)}*200=0	Rs 2000/-
				Loss is unlimited to seller. However, spot can not fall below zero, theoretically			

P&L PAY OFF THROUGH PHYSICAL SETTLEMENT WHEN TRADE IS HELD TILL EXPIRY ASSUMING SPOT @ 800

ON EXPIRATION	PUT BUYER	PUT SELLER
By Exercising right to sell 200 shares	Put buyer has to give delivery to Exchange	Put seller has to take delivery in his Demat a/c
Effective price per share for physical settlement	To sell @ strike minus Prem.paid viz 840—30=810	To buy @ strike minus Prem. recd viz 840—30=810
When spot is 800/ on 28th Jan`21-day of expiry	Profit=810—800=10*200=2000 minus other charges	Loss=810—800=10*200=2000 minus other charges

CONDITIONS TO BE ELIGIBLE FOR MANDATORY PHYSICAL SETTLEMENT
1. Options should be held till expiry to exercise right to buy (for Call) or sell (for Put) for physical settlement
2. Only ITM options are settled physically since OTM Options are worthless on expiry
3. Buyers and sellers should have amount of contract value in their trading account to enable transact physical settlement. Failure to do so will attract penalty
4. Traders of Short Futures, Short ITM Call, Long ITM Put need to hold shares in their Demat a/c to give delivery
5. Traders of Long Futures, Long ITM Call & Short ITM Put will take delivery in their Demat a/c
6. Physical settlement will not be applicable for trades with net-off i.e., if you have multiple positions with the same expiration and in the same underlying with the purpose of hedging

P&L PAY OFF WHEN TRADE IS CLOSED BEFORE EXPIRY

Option	Contract	On 6th Jan`21		On 20th Jan`21		Strike	Lot	Expiry
Put Buy	Right to sell	Spot- 820/-	Prem.Rs 30/-	Spot- 810/-	Prem.Rs 35/-	840/-	2 lot=200	28th Jan`21

PUT BUYER

Assuming up in premium on 20th Jan, due to decrease in price of the underlying and increase in volatility, Put buyer may close the trade with change in premium, by selling back the trade to the market i.e., writing a Put option on the same underlying and on the same expiration His P&L Pay off is:-

Premium Paid as Put Buyer On 6 th Jan	Premium received as Put Seller On 20 th Jan	Difference	P&L Pay off
Rs 30/-	Rs 35/-	Rs 5/-	Rs 5*2*100=Rs 1000/-

NOTE

1. Note that trader need not wait till change in premium is favorable to him to earn profit. Even if it is against him, he may still exit the trade at the time he considers appropriate to minimize the loss

2. By writing a Put, he in effect, cancels the effect of his first trade. Do note to initiate the trade after factoring charges like brokerage etc.

3. By trading on premium, security transaction tax is avoided as buy side having no STT, sell side STT is 0.05% of premium sold. But, if you exercise your right on expiry, you have to pay STT @ 0.125% of intrinsic value. Please get clarified for the current instructions on STT.

4. Note Option value on 20th Jan is 840—810=30 while premium is Rs 35/- which means intrinsic value is Rs 30/- & Time value is Rs 5/-By closing before expiry, trader gets added benefit of Rs 5/- of time value which will be lost if the trader waits till expiration when time value becomes zero.

5. By trading on premium, mandatory physical settlement is avoided. Also, trade is exit with little capital

6. Premium trading is the most preferred trade by option traders because of the above reasons.

PUT SELLER

Put seller can profit on premium trading if premium falls before expiry. In the above example, if the premium, instead of rising, falls say to Rs 25/- he earns profit by buying back the option from the market when his P&l Pay off is:- Rs 10/- per share (Rs 35/- received as seller earlier minus Rs 25/ premium payable now as buyer.) Note buy back means buying a Put option on the same underlying, same expiration and same strike to off-set the effect of his first trade.

SCENERIO-2-WHEN THE PURPOSE OF TRADE IS TO HEDGE

If a trader, having purchased one lot of a stock last week, apprehends that it`s price may fall in a month`s time, he can protect his investments from fall in value by buying Put option in the same stock and for the same lot with expiration of near term. What he has deployed in effect is called hedging that reduces risk of adverse price movements on stocks he has purchased earlier. By buying Put option he pays premium and off sets the effect of likely risk of fall in value. So, hedging may be called as an insurance cover by buying Put as a strategy to mitigate such downside risks.

LONG POSITION

View	Purpose	Term	Stock	On 10th Jan`21	Lot	Capital deployed
Bullish	Portfolio	Long Term	A	Spot -450/-	1 lot=100	Rs 45000/-

PUT BUY POSITION

View	Option	Contract	Stock	On 10th Jan`21		Strike	Break even	Lot	Expiry
Bearish	Put Buy	Right to Sell	A	Spot 450/-	Prem.8/-	Rs 450/–	Rs 450—8=442	1 lot=100	28th Jan`21

P&L PAY OFF WHEN TRADE IS HELD TILL EXPIRY

If Option trade moves in his favor on 28th Jan `21 with spot @ 430/-	If Option trade moves against him on 28th Jan`21 with spot @ 470/-
When spot price is below strike, he will exercises his right to sell @450/-	When spot is above strike, contract is allowed to lapse worthless.

Spot	Strike	Profit- from Put buying	Loss	Spot	Strike	Profit	Loss from Put buying
430/-	450/-	{(450—430)—8}*100=1200	Zero	470/-	450/-	{(450—470)—8}*100=0	Premium paid-Rs 800/-

If he sells from his long position-Loss	Profit from his long position
Profit by selling {(450—450)—8}*100=Loss Rs 800/-	Profit by selling (470—450)*100=2000—800=1200

When Put buy is in his favor

1. If the trader wants to retain his stock A as he anticipates it will rise in a month`s time from now on, he may exercise his right to sell @ 450/-, by buying the same stock from the market @ Rs 430/- and earn profit of Rs 1200/-in the process. Right choice rests with the trader`s risk appetite and his market`s analysis.

2. If he chooses to sell from his long position, he will incur loss of Rs 800/-

When Put buy is not in his favor

1. He incurs loss of premium paid Rs 800/- while retaining his long position intact.

2. If he chooses to sell stock in his long position at current market price @ Rs 470, he earns profit of Rs 1200/-

Note

1. The above indicative example illustrates how buying Put works to protect investment for a small amount of premium and benefits trader to gain irrespective of stock`s price behavior i.e., rise or fall.

2. This strategy is also called Married Put for which trader needs to buy both long and Put buy at the same time, same day and the same underlying and strike selection should be ATM for both long and Put buy. By selecting ATM, rise or fall in prices are covered by profit either under Long or Put buy.

3. Traders can deploy other strategies also like Protective Put.

4. Trading on premiums to close before expiry is not intended to discuss here as they are speculative and not hedging.

9. EUROPEAN OPTION

Our Put buyer decides to buy European option contract as he knows well that it is the only type on offer by Exchanges in India. By opting for European option, he is aware that he can exercise his right to sell only on the last day of expiration. It does not, however, restrict him to close the trade on any day before expiration.

10. SELECTING THE PREMIUM

AS A SELLER OF OPTION

Premium is the price of the option that you are going to pay to buy it or receive to sell it. Premium is expensive if you choose (i) ITM, or ATM strike, (ii) long dated expiration and (iii) when Implied volatility is high. From the view point of high premium, you may decide to write an option if you are otherwise confident of your bullish or bearish view on the underlying in the near term since you are set to receive higher premium as a writer. However, instead of merely being lured by high premium alone, you may try at other things too, like choosing a contract with few days remaining to expiry as this could probably enhance, as a writer, your chances of winning the trade in less number of days. Note that if few days are remaining to expiry for a buyer, his contract is less likely to win because transition to ITM, if not happened in longer days, is less likely to happen in the remaining few days. Moreover, as a writer you benefit by time value which goes to decline buyer's value of option each day, increasing chances of the trade expiring worthless and retaining premium by writer. As a precaution, writer should always enter a contract with advance plan of when to enter and exit the trade because he is the one to face unlimited loss and block his margin amount too. Note that winning the trade is paramount and hence your decision may ride or override the above points that are only suggestive and not sure shot to win.

AS A BUYER OF OPTION

Premium is less expensive or cheap if strike price is OTM, more number of days are there remaining to expire and implied volatility is low or settled to cool. In such scenario, you may decide to buy option if you expect the underlying will behave bullish or bearish in the near term. For a buyer, long duration contract say a month is more advantageous because more days are beneficial for transition from say OTM to ITM. Let it be known that rise in price is slow whereas crash in price is sudden in the market. Another fallacy on the part of buyer is that they think if the market is bullish, price of the underlying will follow suit and move up. Note that about 80% of option buyers leave the trade worthless possibly due to their inappropriate selection of strike rate lured by greedy mindset that profit is unlimited.

10 (i) ASSESSING DELTA AND GAMMA

Delta is rate of change in an option's premium resulting from change in price of the underlying asset. Our Put buyer knows that for Put option, if price of Stock X increases, premium will decrease and if price of stock X decreases, premium will increase. Having selected slight ITM whose delta value is approximately –0.6 for Put option buying, our trader will gain premium if spot price of stock X decreases. This is also in tune with his bearish view on the stock X. Delta value of –0.6 means if price of the underlying rises by one point, premium will fall by 0.6.

1. Delta of Call & Put option is easily predictable. But delta with gamma effect is not so, because gamma`s impact on delta varies, either accelerating delta or slowing delta.

2. Unlike delta, gamma is a positive number. Since delta is changing value due to changes in spot price, Gamma is used to measure delta`s rate of change that will facilitate a trader calculate new delta and new premium with estimation of his contract`s probability of moving to or away from ITM or OTM.

3. If two options have the same delta, but with different gamma, option with higher gamma tends to be riskier than that with low gamma since high gamma will tend to make higher delta and higher premium when the underlying`s price experience higher swings.

4. Gamma is the least at deep ITM i.e., when delta is close to 1. Similarly, gamma is the least when delta is deep OTM. Gamma is at it`s highest at ATM

When longer days are there to expiration, all ITM,OTM,ATM options have lower gamma.

5. Do not short ATM options close to expiry as gamma is at it`s peak at ATM and due to this, delta changes rapidly

10 (ii) ASSESSING DELTA AND GAMMA OF OUR LONG PUT OPTION

Assume Gamma for our Put buy is 0.0012. Delta—0.6, Premium Rs 8/20 Strike rate Rs 840/-

1. An illustration:- Assume If premium of our Put is say Rs 8/20 and our underlying stock`s price decreases by say Rs 10/-, new premium will be Rs 14/20

(–0.6*–10=+6).i.e (8/20+6.0) In put option when spot decreases, premium increases. New delta is = gamma *–10=–0.6120 (0.0012*-10=-0.0120+(–0.6000)

10 (iii) COMPARING VOLATILITY,IMPLIED VOLATILITY, VIX

Implied volatility (IV) is considered the most important determinant of options price since delta of option and theta for duration of contract are selected by trader himself while implied volatility can only be forecast by him. Winning the trade therefore rests mostly with correct forecast of implied volatility. To achieve this, he can do the following;-

1. IV is market`s participators` perception of volatility while VIX is outstanding option contracts for near month. Compare IV with VIX & historical volatility. Wide variation among the three may be an indicator of upcoming change in trends of IV. Know historical data as a reference data. Exercise care if VIX is more than 30%. If IV is extremely high, expect a fall in IV to the lowest and bouncing again or fall to it`s mean level, which indicates change in option price is imminent. High IV means expensive premium and low IV is for relatively less expensive premium. By analyzing premium and remaining days to expire, a trader can decide when to enter the trade and whether to buy or sell option contract which is possible because of IV.

10 (iv) SETTING STOP LOSS, RISK TO REWARD

Few broking firms offer GTT based stop loss for option price. If you buy option for premium of say Rs 100/-, stop loss may be set say at 10% downside meaning your stop loss is Rs 90/- Here risk is 100—90=Rs 10/-. If his target for reward is say Rs130/- reward is 130—90=40. So, risk to reward is 10/40, i.e. 1:4 If SL is triggered@ 90, a limit sell order is sent to exchange and trade closed before expiry. By setting SL, he is set to exit the trade with profit or minimum loss..

11. SCOUTING FOR SELLER/WRITER

Having a positive outlook, our Put option buyer now scouts for writer for the option. He gets a writer ready to join the contract as a counter party. By joining the trade, counter party admits that he has an opposite view on the stock X, meaning he is bullish on the stock X and he expects the stock X`s price will move up or stay at the same rate, but definitely will not move down on 28th Jan `21.

12. SELLER/WRITER`S CONTRACTUAL OBLIGATIONS

Seller is aware of the terms of contract that binds him. They are as under:-

(i) Seller is obligated to buy the two lots of stock X at the agreed strike price from the put buyer, only if the buyer exercises his right to sell on the last day of expiration. Having agreed to fulfill his obligations under the contract, he accepts the cost of contract viz., premium payable by the buyer

(ii) in case the buyer allows the trade to lapse worthless on expiry i.e., by not exercising his right to sell, seller can retain the premium paid by the buyer as his profit.

(iii) he is in full knowledge of the terms of contract that instead of waiting till expiration, buyer may close the trade by trading on premiums if he so wishes, on any day before expiration.

13. OPTION CONTRACT

Both buyer and seller enter into Put option contract by digitally signing it with the following inputs on agreement.

Option	Date of contract	Underlying asset	Spot rate	Strike rate	Expiration	Lot size	Premium
Put	6th Jan`21	Stock X	Rs 820/-	Rs 840/-	28th Jan`21	2 (200)	Rs 30/-
Premium Paid by buyer to seller is Rs 6000/- i.e.,30*200				Premium received by seller from buyer is Rs 6000/-			

1. Note here:- By paying little amount of Rs 6000/- as premium, trader is exposing his sell trade to a contract valued at 1.64 lakhs (Rs 820*200) This is the major difference between delivery trade and option contract.

2. The Put options value is Rs 30*200 that will move on changing, owing to interplay of greek factors influencing the premium

3. The option contract is now identifiable in abbreviation as - X840PE expanding, X for stock X, 840 denotes strike rate, P for Put option & E for European option

4. Below is a chart summarizing the effect of Greeks on option`s value on Call Buy & sell and Put buy & sell

SUMMARIZING THE EFFECT OF GREEKS ON PREMIUM OF OPTIONS						
Option type	If Increase in spot, Delta`s Impact	If Decrease in spot, Delta`s Impact	Longer time to expiry Theta`s Impact	Lesser time to expiry Theta`s Impact	If Increase in Volatility, Vega`s act	If Decrease in Volatility, Vega`s act
Call option	+ Premium	− Premium	+ Premium	− Premium	+ Premium	− Premium
Put option	−Premium	+ Premium	+ Premium	− Premium	+ Premium	− Premium

THE EFFECT OF GREEKS ON PREMIUM OF CALL OPTIONS						
Call option	If Increase in spot, Delta`s Impact	If Decrease in spot, Delta`s Impact	Longer time to expiry Theta`s Impact	Lesser time to expiry Theta`s Impact	Increase in Volatility, Vega`s act	Decrease in Volatility, Vega`s act
Long	+Premium	−Premium	+Premium	−Premium	+ Premium	−Premium
Short	−Premium	+Premium	−Premium	+Premium	−Premium	+ Premium

THE EFFECT OF GREEKS ON PREMIUM OF PUT OPTIONS						
Put option	If Increase in spot, Delta`s Impact	If Decrease in spot, Delta`s Impact	Longer time to expiry Theta`s Impact	Lesser time to expiry Theta`s Impact	Increase in Volatility, Vega`s act	Decrease in Volatility, Vega`s act
Long	−Premium	+Premium	+Premium	−Premium	+Premium	−Premium
Short	+Premium	−Premium	−Premium	+Premium	−Premium	+Premium

+ means premium gains and -ve means premium losses. Gamma is first derivative on Delta & second derivative on spot and hence not shown.

Note the key point:-Buyers of Call & Put lose premium on time value daily by their negative Theta while sellers of Call & Put gain the same by their positive Theta

The effect of each greek shown above is subject to the assumption that all other Greeks are constant

14. CHOICES FOR TRADERS TILL EXPIRATION	
WHAT BUYER OF CALL AND PUT OPTIONS CAN DO ON LAST DAY OF EXPIRY 28th JANUARY`21	
Call option buyer	Put option buyer
1. If the trade is in his favor i.e., bullish, he can exercise his right to buy stock from seller at agreed strike price which is lower than market price and sell the same in the market at higher price. His P&L is settled at (Spot—Strike)*lot—premium paid	1. If the trade is in his favor, i.e, bearish if spot is say at Rs 810/-(below strike rate & bearish) he can exercise his right to sell stock to seller at Rs 840/- by buying the same at Rs 810/-in the market. His P&L is settled at (840–810)*200—premium paid Rs 2,500/- His profit is Rs 3,500/-

2. If the trade is not profitable, he can allow the trade to expire worthless. *1	2. If the trade is not profitable, he can allow the trade to expire worthless*1
WHAT BUYER OF CALL AND PUT OPTIONS CAN DO ON ANY DAY BEFORE EXPIRY	
Call option buyer	Put option buyer
1. If trading on difference of premium is in his favor or if he intends to minimize loss, he can exit the trade before expiry by square off. To square off, he has to **sell aCall option to another trader**on the same stock at the same strike & at the same expiration to offset his position. His profit or loss is (difference between buying and selling price of premium)*lot. Off setting means taking opposite trade to cancel the effect of his first trade. *2	1. If trading on difference of premium is in his favor or not, he can exit the trade before expiry by square off. To square off, he has **to sell Put option to another trader**on the same stock at the same strike & at the same expiration to offset his position. His profit or loss is (difference between buying and selling price of premium) *lot. Assuming premium of 20th Jan`21 is Rs 20/50, he can sell back to profit Rs 1,600/-i.e. (20/50—12/50)*200. Off setting means taking opposite trade to cancel the effect of his first trade. *2

1 Note that only if the trade is zero meaning there is no intrinsic value on expiry, he can allow the trade to become worthless. If the trade on expiry has some intrinsic value, Exchange will value it as ITM and charge STT on sell side.. So, if appropriate, buyer himself may sell it on last day of expiry to avoid higher STT

*2 Most of the traders do not hold the contract till expiry. They prefer to trade and profit on change in premium when time value is left before expiration.

Before settling the above alternatives, factor into the applicable Tax & other Broker charges

* Security Transaction Tax

WHAT SELLERS/WRITERS OF CALL AND PUT OPTIONS CAN DO ON LAST DAY OF EXPIRY 28th JANUARY`21	
As per the terms of contract, sellers/writers of Call and Put option are obligated to sell or buy the asset whenever buyers exercise their rights on the last day of expiry	
WHAT SELLERS/WRITERS OF CALL AND PUT OPTIONS CAN DO ON ANY DAY BEFORE EXPIRY	
Call option seller	Put option seller
1. If trading on difference of premium is in his favor or if he intends to minimize his loss,, he can exit the trade before expiry by square off. To square off, he has to buy back a Call option on the same stock at the same strike & at the same expiration to offset his position. His profit or loss is (difference between buying and selling price of premium)*lot. Off-setting means taking opposite trade to cancel the effect of his first trade.	1. If trading on difference of premium is in his favor or not, he can exit the trade before expiry by square off. To square off, he has to buy back a Put option on the same stock at the same strike & at the same expiration to offset his position. His profit or loss is (difference between buying and selling price of premium)*lot. Off-setting means taking opposite trade to cancel the effect of his first trade.

ASSIGNMENT IN OPTIONS

In assignment, when an option is exercised, stock exchange software randomly select a seller or buyer to honor the contract. Suppose you have sold TATA MOTORS Call @strike Rs 400/- & stock is trading @ Rs 450/- and a buyer exercise his right to buy. If software randomly assigns the trade to you, you have to honor the contract. Assignment in options, however, happens rarely.

STANDARD DEVIATION & VARIANCE

Standard deviation (SD) is a statistical method of finding an asset's volatility in a given period say weekly, monthly or yearly volatility. It helps a trader to predict how short or large an asset's price deviates from it's mean or average price and gauge the asset's price band within which it's price will move up or down in a given period. Note that SD is based on closing price of an asset and hence it is a measure of historical volatility. Standard deviation is the square root of variance.

USEFULNESS OF STANDARD DEVIATION

1. Standard deviation (SD) is useful to find a stock's or index's volatility. A volatile stock has high SD & non volatile has low SD

2. As SD is for measurement of risk, it is widely used in various strategies by Analysts, Investment Managers, Mutual Fund reporters etc, to report deviation from the expected return.

3. SD is used in technical analysis, like Bollinger Bands, which uses two SD from it's Simple Moving Average price

4. Under Normal Distribution Method, Ist SD denotes 68% accuracy of volatility, 2nd SD, 95% & 3rd SD, 99.7%

To calculate SD, trader can use MS Excel or he can do it by himself. Given below is indicative steps to calculate SD.

HOW TO CALCULATE VOLATILITY WITH SD & VARIANCE -AN INDICATIVE METHOD

Step 1:-To calculate mean price, Take down each day's closing price of stock A say for 10 days. Add all closing price and divide it by 10. Result is mean price

Step 2:-To calculate deviation, Subtract mean price from each day's closing price for 10 days. Get deviation for 10 days in %

Step 3:-To get variance, square each day's deviation. Add all deviation and divide it by 10-You get variance in %

Step 4:-To get standard deviation, square root variance. The figure is Ist standard deviation in %

Step 5:-To calculate upper & lower band within which a stock is predicted to move say for one month, multiply mean price with 30. You get mean result in %

Step 6:-To calculate SD for 30 days, multiply SD with square root of 30. You get SD in %

Step 7:-To get upper band of volatility, Add SD in step 6 with Mean in step 5. Get the result. Multiply this with current market price of stock A which is upper band

Step 8:-To get lower band of volatility, subtract SD in step 6 from Mean in step 5. Multiply the result with current market price of stock A which is lower band

Note:-1. Prediction is that volatility of stock A will move in the next 30 days within the maximum of upper band in step 7 & and minimum of lower band in step 8.

2. As we have calculated with Ist SD, volatility accuracy is 68% under Normal Distribution Method.

3. While the above is for one SD, traders may use 2 SD or 3 SD depending on trader's choice. For 2 SD, addition & subtraction in step 7 & 8 be done with SD*2 to get 95% accuracy. Likewise for 3 SD to get 99.7% accuracy.

4. Trader can also calculate the above with MS Excel

CHAPTER 7-A

TRADING OPTIONS II – SINGLE LEG STRATEGY

CONTENTS

1 Long Call Option -with example
2 Short Call Option (Naked Call)-with example
3 Long Put Option -with example
4 Short Put Option (Naked Put)-with example
5 Why Naked Call and Naked Put

LONG CALL	
View	Bullish-expecting rise in price in near future
Strategy	Single Leg
Trade	Buy a Call (ATM, ITM or OTM)
Expiry	At any level
Max. Profit	Unlimited
Max.Loss	Limited to Premium Paid
Break-even	Strike + Premium Paid
How to Exit	(1) Sell the Call on profit or loss before expiry
	(2) Wait for the Call to expire worthless
	(3) Exercise the Call to buy on last day of expiry
Similar strategies*	Protective Put, Covered Put/Married Put
	Bull Call Spread
Risk exposure	Ideal for beginners

Example-Long Call option bought @ strike 9600					
SPOT	STRIKE	PREMIUM	BREAK-EVEN	LOT	Prm.Paid
9700	9600 (ITM)	Rs 100/-	9700	100	Rs 10000/-
SPOT ON EXPIRY	IV (SPOT-STR)	IV*LOT	Net Pay off (IV*LOT)—Prm.Paid		
9900	300	30000		20000	
10000	400	40000		30000	
9700	100	10000	0		
9500	0	0	−10000/-		
9200	0	0	−10000/-		

SHORT CALL (NAKED CALL)	
View (writing)	Bearish-expecting fall in price in near future
Strategy	Single Leg
Trade	Sell a Call (ITM or OTM)
Expiry	At any level
Max. Profit	Limited to Prem.Received
Max.Loss	Unlimited
Break-even	Strike + Premium Received
How to Exit	(1) Buy back Call for profit or loss before expiry
	(2) Wait for option to expire & retain Prem.Recd.
Similar strategies*	Covered Put, Covered Calls, Bear Call Spread
Risk exposure	High risk for beginners

Example-SHORT Call option sold @ strike 500					
SPOT	STRIKE	PREMIUM	BREAK-EVEN	LOT	Prm.Recd
490	500 (OTM)	Rs 10/-	Rs 510/-	75	Rs 750/-
SPOT ON EXPIRY	IV (SPOT-STR)	IV*LOT	Net Pay-off. Prm.Reced—(IV*LOT)		
480	0	0	Rs 750/-		
490	0	0	Rs 750/-		
510	10	750/-	0		
530	30	2250/-	−1500/-		
550	50	3750/-	−3000/-		

*For detailed study, go for multi leg strategies in the next chapter

TRADING OPTIONS-SINGLE LEG STRATEGY

LONG PUT	
View	Bearish-when you expect sharp decline in price or in volatile in near future
Strategy	Single Leg
Trade	Buy a ATM PUT
Expiry	At any level
Max. Profit	Unlimited
Max.Loss	Limited to Premium Paid
Break-even	Strike – Premium Paid
How to Exit	(1) Sell the Put for profit or loss before expiry
	(2) Exercise put to sell on last day of expiry
	(3) Wait for Put to expire worthless
Similar strategies*	Protective Call, Short Put, Long Straddle
Characteristic	Opposite to Long call
Risk exposure	Ideal for beginners

Example-Long Put option bought @ strike 40					
SPOT	STRIKE	PREMIUM	BREAK-EVEN	LOT	Prm.Paid
40	40 (ATM)	Rs 5/-	Rs35/-	100	Rs 500/-
SPOT ON EXPIRY	IV (STR-SPOT)	IV*LOT	Net Pay off. (IV*LOT)—Prm.Paid		
35	5	500	0		
30	10	1000	500/-		
45	0	0	−500/-		
50	0	0	−500/-		
55	0	0	−500/-		

SHORT PUT (NAKED PUT)	
View	Bullish-when you expect asset`s price will not go beyond a certain level
Strategy	Single Leg
Trade	Sell OTM PUT
Expiry	At any level
Max. Profit	Limited to premium received
Max.Loss	Unlimited
Break-even	Strike – Premium received
How to Exit	(1) Buy Put for profit or loss before expiry (2) Wait for Put to expire & retain the premium
Similar strategies*	Bull Put Spread, Covered Call, Short Straddle
Risk exposure	Ideal for beginners

Example-Short Put sold @ strike 600					
SPOT	STRIKE	PREMIUM	BREAK-EVEN	LOT	Prm.Recd
650	600 (OTM)	Rs 10/-	590/-	100	Rs 1000/-
SPOT ON EXPIRY	IV (STR-SPOT)	IV*LOT	Net Pay off. Prm.Recd–(IV*LOT)		
640	0	0	Rs 1000/-		
620	0	0	Rs 1000/-		
590	10	1000	0		
580	20	2000	–Rs 1000/-		
560	40	4000	–Rs 3000/-		

*For detailed study, go for multi leg strategies in the next chapter

NAKED CALL AND NAKED PUT
When Call or Put options are written, i.e., sold, they are termed Naked Call or Naked Put because such single leg option trade has no protection or off setting cover from high risk of unlimited loss. For instance, call option writer has unlimited risk if he does not hold long position to meet his obligation to sell shares. Similarly, Put option seller has unlimited loss of risk if he does not own adequate cash to meet his obligation to buy stock. Note that only writers of call or put are termed so because loss to buyers of call or put is limited to the extent of premium paid. Because of this high risk trade, naked call or naked put are not suited for inexperienced traders or beginners.
KEY POINT TO REMEMBER
Traders are advised to trade multiple strategy option contracts as these contracts are combo trades, meaning simultaneously buying and selling on the same asset to cover and offset unlimited loss.

TRADING OPTION III – MULTI LEG OPTION STRATEGIES

CONTENTS

1 Spreads

2 Vertical Spread & when useful

3 Calendar Spread & When useful

4 Know the difference between Vertical Spread and Calendar Spread

5 Straddle &When to deploy

6 Strangle &When to deploy

7 Know the difference between Straddle and Strangle

8 Net Debit vs Net Credit Strategy

9 Key points to keep in mind before learning Multi Leg Strategies

10 Know the differences between various Combined Strategies

11 Security Transaction Tax on Option trade

12 Multi Legs-with model execution of trades-when, how, conditions to trade, P&L Pay off

13 Bull Call Spread

14 Bear Call Spread

15 Bull Put Spread

16 Bear Put Spread

17 Bear Call Ladder

18 Call Ratio Back Spread

19 Put Ratio back Spread

20 Long Straddle

21 Short Straddle

22 Long Strangle

23 Short Strangle

24 Iron Butterfly

25 Iron Condor

26 Long Call Condor

27 Short Put Condor

28 Long Box Spread

29 Short Box Spread

30 Other Option Strategies You need to know in brief

SPREADS	
Option Spread	Option spread is a strategy that involves simultaneous buying and selling of option on the same asset
Credit spread	Involves selling a high premium option while simultaneously buying a low premium option on the same asset
Debit spread	Involves buying a high premium option while simultaneously selling a low premium option on the same asset
Bullish Trader	He buys Call or Put at certain strike & sells the same number of Call or Put on the same asset & at same expiry but **at HIGHER STRIKE**
Bearish Trade	He buys Call or Put at certain strike & sells the same number of Call or Put on the same asset & at same expiry but **at LOWER STRIKE**

VERTICAL SPREAD		CALENDAR SPREAD	
1. This is an option strategy of simultaneous buying and selling of the option of the **same type** (Put or Call) & **same expiry** but **at different strike price**		1. This is an option strategy of simultaneous buying and selling of the same option type, Put or Call, with **the same strike price** but **at different expiry**	
2. Vertical spread is used when the trader expects a moderate move in the price of the underlying. Strategy is using 2 or more options		2. Purpose is to profit from the passage of time and /or on increase in Implied Volatility. Strategy is using 2 or more options	
3. Strategy for Bullish	**Strategy for Bearish**	**3. Strategy for Bullish**	**Strategy for Bearish**
Buy option with lower strike price **Sell option with higher strike price** **using either both calls or both puts**	**Buy option with higher strike price** **Sell option with lower strike price** **using either both calls or both puts**	**Sell near term Call** **Buy longer term Call** **Using both calls**	**Sell near term Put** **Buy longer term Put** **Using both puts**
4. Vertical spread involves simultaneous selling of an option to partly or fully off-set the premium required to buy an option		4. Strike price should be as near as possible to asset`s price for both options. Preferable but not required is that implied volatility is low	
5. Vertical spreads are tailor made to limit both risk and potential return A Bull vertical spread profits when underlying price rises A Bear Vertical spread profits when underlying price falls		5. Strategy is also to take advantage of different expiration-one near term & another longer term because longer term options are more sensitive to change in volatility due to higher Vega	

6. Below are all vertical spreads. Bullish traders use Bull Call spread & Bull Put spread Bearish traders use Bear Call spread & Bear Put spread	6. Below is calendar spread strategy. Long Calendar Spread

WHEN TO USE VERTICAL SPREAD	1. If you are very Bullish/Bearish, consider Stand-alone Calls/Puts and NOT Spread 2. If you are moderately Bullish, consider Bull Call spread or Bull Put spread 3. If you are moderately Bearish, consider Bear Call spread or Bear Put spread
VOLATILTIY	1. If expecting rise in volatility, buying spread is favorable. 2. Declining volatility is likely to increase the odds for writer
RISK TO REWARD	1. Buyers may opt spread if they prefer limited risk and potentially higher reward 2. Sellers may opt spread if they seek limited reward for greater risk
WHEN TO USE CALENDAR SPREAD	1. Bullish/Bearish outlook & no sign of change over the next few months 2. Short term sentiment should be ideally neutral. 3. Spread between Bid & Ask should be narrow 4. If Bullish, Buy a calendar Call spread and If Bearish, Buy a calendar Put spread
VOLATILTIY	Calendar spread is used to profit from time decay & increase in volatility
RISK TO REWARD	1. Limited risk is Net debit 2. Benefit from increased volatility 3. Earn unlimited profit If market moves as expected.

TRADING OPTION STRATEGIES

STRADDLE	
When to employ	Straddle is a neutral option strategy which refers to two separate transactions in the same asset, off-setting one another. Traders employ Straddles when they anticipate a significant move in asset`s price, but unsure of whether it will move up or down. For Ex. A stock is trading @Rs 60/- @ prm. of Rs 3/- A trader can create a Straddle if he believes that the stock may rise or fall from the current price of Rs 60/-
Strategy	**Simultaneously buying Both Put option & Call option on the same asset, with the same strike price and the same expiration**
Cost of creation	If a trader buys **Put & Call at the same strike** of say @ Rs 60/-for the same expiry say 25th Oct & premium for each Call & Put option is say Rs 2/-, then, adding these is Rs 4/- which is premium paid by him and also cost of creating the straddle

Predicting volatility & Range	Here, asset`s price should rise or fall by 6.6% (4/60)*100 from strike price to earn a profit on expiry viz 25th Oct. This is the prediction for volatility. For range prediction, add cost of creation to strike price ie Rs 60/-+ Rs 4/-=Rs 64/- which is higher range. Subtract cost from strike ie Rs 56/- which is lower range
Profit	If the asset trades within the zone of higher range of Rs 64/- & lower range of Rs 56/-, it is limited Loss. If asset trades above the zone of Rs 64/- & below the zone of Rs 56/-, it is profit. Profit is when the asset`s price rises or falls from the strike price by the amount more than the total premium paid. Profit potential is unlimited when the asset`s price move very sharply

STRANGLE	
When useful	When you expect the asset price will experience a large price movement and unsure of whether it is up or down, but movement will be sharp in price in future
Strategy	**Investor holds both Call & Put option at the same asset, same expiration but at different strike price (For Straddle, it is same strike price)**

DIFFERENCE BETWEEN STRADDLE & STRANGLE	
STRADDLE	**STRANGLE**
1. Straddle is at **SAME strike price for both Call & Put at ATM**	1. Strangle is at **DIFFERENT strike price for both Call & Put at OTM**
2. Premium is expensive than Strangle and straddle is a neutral option strategy	2. Premium is less expensive than Straddle, but carries greater risk.
3. Straddle can be initiated when significant move in price is anticipated	3. Strangle can be initiated if investor anticipates larger price move
4. Profit is when the asset`s price rises or falls from the strike price just by an amount more than the cost of premium paid for both options. So **it does not require a large price jump**	4. Profit is only **when asset`s price makes a larger move**

NET DEBIT vs NET CREDIT STRATEGY	
Net credit	Net credit refers to deploying strategy where trader is selling high premium option and buying low premium option simultaneously, in the same asset so that net flow is receipt or credit of premium to trader`s account when positions are open. When traders use net credit strategies, maximum profit is net credit. By trading a net credit strategy, a trader hopes the value of the option will diminish as opposed to net debit wherein trader holds opposite view
Net debit	Net debit refers to deploying strategy where trader is selling lower premium option and buying higher premium option simultaneously, in the same asset so that net flow is payment or debit of premium from trader`s account when positions are open. Debit spreads are normally used to offset the cost involved in each option.

KEEP THE FOLLOWING IN MIND BEFORE LEARNING MULTILEG STRATEGIES

Given below are 17 multileg strategies with various combinations like Vertical spread, Straddle, Strangle, arbitrage etc wherein more than one leg strategy is deployed like buy and/or sell in Call or Put or both. As these strategies are tailor made with simultaneous trading to cap unlimited loss, it is unavoidable that profit too tends to get capped. Before moving to strategies, traders need to assimilate the following quotes to understand the strategies unambiguously. Multi leg strategies are advantageous to traders in view of it`s combo effect that when loss making, traders suffer pre defined limited loss and when in profit, traders earn limited profit and when deployed appropriately, traders have chances to earn sustained return, though small.

Lot size	Option trading is executed in lots. In the following illustrations, while calculating net pay off, lot size has not been factored into for the purpose of simple and easy calculation. In real trade, traders should multiply the net pay off with the lot size, like 100 or 200 etc, as the case may be. For ex., if the net pay off is shown as + 5 in the workings, then., profit is 500, if lot size is 1 lot (100). If net pay off is shown as –5, then, loss is –500. **In short, P&L pay off is always IV*Lot minus Prem. Paid for lot (to buy)& Prem. Received for lot minus IV*Lot (to sell) Higher the lots, higher the amount of profit or loss. Traders must keep this in mind while going through illustrations below.**
Combo ratio	Multi leg strategies are combo trades, meaning simultaneously buying and selling on the same asset and same expiration, some of them even with same strikes. Combo refers to 1 buy and 1 sell in a 2 leg strategy. In a 3 leg strategy, ratio may be 2:1 meaning for every 2 buys. 1 sell or for every 2 sells 1 buy etc. Ratio needs to be maintained in multi leg strategy, else their neutral effect on P&L may get vanished with the result, options may go the way naked options does where your loss is unlimited without cap.
Exit before expiry	Traders can exit the trade anytime they want. Exiting the trade before expiration means trader is transferring his contractual rights and obligation to someone who is ready to step into his trade, as a result of which the contract is now validated by a new trader and his counter party as opposed to exercising right which can be done only on the last day of expiry. If a trader exits before expiry, he has to do it by taking opposite trades to off-set i.e., to cancel the effect of his first trade. Traders normally do not wait till expiration to avail P& L pay off. Instead, they trade on difference in premiums and exit before expiry. Note, more than 80% of option trades are closed before expiry. Normally writers of option wait till expiry to benefit from retaining the full premium received.
Expiration and exercising	On expiration, trader need not do any off setting transaction. Suffice if the trader lets the contract expire. Exchange itself will settle all contracts on expiry. Here, trader has to distinguish between exercising his right on expiry date and allowing it to expire. On expiry of contract, if trade ends ITM, Exchange deem the trade exercised and settle it accordingly. When a contract expires worthless, i.e. OTM, it is deemed there is no exercise of right. From Security Transaction Tax angle, ITM is taxable while OTM is not. Find below details on STT and it`s applicability.

Pay off before expiry	Strategies are designed to give full pay off only if it is held till expiry. Pay off will vary if closed before expiry. Traders here have to note that while taking opposite trades to off-set their positions, they have to transact quickly, else premiums may vary eroding profit potential.
Margin on writing option	For writers of option, premium received is blocked and kept as margin. Margins are not insisted on buyer of an option as his loss is limited to the extent of premium paid by him whereas seller of an option has unlimited loss potential.
MTM margin in option	There is no margin requirement for buyers of Call & Put option as their loss is limited to the extent of premium paid by them. However, for sellers of Call &Put option their potential loss is unlimited. So, in order to avoid any default by seller in the event of huge loss, Exchanges prescribe margin for Options sellers. Margin requirement for them is approximately similar to Futures contract. Unlike Futures, there is no daily settlement of notional profit or loss as NO margin is required for buyer of option and hence NO mark to market call for buyer while, for seller, margin call may arise if there is increase in the premium after writing the contract.

Trading on spreads	Unlike naked options, trading on spreads like multi leg strategies protect a trader from unfavorable market directions with pre defined losses. However, spread trading needs right selection of strike price. Normally, unless you owe unambiguous view on the asset`s price movements, do not go for deep OTM, lured by cheap premiums. When a strategy is designed to select OTM strikes, select two or less steps higher than ATM for Call & lower than ATM for Puts. If a Strategy is designed for strikes of deep OTM, a trader may go upto three steps. Note that deep OTMs are designed to act as wings in Call & Put to protect from steep downside risk.
Combining strategies	Traders can innovate new strategies and implement, if successful, by combining two strategies listed below. For example, you can combine Bull Call spread and Bear Put spread so as to gain from any one of them because P&L Pay off is always difference between two strikes.
Earning`s season	Traders before initiating any contract have to know earning season of corporate and their timing for release January, April, July, October and their time to settle or cool off to return to normal trading in the market. This will certainly avoid impact cost from high volatility due to these reports.
Back testing & Paper trading	Though few strategies especially, 3 or 4 leg strategies, look apparently simple, it is better to back test it before actual implementation. In back testing, you design the strategy as per your plan and arrive return results before actually deploying it with capital. If the trade is within your projected return and risk, you implement it with real capital. Paper trading, on the other hand, is a simulated trade for a trader to practice buying and selling, without risking real money, in the brokers` trading platform. Paper trading platforms are offered only by a few brokers in India.

Greeks and multi leg strategies	Few multi leg strategies are designed on delta neutral content, meaning impact of delta will off-set P&L pay off. Few are designed with ATM, ITM, OTM moneyness leaving no choice for traders to avoid. If OTM is chosen instead of given ITM, strategy may not yield the desired result. The only greek that a trader has no visibility is implied volatility. Few strategies are designed to beat volatility which a trader can choose to suit his trade.
Conditions	Note to follow the conditions given at the top left corner of each strategy that are essential for strategy to work and give desired results.
Work out	It is good for a trader to work out before initiation of any strategy and arrive expected return on it.

DIFFERENCE BETWEEN VARIOUS COMBINED STRATEGIES				
VERTICAL SPREAD	**CALENDAR SPREAD**	**STRADDLE**	**STRANGLE**	**NET DEBIT/NET CREDIT**
Simultaneously buying & selling with same option, i.e., either both Calls or either both Puts, on the same asset, same expiry, but different strike	Simultaneously buying & selling with same option, i.e., either both Calls or either both Puts, on the same asset, same strike, but different expiry	Simultaneously two buy- both buying with Call and Put, and NO selling, on the same asset, same strike and at same expiry	Simultaneously two buy- both buying with Call and Put, and NO selling, on the same asset, same expiry and at different strike	Simultaneously both buying and/or selling with Call and/or Put, on the same asset, same or different expiry and at same or different strike with net of premium received and paid.
DIFFERENCE	**DIFFERENCE**	**DIFFERENCE**	**DIFFERENCE**	**DIFFERENCE**
1. Either both Call or both Put 2. Different strike	1. Either both Call or both Put 2. Different expiry	1. No selling-Two buys-one Buy Call & one Buy Put 2. Same strike 3. Strike rate at ATM	1. No selling-Two buys-one Buy Call & one Buy Put 2. Different strike 3. Strike rate at OTM	If premium received is more than paid, it is net credit and net debit if paid is more than received.

BRIEF OF MULTI-LEG STRATEGIS

S	Strategy name	Strategy	Outlook	Leg	Option	Trade		Net		Profit	Loss
						Buy	Sell	Dr.	Cr		
1	Bull Call Spread	Vertical	Moderate Bullish	2	Both Call	1	1	Dr	-	Spread—Net Debit	Net Debit
2	Bear Call Spread	Vertical	Moderate Bearish	2	Both Call	1	1	-	Cr	Net Credit	Spread—Net Credit

3	Bull Put Spread	Vertical	Moderate Bullish	2	Both Put	1	1	-	Cr	Net Credit	Spread – Net Credit
4	Bear Put Spread	Vertical	Moderate Bearish	2	Both Call	1	1	Dr.	-	Spread—Net Debit	Net Debit
5	Bear Call Ladder	Combo	Outright Bullish	3	All Call	2	1	—	Cr	Net Credit	Spread—Net credit
6	Call Ratioback Spread	Combo	Outright Bullish	3	All Call	2	1	—	Cr	unlimited	Spread—Net credit
7	Put Ratioback Spread	Combo	Outright Bearish	3	All Put	2	1	Dr	—	Unlimited	Net debit
8	Long Straddle	Straddle	Market Neutral	2	1 Call & 1 Put	2	—	Dr	—	Unlimited	Net Debit
9	Short Straddle	Straddle	Market Neutral	2	1 Call & 1 Put	—	2	—	Cr	Net Credit	Unlimited
10	Long Strangle	Strangle	Market Neutral	2	1 Call & 1 Put	2	—	Dr.	—	Unlimited	Net Debit
11	Short Strangle	Strangle	Market Neutral	2	1 Call & 1 Put	—	2	—	Cr	Net Credit	Unlimited
12	Iron Butterfly	Combo	Market Neutral	4	2 Call & 2 Put	2	2	—	Cr	Net Credit	Spread—Net Credit
13	Iron Condor	Combo	Market Neutral	4	2 Call & 2 Put	2	2	—	Cr	Net Credit	Spread—Net Credit
14	Long Call Condor	Combo	Market Neutral	4	4 Call & NoPut	2	2	Dr	—	Spread—Net Debit	Net Debit
15	Short Put Condor	Combo	Market Neutral	4	4 Put & NoCall	2	2	—	Cr	Net Credit	Spread—Net Credit
16	Long Box Spread	Combo	Arbitrage	4	2 Call & 2 Put	2	2	Dr	—	Spread—Net Debit	Net Debit
17	Short Box Spread	Combo	Arbitrage	4	2 Call & 2 Put	2	2	—	Cr	Spread—Net Credit	Net Credit

NOTE

1. Spread means difference between strike prices of buy & sell. In Profit &Loss "—" denotes minus

2. In 3 or 4 leg strategies, spread noted under profit is difference between different strike prices. For complete details, see the strategy.

SECURITY TRANSACTION TAX (STT) ON OPTION TRADING	
As per circular instructions from NSE/BSE, intrinsic value is the difference between settlement price and strike price of the option.	
When you create a new position by buying an option	No STT
When you close the above position by selling	STT on sell side @ 0.05% of premium value For ex. if you sell one lot of index with Rs 200 as premium, your STT will be 0.05% of (200*75). (75 being 1 lot for index)
When your buy option ends in ITM on expiry	STT @ 0.125% of intrinsic value. For ex., if you have bought an option on index at 7000and if it is 7100 on last day of expiry, your STT charges is 0.125% of (7100—7000)=0.125% of 100*75=Rs 9.38 (1 lot)
When option end ITM on last day of expiry	It is considered option exercised on the last day. So, a buyer of an option need not do any transaction on the last day of expiry. Buyer needs to let the contract expire. Depending on it`s intrinsic value STT is levied.
When your buy option ends OTM on expiry	No STT because option ends worthless

BULL CALL SPREAD (1)

Spread	Strategy	Select strike price	Debit/ Credit	Max.Gain	Max.Loss	Break-even
Bull Call Spread 2 leg	Buy Call (C1) & Write Call (C2) C1-Lower strike & C2 higher strike	C2>C1	Debit	(C2—C1)— Net Prem.	Net Prem.	C1+Net Prem.

Conditions:-	Positive factors
1,Both legs belong to the same underlying	1. Profit or loss is capped regardless of move, up or low, in the stock`s price
2. Both legs belong to the same expiry	2. A Bull Call spread is cheaper than buying a stand alone Call option
3. Ratio 1:1 or 2:2 so on is to be maintained	
Simultaneously- Buy one. Sell one	

1.	Why Bull Call Spread	To reduce the strategy cost-When you expect moderately bullish market	Net debit strategy
2	View- **2 Leg-Bullish**	2 leg spread **traditionally involving ATM & OTM options. Can be created with any two of ITM,ATM,OTM also**	
3.	Strategy trade-**BOTH CALL** **BUY 1 & SELL 1**	**Simultaneously, BUY 1 ATM CALL option at lower strike & SELL 1 OTM CALL option at higher strike** **Condition: Strike for sell Call should be higher than strike for buy Call**	
4.	Market	Market may move to any direction	
5.	Holding period	Till expiration to reap the full pay off. You may close the trade before expiry too.	
6.	Net Cash flow	Net Debit ie Premium Paid minus Premium Received	
7.	Spread	Difference between the higher and the lower strike. Wider the spread, higher the amount one can potentially make	
8.	Net Debit	Premium paid for the lower strike minus Premium received for the higher strike	
9.	Maximum Loss	Net Debit of the strategy if spot moves below lower strike	
10.	Maximum Profit	Difference between Strike minus Net Debit- Profit if spot moves above higher strike	
11,	Break Even	Lower strike + Net Debit	
12.	Exit	Wait for option to expire or if exiting before expiration, buy back the sold call option & sell the bought Call option	

EXECUTION OF TRADE -AN EXAMPLE-USING MARKET INDEX AS ASSET							
Assume strike for ATM long Call is 7000 with prem.paid Rs 82/-& OTM short Call strike 7100 with prem.recd is Rs 30/-Net debit is Rs 52 i.e.,(82—30).							
If Market expires at	IV for ATM Long Call	Prem. Paid	P&L	IV for OTM Short Call	Prem. Reced.	P&L	Net P&L Pay off
8000	8000—7000=1000	82	1000—82=918	8000—7100=900	30	−870	+48
7200	7200-7000=200	82	200—82=+118	7200—7100=100	30	30—100=−70	+48
7100	7100—7000=100	82	100—82=+18	7100—7100=0	30	+30	+48
6900	6900—7000=0	82	−82	6900—7100=0	30	+30	−52
1. Net loss is restricted to net debit 52 (82—30) 2. Net profit is restricted to difference between strike (7100—7000) minus net debit=100—52=48. Note that even if the index soars to 8000, trader`s profit is capped at 48 or if the index falls to 6000, your loss is capped at 52							

BEAR CALL SPREAD (2)

Spread	Strategy	Select strike price	Debit/ Credit	Max.Gain	Max.Loss	Break-even
Bear Call Spread 2 leg	Write Call (C1) & Buy Call (C2) C1-Lower strike & C2 higher strike	C2>C1	Credit	Net Prem.	(C2-C1)—Net Prem.	C1+Net Prem

Conditions:-	Positive factors
1. Both legs belong to the same underlying	1. Bear Call spread is considered less risky with less reward.
2. Both legs belong to the same expiry	2. Loss is capped when market goes up & profit is capped when market goes down
3. Ratio 1:1 or 2:2 so on is to be maintained	
Simultaneously- Buy one, Sell one	

1.	Why Bear Call Spread	Less risk	
2	View **BEARISH**	Moderately Bearish	Net credit strategy
3.	Strategy-**2 leg-BUY 1 & SELL 1**	2 leg spread **involving OTM &ITM options. Can be created withany two of ITM,ATM,OTM also**	
4.	Market	Market may move to any direction	
5.	Holding period	Till expiration to reap the full pay off. You can close the trade before expiry too.	
6.	Trade-**Note BOTH CALL**	**SIMULTANEOUSLY BUY: 1 OTM CALL at higher strike & SELL 1 ITM CALL at lower strike** **Condition: Strike for Sell Call should be lower than strike for Buy Call**	
7.	Net Cash flow	Net credit	
8.	Spread	Difference between the higher and the lower strike. Wider the spread, higher the amount one can potentially make	
9.	Net Credit	Premium received for selling and premium paid for buying	
10.	Maximum Loss	Difference in Strike (spread) minus net credit. Loss is incurred when the spot moves above higher strike	
11.	Maximum Profit	Net Credit. Profit is earned when the spot moves below lower strike	
12,	Break Even	Lower strike + Net credit	
13.	Exit	Wait for option to expire or if exiting before expiration, buy back the sold call & sell the bought Call	

EXECUTION OF TRADE -AN EXAMPLE-ASSUMING ATM 7900

Assuming strike for Buy OTM Call 8000 &prem.paid. is Rs 32/-& strike for Sell ITM Call 7800 & Prem.recd., is Rs 162/-, net credit 162—32=130

If Market expires at	IV for Buy OTM Call	Prem. paid	P&L	IV for Sell ITM Call	Prem.recd.	P&L	Net P&L
8200	8200—8000=200	32	200—32=168	8200—7800=400	162	162—400=—238	−70
8000	8000—8000=0	32	−32	8000—7800=200	162	162—200=−38	−70
7800	7800—8000=0	32	−32	7800—7800=0	162	162—0=+162	+130
7600	7600—8000=0	32	−32	7600—7800=0	162	162—0=+162	+130

Loss is when spot moves at and above higher strike i.e., 8000. It is profit when spot moves below lower strike 7800& below

Net loss is restricted to difference in strike (8000—7800) minus net credit i.e, 200—130=70. Net profit is restricted to Net credit=130

BULL PUT SPREAD (3)

Spread	Strategy	Select strike price	Debit/ Credit	Max. Gain	Max.Loss	Break-even
Bull Put Spread 2 leg	Write Put (P1) & Buy Put (P2) P1-higher strike & P2-lower strike	P1>P2	Credit	Prem Recd	(P1-P2)— Net Prem	P1—Net Prem

Conditions:-	Positive factors
1. Both legs belong to the same underlying	1. Profit & Loss is capped
2. Both legs belong to the same expiry	2. Attractive premium
3. Ratio 1:1 or 2:2 so on is to be maintained	
Simultaneously, buy one, Sell one	

1.	Why Bull PUT Spread	When you expect Market will not go down further	
2	View **BULLISH**	Moderately Bullish	Net credit strategy
3.	Strategy-**2 leg-BUY 1& SELL 1**	**2 leg spread, ALWAYS involving 1 OTM & 1 ITM options simultaneously with one lower & one higher strikes**	
4.	Market	Market may move to any direction	

5.	Holding period	Till expiration to reap the full pay off. You may close the trade before expiry too.
6.	Trade-Note **BOTH PUT**	**Simultaneously BUY: 1 OTM PUT at lower strike & SELL 1 ITM PUT at higher strike.** **Condition: Strike for Sell Put should be higher than strike for Buy Put**
7.	Net Cash flow	Net Credit ie Premium Received minus Premium paid
8.	Spread	Difference between the higher and the lower strike. Wider the spread, higher the amount one can potentially make
9.	Net Credit	Premium received for the higher strike minus Premium paid for the lower strike
10.	Maximum Loss	Spread minus Net Credit. Loss occurs if spot moves below lower strike
11.	Maximum Profit	Net Credit. Profit is earned if spot moves above higher strike
12,	Break Even	Higher strike minus Net Credit
13.	Exit	Wait for option to expire &Retain the prem. Recd Or if exiting before expiration Buy back the short Put & sell the bought Put

EXECUTION OF TRADE-AN EXAMPLE-ASSUMING ATM 9100

Assuming strike for Buy OTM Put is 9000 & prem.paid Rs 92/-& strike for Sell ITM Put is 9200 & prem.recd. is Rs 197/-, net credit is Rs 105 i.e.,(197—92)

If Market expires at	IV for Buy OTM Put	Prem. Paid	P&L	IV for Sell ITM Put	Prem. Recd	P&L	Net pay off
8900	9000—8900=100	92	100—92=+8	9200—8900=300	197	197—300=−103	−103+8=−95
9000	9000—9000=0	92	−92	9200—9000=200	197	197—200=−3	—92−3=−95
9300	9000—9300=0	92	−92	9200—9300=0	197	+197	197—92=+105
9400	9000—9400=0	92	−92	9200—9400=0	197	+197	197—92=+105

If spot moves at or below 9000, loss is incurred. Max.loss is restricted to spread (9200—9000) minus net credit =200—105=95. Trade is profitable when the spot moves at or above higher strike, 9200. Max.profit is capped at net credit=105.

BEAR PUT SPREAD (4)

Spread	Strategy	Select strike price	Debit/ Credit	Max.Gain	Max.Loss	Break-even
Bear Put Spread 2 leg	Buy Put (P1) & Write Put (P2) P1-higher strike & P2-lower strike	P1>P2	Debit	(P1—P2)—Net Prem.	Net Prem.	P1—Net Prem

Conditions:-	Positive factors
1. Option belong to the same underlying	1. Profit and Loss is capped
2. Options belong to the same expiry	2. Less risk
3. Ratio 1:1 or 2:2 so on is to be maintained	
Simultaneously Buy one, Sell one	

1.	Why Bear PUT Spread	Attractive premium.	
2	View -**2 legBEARISH**	Moderately Bearish-expecting the Mkt to go down in the near term	Net debit strategy
3.	Strategy-**BUY 1& SELL 1**	**2 leg spread, by employing any two of ITM, ATM, OTM options simultaneously**	
4.	Expiry	Select strikes based on time to expiry	
5	Trade-**Note BOTH PUT**	**Simultaneously BUY: 1 ITM PUT at higher strike & SELL 1 OTM PUT at lower strike** **Condition: Strike for Sell Put should be lower than strike for Buy Put.**	
6.	Holding period	Till expiration to reap full pay off. Trader can close the trade before expiry too.	
7.	Net Cash flow	Net Debit ie Premium Paid minus Premium received	
8	Spread	Difference between two strikes	
9.	Net Debit	Premium Paid minus Premium received	
10.	Maximum Loss	Net Debit. Loss is incurred if spot moves above higher strike	
11.	Maximum Profit	Spread minus net Debit. Profit if spot moves below lower strike	
12.	Break Even	Higher strike minus Net Debit	
13.	Money Making	When Spot moves below Break even, Larger the spread, larger the reward	
14	Strike selection	Select the strike based on the time to expiry	
15.	Exit	Wait for option to expire OR If exiting before expiration, reverse the trade by buying sold Put & selling bought Call	

EXECUTION OF TRADE ON MARKET INDEX-AN EXAMPLE-ASSUMING ATM 9300

Assuming strike for Buy ITM Put is 9400, prem.paid is Rs 208/- & Strike for Sell OTM Put is 9100, prem.recd.is Rs 86/-. Net debit is Rs 122/-

If Market expires at	IV for ITM Put Buy	Prem.Paid	P&L	IV for OTM Put Sell	Prem.Recd.	P&L	Net Pay off
9000	9400—9000=400	208	+192	9100—9000=100	86	−14	+178
9100	9400—9100=300	208	+92	9100—9100=0	86	+86	+178
9400	9400—9400=0	208	−208	9100—9400=0	86	+86	−122
9500	9400—9500=0	208	−208	9100—9500=0	86	+86	−122

Loss is incurred when index moves at or above higher strike i.e., 9400 & above. Max.loss is net debit i.e 122/- Profit is when the index moves at or below lower strike i.e.,9100 & below. Max. Profit is (9400—9100) minus 122=178. Both profit and loss is capped.

BEAR CALL LADDER (5)

Conditions:-	Important Note
1. Call options belong to the same underlying	**1. This is a bullish strategy**
2. Call options belong to the same expiry	**Positive factor**
3. Ratio 2:1 or 4:2 so on is to be maintained, for every	1. Profit potential is capped if price moves within range and higher when price moves above the range
2 options bought, 1 option to be sold simultaneously	

1.	View **BULLISH**	Implement when you are Outrightly Bullish	Set up : Net credit
2.	Strategy **3 leg- ALL CALL**	3 Leg option. Ratio 1:1:1 meaning for every one 1 ITM Call sold, 1 ATM Call & 1 OTM Call to be bought	
3.	Trade-**SELL 1 CALL & BUY 2 CALL**	**SELL 1 ITM CALL, BUY 1 ATM CALL, BUY 1 OTM CALL simultaneously. Example:-If ATM @ 7800, sell ITM CALL @ 7600 & buy ATM CALL @ 7800, and Buy OTM CALL @7900**	
4.	Market	May move to any direction	
5.	Holding period	Till expiration to reap the full pay off. You may close the trade before expiry too.	
6.	Pay-off	Net Credit, when market goes down	
7.	Spread	Difference between ATM & ITM Strikes. In the below ex.9600—9400=200	
8.	Net Credit	Premium received from ITM minus Premium paid to ATM & OTM	
9.	Maximum Loss	Spread minus Net Credit, occurs at ATM & OTM Strikes	

10.	Maximum Profit	High Profit potential when Market moves above higher BE. Profit is limited to Net Credit, when Market moves below lower BE
11.	Lower Break-even	Lower Strike + Net Credit. In the below example, 9400+79=9479
12.	Higher Break-even	Sum of Long Strikes minus Short Strike minus Net Premium. In the below ex.(9600+9700)—9400—79=9821
13	Exit	Wait for option to expire OR If exiting before expiration, Buy back one call sold earlier and sell two calls bought earlier.

EXECUTION OF TRADE-AN EXAMPLE
Assume ATM Buy Call (1) strike is 9600, prem.paid Rs 125/-, strike for OTM Buy Call (2) is 9700, prm.paid Rs 80/-& strike for sell ITM Call is 9400 & Prem.Recd is 284/-Net credit is 284—80—125=79/-

Market expiry	IV for ATM Buy Call (1)	Pre.Pd	P&L	IV for OTM Buy Call (2)	Pre. Pd	P&L	IV for ITM SELL Call	Pr.Recd	P&L	Net P&L
9479	9479—9600=0	125	−125	9479—9700=0	80	−80	9479—9400=79	284	+205	0
9600	9600—9600=0	125	−125	9600—9700=0	80	−80	9600—9400=200	284	+84	−121
9700	9700—9600=100	125	−25	9700—9700=0	80	−80	9700—9400=300	284	−16	−121
9821	9821—9600=221	125	+96	9821—9700=121	80	+41	9821—9400=421	284	−137	0
9900	9900—9600=300	125	+175	9900—9700=200	80	+120	9900—9400=500	284	−216	+79
10100	10100—9600=500	125	+375	10100—9700=400	80	+320	10100—9400=700	284	−416	+279

Spread here is difference between ITM&ATM (9600—9400)=200, Max.Loss =spread minus net credit=121 i.e., (200—79) Higher BE is (9600+9700)—9400—79=9821. Lower BE is 9400+ 79= 9479. Profit and loss is capped when the price moves within the higher & lower range. Here, between 9400 & 9700. Profit potential is higher when the price moves above higher BE i.e.9821. If the stock does not move, here 9600, loss is high. This strategy offers higher profit potential if deployed on stocks instead of index.

CALL RATIO BACK SPREAD (6)

Conditions:-	Positive factors:-
1. Call options belong to the same expiry	1. Unlimited Profit if the Market goes up and Limited Profit if the Market goes down
2. Call options belong to the same underlying	2. A pre-defined loss if the market stays within the range
3. The Combo ratio 2:1 is to be maintained	3. As it makes money in either direction, it is better than buying a plain Vanilla Call option

4. Ratio of combo means 2 options bought for every 1 option sold- **simultaneously**	4. Call Ratio Back Spread works best when you sell slightly ITM option & buy slightly OTM option combination, when there is ample time to expiry

1.	Why	Profit when market moves either direction and Loss is predefined when market stays within a range
2.	View	Out rightly Bullish — Strategy: Net Credit
3.	Strategy **3 leg**	**3 leg strategy ie 2:1 combo** ie 2 options bought for every one option sold or 4 options bought for every 2 option sold & so on
4.	Trade: **NOTE- SELL 1 CALL& BUY 2 CALL**	**SELL One lot ITM Call option & BUY 2 lots of OTM call option at the same strike, simultaneously. For Ex., If spot is 7700, sell 1 ITM Call @ 7600 & Buy 2 OTM Call @ 7800**
5.	Market	May move to any direction
6.	Holding period	Till expiration to reap the full pay off. You may close the trade before expiry too.
7.	Pay-off	Unlimited profit when Market goes up & limited profit is net Credit when market goes down
8.	Spread	Higher Strike minus lower Strike. In the below example,6000—5800=200
9.	Net Credit	Premium received for lower Strike minus (2 x premium paid for higher strike), here 2 stands for 2 options bought
10.	Maximum Loss	Spread minus Net Credit. Loss occurs at higher strike and below. Max. loss in the example below, 200—52=148
11.	Maximum profit	Profit is unlimited when the spot moves up.
12.	Break even (B.E)	Two B.E.-one on the lower side and another on the upper side
13.	Lower B.E	Lower Strike + Net Credit. In the example below,5800+52=5852
14.	Higher B.E.	Higher Strike + Maximum Loss. In the example below, 6000+148=6148
15	Exit	Wait for option to expire OR If exiting before expiration, Buy back call sold & sell calls bought

<table>
<tr><th colspan="11" style="text-align:center">EXECUTION OF TRADE-AN EXAMPLE</th></tr>
<tr><td colspan="11">Assuming ATM is 5900, strike for Ist OTM Buy Call is 6000, Prem.paid is 80/-, 2nd OTM Buy Call is also 6000 & Prem.Paid is 80/-& ITM Sell Call is 5800, prem.recd is 212/- Net credit is 212—160=52</td></tr>
<tr><th>Mkt.at</th><th>IV for OTM Buy Call</th><th>Prm.Pd</th><th>P&L</th><th>IV for OTM Buy Call</th><th>Prm. Pd</th><th>P&L</th><th>IV for sell ITM Call</th><th>Pr.Rcd</th><th>P&L</th><th>Net P&L</th></tr>
<tr><td>5800</td><td>5800—6000=0</td><td>80</td><td>−80</td><td>5800—6000=0</td><td>80</td><td>−80</td><td>5800—5800=0</td><td>212</td><td>+212</td><td>+52</td></tr>
<tr><td>5900</td><td>5900—6000=0</td><td>80</td><td>−80</td><td>5900—6000=0</td><td>80</td><td>−80</td><td>5900—5800=100</td><td>212</td><td>+112</td><td>−48</td></tr>
<tr><td>6000</td><td>6000—6000=0</td><td>80</td><td>−80</td><td>6000—6000=0</td><td>80</td><td>−80</td><td>6000—5800=200</td><td>212</td><td>+12</td><td>−148</td></tr>
</table>

6148	6148—6000=148	80	+68	6148—6000=148	80	+68	6148—5800=348	212	−136	0
6200	6200—6000=200	80	+120	6200—6000=200	80	+120	6200—5800=400	212	−188	+52
6400	6400—6000=400	80	+320	6400—6000=400	80	+320	6400—5800=600	212	−388	+252

Max. Loss occurs at 6000&below. Maximum loss is spread minus net credit i.e, 6000—5800=200 minus 52=148. Loss is pre defined within the range 5900 to 6149 Limited Profit is earned even when the market goes down i.e., 5800. Profit potential is unlimited when the price moves above higher break even i.e., 6148

PUT RATIO BACK SPREAD (7)

Conditions:-	Positive factors:-
1. Put options belong to the same expiry	1. Unlimited Profit if the Market goes down
2. Put options belong to the same underlying	2. Limited Profit if the Market goes up
3. The Combo ratio 2:1 is maintained	3. A pre-defined loss if the market stays within the range
4. Ratio of combo means 2 options bought for every 1 option sold	4. Irrespective of time to expiry, opt for ITM & OTM combination
Simultaneously	

1.	Why Put Ratio Back spread	Profit when market moves either direction and Loss is predefined when market stays within a range
2.	View	**Out rightly Bearish** — **Net credit strategy**
3.	Strategy **3 leg-ALL PUT**	**3 leg strategy 2:1 combo** ie 2 options bought for every one option sold or 3 options bought for every 2 option sold & so on
4	Trade-**NOTE-SELL 1 PUT & BUY 2 PUT**	**SELL One lot ITM PUT option & BUY 2 lots of OTM PUT option simultaneously-Care BUY 2 OTM PUT at the same strike. For ex. If Spot @ 7500, SELL 1 ITM @ 7600 & BUY 2 OTM at 7200**
5.	Market	May move to any direction
6.	Holding period	Till expiration to reap the full pay off. Trader can close the trade before expiry too.
7.	Spread	Higher Strike minus lower Strike. In the example below,8100—7800=300
8.	Net Credit	Premium received minus 2 x premium paid, here 2 stands for 2 options bought
9.	Maximum Loss	Spread minus Net Credit. In the example below, 300—77=223
10.	Maximum Loss	Occurs at lower Strike i.e., at 7800 in the example below
11.	Maximum profit	Profit is unlimited when the price moves down
12	Break even (B.E)	Two B.E.-one on the lower side and another on the upper side

13.	Lower B.E	Lower Strike minus Maximum Loss 7800—223=7577
14.	Higher B.E.	Lower Strike + Maximum Loss 7800+223=8023
15.	Money Making	Profit unlimited when Market moves below lower B.E 7577 & limited profit when market moves above higher B.E. 8023
16.	Exit	Wait for option to expire OR if exiting before expiration, buy back put sold and sell to market puts bought

EXECUTION OF TRADE-AN EXAMPLE

Assume ATM is 8000, strike for each Buy OTM Put is 7800 & Premium paid is each at Rs 64/-, strike for sell ITM Put is 8100 & Premium received is Rs205/- Net credit is 205—128=77

Mkt. At	IV for Buy OTM Put-I	Pre. Pd	P&L	IV for Buy OTM Put-II	Pre. Pd	P&L	IV for Sell ITM Put	Pre. Rcd.	P&L	Net P&L
8200	7800—8200=0	64	−64	7800—8200=0	64	−64	8100—8200=0	205	+205	+77
8100	7800—8100=0	64	−64	7800—8100=0	64	−64	8100—8100=0	205	+205	+77
7800	7800—7800=0	64	−64	7800—7800=0	64	−64	8100—7800=300	205	−95	−223
7700	7800—7700=100	64	+36	7800—7700=100	64	+36	8100—7700=400	205	−195	−123
7400	7800—7400=400	64	+336	7800—7400=400	64	+336	8100—7400=700	205	−495	+177

Profit is unlimited @ 7577& below and limited @ 8023& above Maximum loss occurs at Lower strike @ 7800 and capped @223 which is spread minus net crdit.

LONG STRADDLE (8)

Conditions:-	Positive factors
1,Both options belong to the same underlying	1. Ideal to deploy around major event or when asset is predicted to rise or fall with increased volatility
2. Both options belong to the same expiry	2. The gain in one option will offset the loss in another option
3. Both options belong to ATM strike	3. Profit is unlimited
4. Ratio of 1:1 or 2:2 is to be maintained, i.e.,	**Note to know before execution**
One lot of Call to one lot of Put etc	1. The asset`s price direction, up or down, predicts implied volatility
	2. Cost of implementing strategy is decisive in assessment of profitability

1	View-**MARKET NEUTRAL**	To take advantage of market`s potential sudden or larger move in price-up or down	
2	Strategy **2 leg**	Strategy - Delta Neutral and is insulated against the movement of market in any direction	Net debit strategy
3	Trade-NOTE BOTHBUY- 1 CALL& 1 PUT- Both @ ATM	**Simultaneously BUY ONE LOT ATM CALL& BUY ONE LOT ATM PUT –AT SAME STRIKE, same asset, same expiry FOR BOTH CALL & PUT option. For Ex., If Spot @ 7600, BUY BOTH CALL &PUT @ 7600 i.e., ATM. Find upper range by adding amount of net premium paid with strike rate. Find lower range by deducting amount of net premium paid from strike rate.**	
4	Market	May move to any direction	
5	Holding period	Till expiration to reap the full pay off. You can close the trade before expiry too.	
6	Pay-off	Profit when market moves in either direction	
7	Maximum Loss	Net premium paid. This happens when the market stays at ATM. Max. loss if spot moves within the upper and lower range	
8	Maximum profit	Profit is unlimited when spot rises or falls outside the upper and lower range i.e., out of 8061 to 8339	
8	Net Debit	Premium paid for both buy options	
9	Two Break even (BE)	On either side, equidistance from ATM	
10	Lower BE	Strike minus Net Premium-In the example below,8200—139= 8061	
11	Higher BE	Strike + Net premium-In the example below,8200+139= 8339	
12	Exit	Wait for option to expire OR If exiting before expiration, reverse the trade by selling the Call and the Put	

EXECUTION OF TRADE-AN EXAMPLE

Assuming prem.paid for Call & Put is Rs 77/ & Rs 62/- respectively, total prem.paid is Rs 139/-. To arrive upper and lower trading range, assume Strike for both Buy Call & Buy Put is 8200. Then, Upper trading range is 8200+139=8339 & lower trading range is 8200—139=8061. If the asset`s price moves above the upper range or below the lower range on expiration, the trade is profitable. It is loss if asset moves within the upper & lower range. Max.loss is net prem.paid i.e,139

Market expires at	IV for Buy ATM Call	Pre. Paid	P&L	IV for Buy ATM Put	Pre. Paid	P&L	Net P&L
8000	8000—8200=0	77	−77	8200—8000=200	62	+138	+61
8061	8061—8200=0	77	−77	8200—8061=139	62	+77	0
8200	8200—8200=0	77	−77	8200—8200=0	62	−62	−139
8339	8339—8200=139	77	+62	8200—8339=0	62	−62	0
8500	8500—8200=300	77	+223	8200—8500=0	62	−62	+161

Trade earns profit if spot rises or falls outside the range i.e, to move by more than 1.70% (139/8200) up or down on the date of expiration. If the trader is confident that the stock will move more than 1.70% up or down on expiration, he can initiate long straddle. Long straddle should be set up around major events. Volatility is a vital factor in deciding the quantum of profitability.

SHORT STRADDLE (9)

Conditions:-	Positive factors	
1,Both options belong to the same underlying	1. To deploy when asset is predicted to rise or fall within a range or stay flat in low or nil volatility	
2. Both options belong to the same expiry	2. The gain in one option will offset the loss in another option	
3. Both options belong to ATM strike	**Negative factor**	
4. Ratio of 1:1 or 2:2 is to be maintained, i.e., One lot of Call to one lot of Put etc	Loss is unlimited	
1	View **MARKETNEUTRAL**	Market will not move and stay at a range	Net credit strategy
2	Strategy- **2 leg**	2 leg selling as opposed to 2 leg buying in Long Straddle	
3	Trade-**NOTE- BOTH SELL** **1 CALL & 1 PUT–** **Both @ ATM**	**Simultaneously SELL 1 ATM CALL & SELL 1 ATM PUT @ same strike, same stock and same expiration. For Ex. If Spot @ 7600, both CALL & PUT Sell @ 7600. Find upper range by adding amount of net premium received with strike rate. Find lower range by deducting amount of net premium received from strike rate.**	
4	Market	For the strategy, market is anticipated to stay or move within a range	
5	Holding period	Till expiration to reap the full pay off. You can close the trade before expiry too.	
6	Pay-off	Net credit	
7	Maximum Loss	Uncapped in either direction	
8	Maximum Profit	Net credit. Profit is when the spot moves between the lower and upper range	
8	Net Credit	Premium received for both sell options	
9	Two Break even (BE)	On either side	
10	Lower BE	Strike minus Net Premium	
11	Higher BE	Strike + Net premium	
12	Exit	Wait for the option to expire and retain the prem. Recd OR if exiting before expiration buy back Call & Put option	

TRADE EXECUTION-AN EXAMPLE

Assuming prem.received for Call & Put is Rs 80/ & Rs 65/- respectively, total prem.received is Rs 145/-, arrive upper and lower trading range. Assuming strike for both ATM Buy Call & ATM Buy Put is 9000. Here, Upper trading range is 9000+145=9145 & lower trading range is 9000—145=8855. If the asset`s price moves within this range on expiration, the trade is profitable. Max. profit is net credit. It is loss if asset moves outside the upper & lower range. Max loss is unlimited.

Market expires at	IV for sell ATM Call	Pre.Recd	P&L	IV for sell ATM Put	Prem.Recd	P&L	Net P&L
8700	8700—9000=0	80	+80	9000—8700=300	65	−235	−155
8855	8855—9000=0	80	+80	9000—8855=145	65	−80	0
9000	9000—9000=0	80	+80	9000—9000=0	65	+65	+145
9145	9145—9000=145	80	−65	9000—9145=0	65	+65	0
9200	9200—9000=200	80	−120	9000—9200=0	65	+65	−55

Trade earns profit only if spot rises or falls within the range i.e, price to move less than 1.61% (145/9000) up or down. If the trader is confident that the stock will move less than 1.86% up or down on expiration or within the range, he can initiate short straddle. Short straddle should not be set up around major events that may drastically alter the market's move beyond 1.91%. Volatility is a vital factor in deciding the profitability. Short straddle is exactly the opposite of long straddle.

LONG STRANGLE (10)

Conditions:-	Positive factors:-	Others factors to note before execution:-
1,Both options belong to the same underlying	1. Premiums are cheap compared to Straddles	1. Market should make a large move before expiry
2. Both options belong to the same expiry	2. Profit is unlimited	2. Strategy to be set up around major events
3. Strike rates are @OTM for Call & Put	3. Strangles are improvisation of Straddles	
4. Ratio of 1:1 or 2:2 is to be maintained, i.e.,	4. The gain in one option will offset the loss in another	
One lot of Call to one lot of Put etc		

1	View- **MKT NEUTRAL**	Market is expected a large move. Profitability is not dependent on market direction & so, called Market Neutral or Delta Neutral
2	Strategy- **2 leg**	Choose 200 or 300 points either way, for example, for call, choose Spot+200, for Put, choose Spot minus 200, Spot means ATM
3	Trade- **BOTH BUY** **1 CALL & 1 PUT** **Both @ OTM**	**Simultaneously Buy 1 OTM Call & Buy 1 OTM Put-EX-If ATM is 7900, choose PUT OTM at 7700 and Call OTM at 8100** **Net debit strategy- Find upper range by adding amount of net premium paid with Call strike rate. Find lower range by deducting amount of net premium paid from Put strike rate.**
4	Market	May move to any direction
5	Holding period	Till expiration to reap the full pay off. Trader can close the trade before expiry too.
6	Maximum Profit	Unlimited when spot moves above the upper range or below the lower range.

7	Maximum Loss	Net premium paid & if price moves within the upper and lower range.
8	Debit	Premium paid for both buy
9	Break even (BE)	Two BE
10	Lower BE	PE Strike—Net premium paid. In the example below,5800—137=5663
11	Higher BE	CE Strike+ Net premium paid. In the example below,6200+137=6337
12	Exit	Wait for option to expire OR before expiration If the asset`s price moves up, sell the Call & profit from Put and If the asset`s price moves down, sell the Put & profit from Call

EXECUTION OF TRADE- AN EXAMPLE

Assume ATM is 6000 for Buy OTM call is 6200, premium paid is Rs 72/-. Strike for Buy OTM Put is 5800, premium paid is Rs 65/-. Net debit is 137/- Arrive upper & lower range. Here, upper range is 6200+137=6337, lower range is 5800—137=5663

Market expiry at	IV for Buy OTM Call	Pre.Paid	P&L	IV for Buy OTM Put	Prem.Paid	P&L	Net P&L
5500	5500—6200=0	72	−72	5800—5500=300	65	+235	+163
5663	5663—6200=0	72	−72	5800—5663=137	65	+72	0
5800	5800—6200=0	72	−72	5800—5800=0	65	−65	−137
6337	6337—6200=137	72	+65	5800—6337=0	65	−65	0
6500	6500—6200=300	72	+228	5800—6500=0	65	−65	+163
6600	6600—6200=400	72	+328	5800—6600=0	65	−65	+263

Loss is maximum If the price moves within the range viz 5663 to 6337. Max.loss is net premium paid i.e.,137. Profit is unlimited if the price moves either direction, above the upper range 6337 or below the lower range 5663. Trade can be executed when a major event is anticipated.

SHORT STRANGLE (11)

Conditions:-	Positive factors:-
1. Both options belong to the same underlying	1. To deploy when asset is predicted to rise or fall within a range or stay flat in low or nil volatility
2. Both options belong to the same expiry	2. Strangles are improvisation of Straddles
3 Strike rates are @OTM for Call & Put	3. The gain in one option will offset the loss in another
4. Ratio of 1:1 or 2:2 is to b maintained, i.e.,	4. Premiums are cheap compared to Straddles
One lot of Call to one lot of Put etc	**Negative factor**
	Loss is unlimited

1	View **MARKET NEUTRAL**	Asset is predicted to stay flat or move within a narrow range.	Net credit strategy
2	Strategy **2 leg**	Choose 200 or 300 points either way, for ex., for call, choose Spot+200, for Put, choose Spot minus 200, Spot means ATM	
3	Trade-note BOTH SELL 1 CALL & 1 PUT	**Simultaneously SELL ONE LOT OTM CALL& SELL ONE LOT OTM PUT. Say if ATM is 7900, choose OTM Put at 7700 & OTM Call at 8100. Find upper range by adding amount of net premium received with Call strike rate. Find lower range by deducting amount of net premium received from Put strike rate.**	
4	Market	may move to any direction	
5	Holding period	Till expiration to reap the full pay off. Trader can also close the trade before expiry too.	
6	Maximum Profit	Net premium received. Profit is limited as long as the market stays between the lower & upper BE	
7	Maximum Loss	Unlimited. Max. Loss occurs when market moves away from the range of lower & upper BE	
8	Net Credit	Premium received for both sell options	
9	Break even (BE)	Two B.E.,On either side	
10	Lower BE	Put option strike minus Net Premium received	
11	Higher BE	Call option strike + Net premium received	
12	Exit	Wait for option to expire & retain the premium received OR if exiting before expiration, reverse the trades both by buy back	

EXECUTION OF TRADE- AN EXAMPLE

Assume ATM is 8200,strike for OTM Sell Call is 8400, prem.received is 39/-, strike for OTM Sell Put is 8000 & prem.received is Rs 23/-, net credit is Rs 62/-

Arrive upper & lower range. Upper range is 8400+62=8462, lower range is 8000—62=7968

Market expiry at	IV for Sell OTM Call	Pre. Recd.	P&L	IV for Sell OTM Put	Prem. Recd.	P&L	Net P&L
7700	7700—8400=0	39	+39	8000—7700=300	23	−277	−238
7968	7968—8400=0	39	+39	8000—7968=32	23	−9	+30
8300	8300—8400=0	39	+39	8000—8300=0	23	+23	+62
8462	8462—8400=62	39	−23	8000—8462=0	23	+23	0
8600	8600—8400=200	39	−161	8000—8600=0	23	+23	−138

Profit is maximum to the extent of net credit when the spot stays within the upper or lower range i.e,7968 to 8462. Maximum loss occurs when the price moves above the upper range 8462 or below the lower range 7968. Strategy may be deployed when volatility is low or major events are not expected.

IRON BUTTERFLY (12)

Conditions:-	Positive factors:-	Others factors to note before execution:-
1. All options belong to the same underlying	1. Startegy protects from upward or downside movements	1. Know impact of trading charges as this is 4 leg
2. All options belong to the same expiry	2. Benefits when price moves within a defined range	2. Profit is when the price is fairly stable
3. Ratio 1:2:1,2:4:2 on is to be maintained	3. Usually initiated during declining implied volatility	3. Success occurs during period of sideway market or mild upward trend
@ Buy one, Sell two, Buy one	4. Market neutral strategy	

1	View	Price to move slightly up.
2	Strategy-**4 leg**	Net credit strategy -**4 leg with 3 strikes, all with the same expiration**
3	Trade-**Note 2 Calls & 2 Puts-Buy 2 & sell 2 & 3 Strike prices**	**1. Buy 1 OTM Call at expiration (A)** **2. Sell 1 ATM Call & Sell 1 ATM Put both at same strike price (B) which is lower than (A) & higher than (C)** **3. Buy 1 Put OTM at expiration (C)**
3A	Condition	**Difference between two outer strikes viz (A)&(C) and middle strike (C) should be equal. For Ex. If (A) is 200, (B) shall be 190 & (C) shall be 180, difference being 10 between (A) &(B),(B) & (C)**
4	Market	may move to any direction
5	Holding period	Normally till expiration
6	Maximum loss	(Difference between highest strike& middle strike OR lowest strike & middle strike) minus net credit
7.	Maximum loss	Occurs when the price is above highest strike or below the lowest strike
8	Maximum Profit	Net credit when price moves between lower BE and upper BE
9	Higher BE	Middle strike + net credit i.e., 250+5=255
10	Lower BE	Middle strike minus ner credit i.e., 250—5=245
12	Exit	Wait for option to expire OR Can close the trade for profit before expiration, by selling Call & Put & Buying back Call & Put options. Place single order, if permitted.

EXECUTION OF TRADE- AN EXAMPLE ASSUMING ATM 250		
Assume strike for OTM Buy Call (A) 260, prem Paid Rs18/- Strike for ATM Sell Put (B) 250, Prem.Recd. is Rs19 /-	Assume strike for ATM Sell Call (B) 250, prem.Recd.is Rs21 /- Strike for OTM Buy Put (C) 240 Prem. Paid is Rs17 /-	Net credit 5 (19+21—18—17)

Stk	IV for Buy Call (A)	P.Pd	P&L	IV for Sell Put (B)	P.Rd	P&L	IV for Sell Call (B)	P.Rd	P&L	IV Buy Put (C)	P.Pd	P&L	Pay of
230	230—260=0	18	−18	250—230=20	19	−1	230—250=0	21	+21	240—230=10	17	−7	−5
245	245—260=0	18	−18	250—245=5	19	+14	245—250=0	21	+21	240—245=0	17	−17	0
246	246—260=0	18	−18	250—246=4	19	+15	246—250=0	21	+21	240—246=0	17	−17	+1
247	247—260=0	18	−18	250—247=3	19	+16	247—250=0	21	+21	240—247=0	17	−17	+2
250	250—260=0	18	−18	250—250=0	19	+19	250—250=0	21	+21	240—250=0	17	−17	+5
270	270—260=10	18	−8	250—270=0	19	+19	270—250=20	21	+1	240—270=0	17	−17	−5

Highest & lowest range is 260 to 240. When the price moves out of this range, Max. loss occurs. Max. loss is difference between highest strikes & middle strike minus net credit. Here, 260—250, So max.loss is 5 i.e.,(10—5) Max. profit is net credit. When the price moves within the range,i.e 245 to 255, profit is earned..

IRON CONDOR (13)

Conditions:-	Positive factors:-
1. Both Call &Put options belong to the same expiry	1. Strategy earns profit when asset goes up or down or sideway movement
2. Both Call &Put options belong to the same underlying	2. A pre-defined loss if the market stays within the range
3. The Combo ratio 2:2 is to be maintained	3. Neutral strategy and suited for assets of low volatility
4. Ratio of combo means 2 options bought for every 2 options sold	4. Strategy is claimed to give consistent return if deployed correctly
	5. Iron condor is extension of Iron Butterfly

1	Why iron Condor	Uniqueness for it`s neutral strategy and being suitable for options on assets of low volatility	
2	View	Assets do not move much or remain flat	Net credit strategy
3	Strategy 4 leg	**4 leg strategy -2 Puts & 2 Calls all with same expiration and 4 different strike prices**	
4	**Trade-NOTE-SELL 2 PUT & BUY 2 CALL**	**1 Long Put further OTM-Strike below the current price & 1 short Put OTM/ATM-Strike close to the current price** **1 Long Call further OTM-Strike above the current price & 1 short Call OTM/ATM- Strike above the current price**	
4A	Condition	**Call Spread and Put spread should be equal. For Ex., If spread between buy Call & sell Call is 20, then, spread between buy Put & sell Put should also be 20.**	
5	Spread	Highest minus lowest strikes either in Call or Put	
6	Market	May move to any direction	
7	Holding period	Till expiration to reap full pay off. Trader can close the trade before expiry too.	
8	Pay-off	Net credit from 4 legs.i.e., Net of all premiums paid and received	
9	Maximum Loss	Capped which is (the difference between long & short Call OR long & short Put) minus net credit	
10	Maximum Loss	Occurs when price moves above further OTM Call or below further OTM Put	
11	Maximum profit	Capped at net credit	
12	Characteristic	Iron condor deploys both Call & Put opposed to Condor Spread which deploys only Call Or only Put.	
13	Exit	Wait for option to expire & retain the premium received OR if to exit before expiration, reverse the trade	

EXECUTION OF TRADE- AN EXAMPLE ASSUMING ATM AT 160

Strike for short OTM Call is 175, prem. recd. is Rs 8 /-	Strike for short OTM Put is 155 -Prem.recd. is Rs 7/-	Net Credit is 4 (8+7—5—6)
Strike for long further OTM Call is 180, prem paid is Rs 5/-	Strike for long further OTM Put is,150 prem.paid is Rs 6/-	

Stk	Short OTM Call	P.Rd	P&L	Long further OTM Call	P.Pd	P&L	Short OTM Put	P.Rd	P&L	Long further OTM Put	P.Pd	P&L	Pay-off
185	185—175=10	8	−2	185—180=5	5	0	155—185=0	7	+7	150—185=0	6	−6	−1
160	160—175=0	8	+8	160—180=0	5	−5	155—160=0	7	+7	150—160=5	6	−6	+4

168	168—175=0	8	+8	168—180=0	5	−5	155—168=0	7	+7	150—168=0	6	−6	+4
170	170—175=0	8	+8	170—180=0	5	−5	155—170=0	7	+7	150—170=0	6	−6	+4
145	145—175=0	8	+8	145—180=0	5	−5	155—145=10	7	−3	150—145=5	6	−1	−1

Highest & lowest range is 180 to 150. Difference between long & short Call or long & short Put is 5. Max.loss occurs when price rises or falls out of highest and lowest range, here, above 180 or below 150. Loss is pre defined i.e., difference between strikes of Call or Put minus net credit i.e, 1 (5-4) Max. profit is when price moves within the range, 180 to 150 and is caped at net credit, here, 4.

LONG CALL CONDOR (14)

Conditions:-	Positive factors:-	Others factors to note before execution:-
1. Call option belong to the same underlying	1. This is a non-directional strategy	1. Strategy is reduced risk and hence reduced profit
2. Call option belong to the same expiry	2. Strategy is suited when asset`s volatility is low	
3. Ratio 2:2 so on is to be maintained	3. Deployed when price moves less or no movement	
	4. Less cost to implement	

1	View	Marginally bullish in low volatility with expectations of less or no move in asset`s price	Net debit strategy
2	Strategy-**4leg**	Uses all call options with **4 different strike prices**	
3	Trade-**Note ALL Calls** **Buy 2 & sell 2**	**(1) Buy a Call at the lowest strike (A) (2) Sell a Call at the second lowest strike (B)** **(3) Sell a Call at the second highest strike (C) (4) Buy a Call at highest strike (D)**	
4	Market	may move to any direction	
5	Holding period	Till expiration to reap full pay off. Trader can close the trade before expiry too.	
6	Maximum Profit	When the price falls within the range of (B) & (C) i.e, middle strikes minus Net debit	
7	Maximum Loss	Net debit	
8	Debit	Premiums paid minus premiums received	
9	Lower BE	Lowest strike plus net debit, i.e., 495+4=499	
10	Higher BE	Highest strike minus net debit i.e.,505—4=501	
11	Behaviour	Limits gains or losses	

12	Characteristic	Buy and sell the options at the same time	Buy and sell the options at the same time
12	Exit	Wait for option to expire OR If exiting before expiration, buy back all call sold and sell to the market all calls bought	

EXECUTION OF TRADE- AN EXAMPLE ASSUMING ATM AT 500		
Assume strike for Buy Call 495 (A) prem.paid Rs 9/- Strike for Sell Call 499 (B) Prem.recd. is Rs 5/-	Assume strike for Sell Call 501 (C) prem. Recd.is Rs 6/- Strike for Buy Call 505 (D) Prem.Paid. is Rs 4/-	Net Debit 2 (9+4—5–6)

Stk	IV for Buy Call (A)	P.Pd	P&L	IV for Sell Call (B)	P.Rd	P&L	IV for Sell Call (C)	P.Rd	P&L	IV Buy Call (D)	P.Pd	P&L	Pay of
488	488-495=0	9	−9	488-499=0	5	+5	488-501=0	6	+6	488-505=0	4	−4	−2
494	494-495=0	9	−9	494-499=0	5	+5	494-501-0	6	+6	494-505=0	4	−4	−2
499	499—495=4	9	−5	499—499=0	5	+5	499—501=0	6	+6	499—505=0	4	−4	+2
500	500—495=5	9	−4	500—499=1	5	+4	500—501=0	6	+6	500-505=0	4	−4	+2
508	508-495=13	9	+4	508-499=9	5	−4	508-501=7	6	−1	508-505=3	4	−1	−2

Max.profit is when the price falls within 499–501 range. Profit is spread minus net debit; Here, spread is 4 i.e., (505—501) or (499—495)

Profit is 2 i.e.,(4-2). Max. loss occurs when price falls out of the highest and the lowest strikes. Max loss is is 2.i.e, net debit.

SHORT PUT CONDOR (15)

Conditions:-	Positive factors:-	Others factors to note before execution:-
1. Put option belong to the same underlying	1. This is a non-directional strategy	1. Strategy is reduced risk and hence reduced profit
2. Put option belong to the same expiry	2. Strategy is suited when asset`s volatility is high	
3. Ratio 2:2 so on is to be maintained	3. Deployed when price moves sharply	
	4. Less cost to implement	

1	View	Bearish in high volatility with expectations of sharp movement in asset`s price	Net credit strategy
2	Strategy-**4leg**	Uses all Put options with **4 different strike prices**	
3	Trade-**Note ALL Puts** **Buy 2 & sell 2**	**(1) Sell a Put at the highest strike (A) (2) Buy a Put at the second highest strike (Bsss)** **(3) Buy a Put at the second lowest strike (C) (4) Sell a Put at the lowest strike (D)**	
4	Market	May move to any direction	
5	Holding period	Till expiration to reap full pay off. Trader can close the trade before expiry too.	
6	Maximum loss	Difference between strikes of (A & B) or (C& D) minus Net credit	
7	Maximum Profit	Net credit	
8	Credit	Premiums received minus premiums paid.	
9	Lower BE	Lowest strike plus net credit. In the example below, 390+2=392	
10	Higher BE	Highest minus net credit. In the example below,410—2=408	
11	Characteristic	Buy and sell the options at the same time	
12	Behavior	Works in high volatility environment	
13	Exit	Wait for option to expire OR Can close the trade for profit before expiration, by selling & Buying back Put options.	

EXECUTION OF TRADE- AN EXAMPLE ASSUMING ATM AT 400		
Assume strike for Sell Put 410 (A) prem received Rs 4/- Strike for Buy Put 405 (B) Prem.paid. is Rs 4/-	Assume strike for Buy Put 395 (C) prem. paid.is Rs 6/- Strike for Sell Put 390 (D) Prem.recd is Rs 8/-	Net credit 2 (4+8—4—6)

Stk	IV for Sell Put (A)	P.Rd	P&L	IV for Buy Put (B)	P.Pd	P&L	IV for Buy Put (C)	P.Pd	P&L	IV Sell Put (D)	P.Rd	P&L	Pay of
385	410—385=25	4	−21	405—385=20	4	+16	395–385=10	6	+4	390—385=5	8	+3	+2
415	410—415=0	4	+4	405—415=0	4	−4	395—415=0	6	−6	390—415=0	8	+8	+2
398	410—398=12	4	-8	405—398=7	4	+3	395—398=0	6	−6	390—398=0	8	+8	−3
402	410—402=8	4	-4	405—402=3	4	−1	395—402=0	6	−6	390—402=0	8	+8	−3

Highest and lowest range is 410 to 390. When the price falls out of this range, Max. profit is gained. Max. profit is net credit. When the price falls within this range, loss is incurred. Loss is spread minus net credit. Here, it is 3 i.e.,(5—2), 5 being the spread (difference between buy & sell strikes) & 2 being net credit.

LONG BOX SPREAD (16)

Conditions:-	Positive factor
1. All options belong to the same underlying	1. This is an arbitrage strategy that combines buying Bull Call spread with matching Bear Put spread
2. All options belong to the same expiry	2. No risk strategy and earns profit regardless of the market`s direction
3. Ratio 2:2 to be maintained	3. Before initiation of the strategy, back-test it for P&L
	Factors to note before execution
1. Trading on arbitrage is possible when premiums are underpriced or overpriced with reference to spread and valuation on expiration	
2. Before initiation of strategy, back-test for P&L and/or ensure that arbitrage exists to profit after meeting other charges, like STT, brokerage etc.	
3. This strategy is used when spreads are underpriced with reference to their expiration values.	

1	View	**Arbitrage 4 leg strategy-** Pofit or loss regardless of the market direction
2	Trade-**Note 2 Calls &** **2 Puts-Buy 2 & sell 2**	**(1) Buy 1 ITM Call (A) (2) Sell 1 OTM Call (B) (3) Buy 1 ITM Put (B) (4) Sell OTM Put (A)** **Note (1) & (4) have same strike rate (A) (2) & (3) have same strike rate (B)** **First, select ITM Call strike (which will be lower than ATM) and fix it for sell OTM Put.** **Second, select ITM Put strike (which will be higher than ATM) and fix it for sell OTM Call**
3	Market	may move to any direction
4	Holding period	Till expiration. Trader can close the trade before expiry too.
5	Identify Profit zone	If positive after difference between (B) & (A) minus net premium paid minus Broker charges, STT etc., meaning underpriced
6	Maximum profit	Riskless profit is (Difference between higher & lower strike) minus net premium paid
7.	Maximum loss	Net premium paid + other transaction charges
8	Box value at expiration	Higher strike minus lower strike i.e, (B) minus (A)
9.	Exit	Wait for option to expire OR if exiting before expiration, reverse the trade –Buy back & sell to market Call & Put options

INDICATIVE EXECUTION OF TRADE- AN EXAMPLE ASSUMING ATM AT 348		
Assume strike for Buy ITM Call is 346, (A) prem.pd is Rs 11/-	Assume strike for Sell OTM Call is 350,(B) prem.recd. is Rs 10/-	Net debit 3 (11+11—10—9)
Then, strike for Buy ITM Put is 350 (B), prem, paid is Rs 11/-	Then strike for Sell OTM Put is 346,(A) prem.reced is Rs 9/-	If trade is 1 lot, net debit is 300
Assume trade is 1 lot (100)	Assume trade is 1 lot (100)	

1. Difference between higher & lower strike (350—346)=4*100=400
2. Cost of implementation charges =Net debit + Broker`s charges + STT=300+20+1 (1900*0.05%)=321.
3. Maximum Profit= Rs 79/- for one lot (400—321) Here it is underpriced. So Long Box Spread is deployed.
4. If price of box is higher, i.e., net premium is higher than the difference between higher & lower strike, then, it is overpriced in which case you initiate Short Box Spread by selling ITM call & buying OTM put. See below more on Short Box Spread.
5. It is good for trader if the strategy is back-tested before initiation

SHORT BOX SPREAD (17)

Conditions:-	Positive factor
1. All options belong to the same underlying	1. This is an arbitrage strategy that combines buying Bull Call spread with matching Bear Put spread
2. All options belong to the same expiry	2. No risk strategy and earns profit regardless of the market`s direction
3. Ratio 2:2 to be maintained	3. Before initiation of the strategy, back-test it for P&L
	Factors to note before execution
1. Trading on arbitrage is possible when premiums are underpriced or overpriced with reference to spread and valuation on expiration	
2. This strategy is used when spreads are overpriced with reference to their expiration values.	
3. Before initiation of strategy. Back test for P&L	

1	View	**Arbitrage 4 leg strategy-** Profit or loss regardless of the market direction
2	Trade-**Note 2 Calls &** **2 Puts-Buy 2 & sell 2** **& 2 Strike prices**	**(1) Buy 1 OTM Call (A) (2) Sell 1 ITM Call (B) (3) Buy 1 OTM Put (B) (4) Sell ITM Put (A)** **Note (1) & (4) have same strike rate (A) (2) & (3) have same strike rate (B)** **First, select ITM Call strike (which will be lower than ATM) and fix it for buy OTM Put too.** **Second, select ITM Put strike (which will be higher than ATM) and fix it for buy OTM Call too**
3	Market	may move to any direction
4	Holding period	Till expiration. Trader can close the trade before expiry too.
5	Identify Profit zone	If positive after (Net premium received minus difference between (A) & (B) minus Broker charges, STT etc) meaning overpriced
6	Maximum profit	Riskless profit is Net premium received minus difference between (A) & (B) minus Brokers charges, STT etc
7.	Maximum loss	Net premium received +Transaction charges

8	Box value at expiration	Higher strike minus lower strike i.e, (A) minus (B)
9.	Exit	Wait for option to expire OR if exiting before expiration, reverse the trade –Buy back & sell to market Call & Put options

INDICATIVE EXECUTION OF TRADE-AN EXAMPLE

Assume strike for Buy OTM Call is 648 (A) & prem paid is Rs 17/- Then, strike for Buy OTM Put is 643 (B) & Prem.paid is Rs 14/- Assume 1 lot (100) is traded	Assume Sell ITM Call is 643 (B) & prem.recd., is Rs 19/- Then, strike for ITM Put is 648 (A) & Prem. Recd., is Rs 18/- Assume 1 lot (100) is traded	Net credit 6 (19+18—17—14) Assume 1 lot (100) is traded
1. Difference between higher & lower strike (648—643)=5*100=500		
2. Cost of implementation charges = Net premium received minus Broker`s charges + STT=(6*100)–20+3=577		
3. Net profit is 77 (577—500) for1 lot		
4. It is good for trader if the strategy is back tested before initiation.		

OTHER OPTION STRATEGIES YOU NEED TO KNOW

COVERED CALL

USEFUL WHEN	STRATEGY	ADVANTAGE	DISADVANTAGE
When you own stock on long position, neutral opinion on it`s direction in short term but wants to retain stock on long term	Write/sell a Call option on the same stock. If the buyer of option exercises his right, writer can deliver it from his long position. This is a short term hedge and also a cover to his long.	1. Protection against the potential decline in stock`s price 2. Generate income through receipt of call premium	Investor should be willing to sell the stock at set price of Call option When Stock`s price goes up, opportunity to sell at higher price is lost

MARRIED PUT

USEFUL WHEN	STRATEGY	ADVANTAGE	DISADVANTAGE
When you are long on a stock and want to protect from downside risk	Purchase stock as normal and simultaneously buy ATM PUT option for equivalent number of shares both on the same day. If exercised, trader can deliver from his long position.	1. Protects like an insurance cover if stock`s price falls  2. Investor will be able to participate in  every upside opportunity if stock`s price gains in value	If the stock does not fall in value, investor loses the amount of premium paid.

PROTECTIVE PUT			
USEFUL WHEN	**STRATEGY**	**ADVANTAGE**	**DISADVANTAGE**
When an investor is long and wants to protect from it`s fall from purchase price, in short term while willing to retain the stock on long term	Purchase 1 OTM/ATM PUT. If ATM, 100% protection from downside risk with expensive premium & if OTM, inexpensive premium with less than 100% protection.OTM option may be bought on any day while ATM option to be bought on the same day of stock bought for long	1. If stock keeps on rising, full upside gain benefits trader 2. If stock falls, protection from Put works as an insurance from huge loss	When price rises steeply, profit is reduced to the extent of premium paid.

LONG CALENDAR SPREAD			
USEFUL WHEN	**STRATEGY**	**ADVANTAGE**	**DISADVANTAGE**
When a trader has a short term sentiment of neutral forecast and expects a gradual or side way movement in the short term & direction bias over long term dated expiry	Buy & Sell a Call or Buy & Sell a Put at same strike price but at different expiration. Strike price should as near as possible to asset`s price. If Bullish, Buy a Calendar Call spread. If Bearish, Buy a Calendar Put spread. For ex:-If spot is 113.82,Buy longer term & Sell near term Viz Buy Sept 113 Put & Sell July 113 Put	Though initially neutral strategy, when near term option expires, long term option has unlimited potential to gain. Generates profit as time decays. Limits risk to net Debit. Benefit from increase in volatility. Provides additional leverage to make excess return	As expiration date approaches, trader must watch for near term expiry and allow long term option to play Timing to enter and exit the market is necessary with in advance plan for exit strategy.

CHAPTER 8

ECONOMIC CALENDAR OF EVENTS THAT IMPACT INDIAN STOCK MARKET

CONTENTS

1 Monetary Policy
2 Consumer Price Index (CPI)
3 Wholesale Price Index (WPI)
4 Periodic Labor Force Survey (PLFS)
5 Govt., of India`s Budget
6 Index of Industrial Production (IIP)
7 Purchasing Managers Index (PMI)
8 Gross Domestic Product (GDP)
9 Other events- import of Crude Oil
10 Parliament/Assembly Elections
11 Other Asian Stock Markets
12 US FED Interest rate
13 October effect

A successful trader needs to know that certain events make significant impact on prices of certain stocks or the market as a whole either before or after the event. Following the chart of these events and being alert is helpful for successful trades. Note to never ignore these events.

Monetary Policy	Event-When
Before studying what is Monetary Policy, a trader ought to know the role and responsibilities of RBI as a Central Bank under The Reserve Bank of India Act 1934. It`s primary responsibility is to regulate money supply aimed at controlling inflation to achieve sustained growth of economy, through demand and supply mechanism. To illustrate, if you have bought grain for Rs 100/- last year and if the same money Rs 100/-could buy in the current year less quantity of grain than what you have bought last year, then value of your money has eroded due to inflation which is due to excess money supply that causes decline in purchasing power. When production capacity (i.e, supply of goods and services) is not adequate enough to keep pace with the rising money supply, excess money supply increases demand forcing prices to rise. Money supply takes the form of issue of paper currency by RBI and flow of credit by Banks. RBI monitors and controls money supply from Bank credits, by increasing or decreasing interest rates that form base rate for lending by Banks to general public. A committee called Monetary Policy Committee (MPC) formed by RBI to track and control inflation, changes Repo rate and Reverse Repo rate, Cash reserve ratio, Statutory Liquidity Reserve ratio, Bank rate and others with the intention of providing or absorbing liquidity in the economy. Liquidity refers to lendable money with Banks that either expands or shrinks depending upon the changes in repo rates and others. MPC`s announcements will have major impact on stock market trending. RBI`s Monetary Policy Committee consists of 6 members that meet once in two months and review the rates. The last scheduled meet was held in April `22. RBI convened an unscheduled MPC meet and announced MPC report in May`22 since in it`s perspective inflation has surpassed their tolerance level that needs urgent appropriate corrective measures. Inflation as on May`22 is at 7.9% which is higher than 6 %, the upper tolerance level for inflation.	Every two months – usually 6th to 8th of the month
What to read in MPC	
Whenever repo rates and reverse repo rates are hiked, it is a measure to absorb and reduce excess lendable money or liquidity available with Banks. So it tends to increase the interest rates for borrowing by public from banks. Corporate normally postpone their expansion plans in such dear money economy. Stock markets normally dip when interest rates are hiked. Conversely, reduction in rates lead to buoyancy in stock market	

Consumer Price Index (CPI)	
CPI is one of useful tools for analysis of the economy to track average changes in retail prices across India, based on every households` consumption expenditure on basket of essential goods and services classified under broad 6 heads viz Food and beverages, Pan, Tobacco and intoxicants, clothing and footwear, Housing, fuel and lighting, and miscellaneous items, the prices of each of which are given weighted average according to the preferences of consumers for livelihood in rural and urban centers selected based on their population in each State/UT. The changes in retail prices are computed with 2012 as base year for 100 points. Consumer price increase or decrease is thus factored to measure inflation in retail prices. Simply put, CPI is an index of changes in cost of living compiled in terms of consumer spending on basket of goods and services. CPI report is compiled by Ministry of Statistics and released in 2nd week of every month.	Every month- 2nd week
Wholesale Price Index (WPI)	
WPI is a similar tracking process as CPI to study average changes in wholesale prices in order to measure inflation. WPI is compiled and released by Ministry of Commerce and Industry. In WPI, wholesale first stage transactions between wholesalers and manufacturers traded on basket of goods, excluding services, are tracked for changes in wholesale prices as against final stage consumers` retail price paid by end consumers under CPI. Base year for WPI is 2011-12. Report is released on 14th of every month. WPI is at 9 year high of 15.08% as on Ap`22	Every mont- 14 th

What to watch in CPI & WPI	Event-When
CPI & WPI are tools to assess the rate of inflation. So, CPI & WPI are not themselves, policy announcements, but help formulate and review Monetary policy. If these indices reveal inflation on sustained level, i.e., more than a quarter or exceeding tolerance level, RBI through MPC is bound to intervene and change interest rates.	
Periodic Labor Force Survey (PLFS)	
PLFS is a quarterly bulletin report compiled and released by NSO (National Statistical office) incorporating labor force participation rate, Worker population Ratio, Unemployment rate, distribution of labor in urban areas for male and female, conducting sample household survey on employment in agricultural and other sectors. Reports are compiled quarterly and annually and released by NSO. Traders may note that though this report is not as important as CPI & WPI for tracking inflationary pressures, PLFS do play a role in policy formulation by Govt. of India like increasing Govt`s spending to create more jobs and stimulate economy.	Quarterly Bulletin and Annual report
What to read in PLFS	
PLFS is nothing but a warning symptom of spiraling unemployment and decreasing demand for goods and services. The report is a tool in the hands of Govt., to modify existing labor policy or announcing new Policy measures to create more jobs.	

Govt.of India`s Budget	
Financial Budget is an important document of report by Govt., that is presented by Finance Minister in the Parliament in the month of February every year, detailing the Govt`s actual and estimated revenue and expenditure for the previous year and current year respectively and arriving surplus or deficit in revenues over expenditure or vice versa. The budget is a balancing exercise done annually by the Govt., for a year, presenting how much it has collected by way of taxes, duties, fees, interest etc., from various sources of revenue and how much it proposes to spend them on various sectors, in tune with it`s avowed policy of good governance. While RBI is responsible for monetary policy of controlling inflation and growth of economy through money supply, Govt` is responsible for fiscal policy of stimulating economy through Govt. spending and appropriate direct and indirect taxation policy measures.	Every year – February
What to read in Budget	
In simple terms, any measure to incentivize manufacturing goods and services including export of goods and services, corporate earnings, industrial policy to ease of doing business, higher allocation for infrastructure creation, reducing personal Income Tax and Corporate Tax, efficient collection of revenues, maintaining fiscal deficits within the prescribed limits, are all positive signals of growing economy and stock market as well.	
Index of Industrial Production (IIP)	
IIP is a monthly exercise being undertaken by the Ministry of Statistics and Programme implementation to measure changes in the volume of products in industrial production in a given period. The Ministry collects information on production data from manufacturing industries, Mining industries, Electricity and Gas industries with level of growth on basic, intermediate and capital goods. The changes are expressed in percentage terms over the previous period with base year as 2011-12. The changes so collected are released monthly by the Ministry as index that indicates positive or negative growth of economy. The report is helpful in knowing advance estimates of GDP and framing policy corrections by Finance Ministry and RBI.	Monthly- 12th of every month
What to note in the report	
Positive changes signal upswing in industrial production and negative changes show sluggish or stagnant economy. Watch for any corrective action from Govt., to stimulate industrial production	

Purchasing Managers Index (PMI)	
PMI is a monthly exercise of capturing the business performance based on survey from Purchasing Managers data of prime manufacturing industries and services with reference to new orders received and their requirement of inputs like Inventories, Production, supply, employment etc to meet such new orders that go to sum up the business conditions in the views of Purchasing Managers as improving, stagnating, and deteriorating compared to the previous month. PMI is an economic indicator that helps economists and analysts assess the direction of economy and take corrective measures if necessary.	Monthly-First week
What to note in the report	
PMI is a reading between 1 to100. If PMI is above 50, it is expanding, below 50 indicates contraction and at 50 indicates no change. If PMI is below 50 for the current month and above 50 for the previous month, business condition is in contraction. Contrary is true for expansion. PMI is compiled by IHS MARKIT, a global survey institution.	
Gross Domestic Product (GDP)	
GDP is the monetary value of total output of goods and services produced in a country by public and private sectors annually. If GDP is calculated, adjusted to inflation, it gives you real GDP. It is thus an indicator of a nation's economic health. Note that unlike CPI where change in prices is compiled only on basket of commodities, GDP accounts for all the output produced within the boundary of a country Though GDPs are calculated in different ways to arrive it accurately, narrating them is beyond the scope of this book. GDP is the most important reliable data for the Govt., Economists, Analysts, Law makers and Corporate to know such as the Nation's economic health, if expanding or contracting, the prime driver of economic growth and necessity for policy Correction if any. GDP does not include output of secondary goods and services in use, those of intermediary goods to produce final goods, goods and services produced out of country, pure financial transactions that do not end in creation of final output of goods and services like remittances between persons for consumption, investment in stocks, bonds etc. Though it is compiled annually, advanced estimates of GDP are also done quarterly. Note that while output of final goods and services produced by Corporate are factored for GDP, it's stock is not because it's stock is a financial tradable security that represents ownership in Corporate and not in products that Corporate produce.	Annually April-May
What to note in GDP	
By comparing year-on-year, expansion or contraction is assessed. Expansion is a positive signal of economic growth for Corporate to plan their investments for expansion and increase their earnings leading to buoyancy in stock market.	

This section illustrates how stock market is affected by various other major events		
Event-Crude oil	**Why it causes**	**Impact on Indian stock market**
India, being import dependant for 80% of it's crude oil needs, even a slight increase in the price leads to higher outgo of foreign exchange. (1) Price of crude oil rising abnormally or to new high like it reached to USD 130/-in May `22. (2) Supply chain of oil delivery is interrupted like Ukraine and Russia war or like block in sea route in Suez Canal due to war in Gulf region	Organization of Petroleum Exporting Countries (OPEC) is an organization of 13 major petroleum producing Countries that fix it's price depending on crude supply from member Countries and international demand. Though OPEC is said to have been formed to avoid price war among member counties, OPEC is said to behave like a cartel in price fixing.	Higher crude oil price leads to heavy drain on Foreign Exchange reserve, surpassing our estimate of footing the import bill. It leads to weaken Rupee to US Dollar resulting in withdrawal of heavy funds from market by FII/ FPI that creates volatility and perhaps crash. Hence watch for FII/ FPI`s` reaction to market trend.
Parliamentary/Assembly Elections	**Why it causes**	**Impact on Indian stock market**
Elections to Parliament and Assembly every five years	People tend to think that new Govt.,/new head of State may change policies that were followed till now.	Stock market reacts cautiously. If market participants believe the new Govt is market friendly, market rises.
Other Asian Stock Markets	**Why it matters**	**Impact on Indian stock market**
Singapore and Hong Kong time zones are +2.30 hours from IST. So, when Indian time is 7.00 am, these Countries stock markets start trading session by opening at by 9.30 am. i.e., earlier than ours by 2.30 hours. So what?	Just have a glance on these markets to watch if market is moving normally. May be any rise or fall in these markets is a prelude to what to follow in Indian Market too.	If Asian markets indicate bullish or bearish trend in the opening session of the day, Indian Market too is **likely** to follow the trend. Note while bullish trend may offer you time to grab opportunities, market `s crash happens suddenly.
US FED`s interest rate	**Why it matters**	**Impact on Indian stock market**
Federal Reserve System, shortly called FED, is Central regulatory Bank to USA., like RBI to India. Frankly speaking, Indian stock market is sensitive to changes in US FED`s interest rate. In general, change in interest rate is inversely related to stock market., i.e., higher	1. USA is home to one of the most developed stock markets in the world 2. US Dollar is global currency representing the powerful economy of US Govt that has an enviable record of no default in it's repayment history.	So, when US FED lowers interest rate, you may expect flight of funds of FII/FPI from Indian stock market to US, making Indian market vulnerable to fall for few sessions.

rate tends to fall in stock market and lower rate tends to rise stock market. International Govts., Funds, Foreign Portfolio Investors (FPI), Foreign Institutional Investors (FII) etc prefer investing in US Dollar denominated US Govt., backed securities for the reasons mentioned herewith.	3 US stock markets are highly developed one with listing of billion dollar asset worth Companies. Theoretically, fall in FED rate leads to cheaper borrowing that boosts consumers spending due to low cost of loans from Banks. This tends to rise stock market.	

The October effect	Why it matters	Impact on Indian Stock Market
According to Investopedia, US stock markets decline in the month of October, as most of their market crash happened in Oct. However, it is said to be a myth as many other market fall happened in the month of September and other months too.	The report says that it could be the effect of US presidential Election efforts, normally taking place in the month of Sept. Whatever be the reason, if markets fall normally in the month of Oct, let us be prepared to trade in Oct cautiously.	As said earlier, our market is sensitive to US market's behavior. So, let us be little more alert. After all, it is our money at stake.